Key Concepts in the Practice of

SUFISM

Emerald Hills of the Heart

2

Key Concepts in the Practice of

SUFISM

Emerald Hills of the Heart

2

M. Fethullah Gülen

Translated by Ali Ünal

Light

New Jersey

10 09 08 07   2 3 4 5
First published 2004

Published by The Light, Inc.
26 Worlds Fair Dr. Unit C
Somerset, New Jersey, 08873, USA

www.thelightpublishing.com

Library of Congress Cataloging-in-Publication Data for the first volume
Gulen, M. Fethullah
  [Kalbin zümrüt tepelerinde. English]
  Key concepts in the practice of Sufism / M. Fethullah Gulen.
  [Virginia] : Fountain, 2000.
  Includes index.
  ISBN 1-932099-23-9
  1. Sufism - - Doctrines. I. Title.
  BP189.3 .G8413 2000
  297.4 - - dc21

                                                              00-008011

ISBN-13 (paperback): 978-1-932099-75-1
ISBN-13 (hardcover): 978-1-932099-77-5

Printed by
Çağlayan A.Ş., Izmir - Turkey
April 2007

TABLE OF CONTENTS

SUFISM AND ITS ORIGIN

Sufism (*tasawwuf*) is the path followed by Sufis to reach the Truth—God. While Sufism usually expresses the theoretical or philosophical aspect of this search, the practical aspect is usually referred to as "being a dervish."

WHAT IS SUFISM?

Sufism has been defined in many ways. Some see it as the annihilation of the individual's ego, will, and self centeredness by God and the subsequent spiritual revival with the light of His Essence.[1] Such a transformation results in the direction of the individual's will by God in accordance with His Will. Others view it as a continuous striving to cleanse one's self of all that is bad or evil in order to acquire virtue.

Junayd al-Baghdadi, a famous Sufi master, defines Sufism as a method associated with "self-annihilation in God" and "permanence or subsistence with God." Shibli summarizes it as always being together with God or in His presence, so that no worldly or otherworldly aim is even entertained. Abu Muhammad Jarir describes Sufism as resisting the temptations of the carnal, (evil-commanding) self (*nafs al-ammara*) and evil qualities, and acquiring laudable moral qualities.

There are some who describe Sufism as seeing behind the "outer" or surface appearance of things and events, and interpreting whatever happens in the world in relation to God. This means that a person regards every act of God as a window through which to

---

[1] God's Essence (*Zat*) is the Divine Being Himself. The phrase "lights of His Essence" refers to the lights of His Being. (Trans.)

"see" Him, and lives his life as a continuous effort to view or "see" Him with a profound, spiritual "seeing," indescribable in physical terms, and with a profound awareness of being continually overseen by Him.

All of these definitions can be summarized as follows: Sufism is the path followed by an individual who, having been able to free himself or herself from human vices and weaknesses in order to acquire angelic qualities and conduct pleasing to God, lives in accordance with the requirements of God's knowledge and love, and in the resulting spiritual delight that ensues.

Sufism is based on observing even the most "trivial" rules of the Shari'a[2] in order to penetrate their inner meaning. An initiate or traveler on the path (*salik*) never separates the outer observance of the Shari'a from its inner dimension, and therefore observes all of the requirements of both the outer and the inner dimensions of Islam. Through such observance, the traveler heads toward the goal in utmost humility and submission.

Sufism, a demanding path that leads to knowledge of God, has no room for negligence or frivolity. It requires the initiate to strive continuously, like a honeybee flying from hive to flowers and from flowers to hive, to acquire this knowledge. The initiate should purify his or her heart from all other attachments; resist all carnal inclinations, desires, and appetites; and live in a manner reflecting the knowledge with which God has revived and illumined his or her heart, always ready to receive divine blessing and inspiration; as well as in strict observance of the Prophet Muhammad's example. Convinced that attachment and adherence to God is the greatest merit and honor, the initiate should renounce his or her own desires for the demands of God, the Truth.

After these (preliminary) definitions, we should discuss the aim, benefits, and principles of Sufism.

---

2   The body of Islamic law, based on the Qur'anic commands and the actions and sayings of the Prophet, and then further developed by legal scholars to apply Islamic concepts to daily life. (Trans.)

Sufism requires the strict observance of all religious obligations, an austere lifestyle, and the renunciation of carnal desires. Through this method of spiritual self-discipline, the individual's heart is purified and his or her senses and faculties are employed in the way of God, which means that the traveler can now begin to live on a spiritual level.

Sufism also enables individuals, through the constant worship of God, to deepen their awareness of themselves as devotees of God. Through the renunciation of this transient, material world, as well as the desires and emotions it engenders, they awaken to the reality of the other world, which is turned toward the Beautiful Divine Names of God.[3] Sufism allows individuals to develop the moral dimension of one's existence, and enables the acquisition of a strong, heartfelt, and personally experienced conviction of the articles of faith that before had only been accepted superficially.

The principles of Sufism may be listed as follows:

- Reaching true belief in God's Divine Oneness and living in accordance with its demands.
- Heeding the Divine Speech (the Qur'an), discerning and then obeying the commands of the Divine Power and Will as they relate to the universe (the laws of creation and life).
- Overflowing with Divine Love and getting along with all other beings in the realization (originating from Divine Love) that the world is the cradle of brotherhood and sisterhood.
- Giving preference or precedence to the well-being and happiness of others.
- Acting in accordance with the demands of the Divine Will—not with the demands of our own will—and living

---

3   The world has three "faces." The first face is turned toward the transient, materialistic world, in which people seek the satisfaction of their bodily (animalistic) desires. The second face is turned toward the "arable field" of the Hereafter, in which a person's "seeds of action" are sown and, at the proper time, harvested in the Hereafter. The third face is the area in which the Beautiful Divine Names of God are manifested. Sufism requires the awakening to the last two "faces" of the world. (Trans.)

in a manner that reflects our self-annihilation in God and subsistence with Him.

- Being open to love, spiritual yearning, delight, and ecstasy.
- Being able to discern what is in the hearts or minds of others through facial expressions and the inner, Divine mysteries and the meanings of surface events.
- Visiting spiritual places and associating with people who encourage the avoidance of sin and striving in the way of God.
- Being content with religiously permitted pleasures, and not taking even a single step toward that which is not permitted.
- Struggling continuously against worldly ambitions and illusions, which lead us to believe that this world is eternal.
- Never forgetting that salvation is possible only through certainty of or conviction in the truth of religious beliefs and conduct, sincerity or purity of intention, and the sole desire to please God.

Two other elements may be added: acquiring knowledge and understanding of the religious and gnostic sciences, and following a perfected, spiritual master's guidance. Both of these are of considerable significance in the Naqshbandiyah Sufi order.

It may be useful to discuss Sufism according to the following basic concepts, which often form the core of books written on good morals, manners, and asceticism, and which are viewed as the sites of the "Muhammadan Truth"[4] in one's heart. They can also be considered as lights by which to know and follow the spiritual path leading to God.

The first and foremost of these concepts is wakefulness (*yaqaza*), which is alluded to in the Prophetic saying (hadith): *My eyes sleep*

---

[4] This term is essential to Sufism. It may be translated as the "reality of Muhammad" as God's Messenger, the most beloved of God, the best example for all creation to follow, the embodiment of Divine Mercy, and the living Qur'an or embodiment of the Qur'anic way of life. (Trans.)

but my heart does not, and in the saying of 'Ali, the fourth Caliph: *Men are asleep. They wake up when they die.* The many other stages on this path will be discussed, at some length, in this book.

THE ORIGIN OF SUFISM

As the history of Islamic religious sciences tells us, religious commandments were not written down during the early days of Islam; rather, the practice and oral circulation of commandments related to belief, worship, and daily life led the people to memorize them.

Thus it was easy to compile these in books later on, for what had been memorized and practiced was simply written down. In addition, since religious commandments were the vital issues in a Muslim's individual and collective life, scholars gave priority to these and compiled books. Legal scholars collected and codified books on Islamic law and its rules and principles pertaining to all fields of life. Traditionists[5] established the Prophetic traditions (*Hadith*s) and way of life (Sunna), and preserved them in books. Theologians dealt with issues concerning Muslim belief. Interpreters of the Qur'an dedicated themselves to studying its meaning, including issues that would later be called "Qur'anic sciences," such as *naskh* (abrogation of a law), *inzal* (God's sending down the entire Qur'an at one time), *tanzil* (God's sending down the Qur'an in parts on different occasions), *qira'at* (Qur'anic recitation), *ta'wil* (exegesis), and others.

Thanks to these efforts that remain universally appreciated in the Muslim world, the truths and principles of Islam were established in such a way that their authenticity cannot be doubted.

While some scholars were engaged in these "outer" activities, Sufi masters were mostly concentrating on the pure spiritual dimension of the Muhammadan Truth. They sought to reveal the es-

---

5   This term refers to scholars who have devoted themselves to the study of the *Hadith*s. Especially when used in the same sense as Sunna, the *Hadith*s are classified into three groups: The Prophet's words, his actions or daily life, and the sayings or actions of his Companions of which he approved explicitly or tacitly. They have been transmitted to succeeding generations through verified chains of narrators. (Trans.)

sence of humanity's being, the real nature of existence, and the inner dynamics of humanity and the cosmos by calling attention to the reality of that which lies beneath and beyond their outer dimension. Adding to Qur'anic commentaries, narrations of Traditionists, and deductions of legal scholars, Sufi masters developed their ways through asceticism, spirituality, and self-purification—in short, their practice and experience of religion.

Thus the Islamic spiritual life, based on asceticism, regular worship, abstention from all major and minor sins, sincerity and purity of intention, love and yearning, and the individual's admission of his or her essential impotence and destitution became the subject matter of Sufism, a new science possessing its own method, principles, rules, and terminology. Even if various differences gradually emerged among the orders that later were established, it can be said that the basic core of this science has always been the essence of the Muhammadan Truth.

The two aspects of the same truth—the commandments of the Shari'a and Sufism—have sometimes been presented as mutually exclusive. This is quite unfortunate, as Sufism is nothing more than the spirit of the Shari'a, which is made up of austerity, self-control and criticism, and the continuous struggle to resist the temptations of Satan and the evil-commanding self in order to fulfill religious obligations.[6] While adhering to the former has been regarded as exotericism (self-restriction to Islam's outer dimension), following the latter has been seen as pure esotericism. Although this discrimination arises partly from assertions that the commandments of the Shari'a are represented by legal scholars or muftis, and the other by Sufis, it should be viewed more as the result of the natural, human tendency of assigning priority to that way which is most suitable for the individual practitioner.

---

6   Sufism is based on the purification of the carnal self (*nafs*). The self needs to be trained and educated, for in its "raw" form it is evil. The Qur'an calls it *nafs ammara (bi al-su')*: the evil-commanding self. (Trans.)

Many legal scholars, Traditionists, and interpreters of the Qur'an produced important books based on the Qur'an and the Sunna. The Sufis, following methods dating back to the time of the Prophet and his Companions, also compiled books on austerity and spiritual struggle against carnal desires and temptations, as well as states and stations of the spirit. They also recorded their own spiritual experiences, love, ardor, and rapture. The goal of such literature was to attract the attention of those people who the Sufis regarded as having restricted their practice and reflection to the "outer" dimension of religion, and to direct their attention to the "inner" dimension of religious life.

Both Sufis and scholars sought to reach God by observing the Divine obligations and prohibitions. Nevertheless, some extremist attitudes—occasionally observed on both sides—caused disagreements. Actually, there was no substantial disagreement, and such conflicts should not have been viewed as disagreements, for they only involved dealing with different aspects and elements of religion under different titles. The tendency of specialists in jurisprudence to concern themselves with the rules of worship and daily life and how to regulate and discipline individual and social life, while Sufis chose to provide a way to live at a high level of spirituality through self-purification and spiritual training, cannot be considered a disagreement.

In fact, Sufism and jurisprudence are like the two colleges of a university that seeks to teach its students the two dimensions of the Shari'a, enabling them to practice it in their daily lives. One college cannot survive without the other, for while one teaches how to pray, be ritually pure, fast, give charity, and how to regulate all aspects of daily life, the other concentrates on what these and other actions really mean, how one can make worship an inseparable part of one's existence, and how to elevate each individual to the rank of a universal, perfect being (*al-insan al-kamil*)—a true human being.[7] That is why neither discipline can be neglected.

---

[7]   This very famous Sufi term denotes an individual's final "spiritual" perfection, which causes him or her to have a universal "nature" that can represent the entire creation and reflect all that is best in it. (Trans.)

Although some self-proclaimed Sufis have labeled religious scholars as "scholars of ceremonies" and "exoterists", real, perfected Sufis have always depended on the basic principles of the Shari'a and have based their thoughts on the Qur'an and the Sunna. They have derived their methods from these basic sources of Islam. *Al-Wasaya wa'l-Ri'aya* (The Advices and Observation of Rules) by al-Muhasibi, *Al-Ta'arruf li-Madhhab Ahl al-Sufi* (A Description of the Way of the People of Sufism) by Kalabazi, *Al-Luma'* (The Gleams) by al-Tusi, *Qut al-Qulub* (The Food of Hearts) by Abu Talib al-Makki, and *Al-Risala al-Qushayri* (The Treatise) by al-Qushayri are among the precious sources that discuss Sufism according to the Qur'an and the Sunna. Some of these sources concentrate on self-control and self-purification, while others elaborate upon various topics of concern to Sufis.

After these great compilers came Hujjat al-Islam Imam al-Ghazzali, author of *Ihya' al-'Ulum al-Din* (Reviving the Religious Sciences), his most celebrated work. He reviewed all of Sufism's terms, principles, and rules, and, establishing those that were agreed upon by all Sufi masters and criticizing others, united the outer (Shari'a and jurisprudence) and inner (Sufi) dimensions of Islam. Sufi masters who came after him presented Sufism as one of the religious sciences or a dimension thereof, promoting unity or agreement among themselves and the so-called "scholars of ceremonies." In addition, the Sufi masters made several Sufi subjects, such as the states of the spirit, certainty or conviction, sincerity and morality, part of the curriculum of *madrassas* (institutes for the study of religious sciences).

Although Sufism mostly concentrates on the individual's inner world and deals with the meaning and effect of the religious commandments on one's spirit and heart, and is therefore abstract, it does not contradict any of the Islamic ways based on the Qur'an and the Sunna. In fact, as is the case with other religious sciences, its source is the Qur'an and the Sunna, as well as the conclusions drawn from the Qur'an and the Sunna via *ijtihad* (deduction) by the verifying scholars of the early period of Islam. It dwells on knowledge, knowledge of God, certainty, sincerity, perfect goodness, and other similar, fundamental virtues.

Defining Sufism as the "science of esoteric truths or mysteries," or the "science of humanity's spiritual states and stations," or the "science of initiation" does not mean that it is completely different from other religious sciences. Such definitions have resulted from the Shari'a-rooted experiences of various individuals, all of whom have had different characters and dispositions, and who lived at different times.

It is a distortion to present the viewpoints of Sufis and the thoughts and conclusions of Shari'a scholars as essentially different from each other. Although some Sufis were fanatic adherents of their own ways, and some religious scholars (i.e., legal scholars, Traditionists, and interpreters of the Qur'an) did restrict themselves to the outer dimension of religion, those who follow and represent the middle, straight path have always formed the majority. Therefore, it is wrong to conclude that there is a serious disagreement (which most likely began with some unbecoming thoughts and words uttered by some legal scholars and Sufis against each other) between the two groups.

When compared with those who speak for tolerance and consensus, those who have started or participated in such conflicts are very few indeed. This is natural, for both groups have always depended on the Qur'an and the Sunna, the two main sources of Islam.

In addition, the priorities of Sufism have never been different from those of jurisprudence. Both disciplines stress the importance of belief and of engaging in good deeds and good conduct. The only difference is that Sufis emphasize self-purification, deepening the meaning of good deeds and multiplying them, and attaining higher moral standards so that one's conscience can awaken to the knowledge of God and thus embark upon a path that leads to the required sincerity in living Islam and obtaining God's good pleasure.[8]

---

[8] The phrase "God's (good) pleasure" means that God has accepted the action of His servant. It does not reflect emotion, and therefore does not resemble human pleasure. (Trans.)

By means of these virtues, men and women can acquire another nature, "another heart" (a spiritual intellect within the heart), a deeper knowledge of God, and another "tongue" with which to mention God. All of these will help them to observe the Shari'a commandments based on a deeper awareness of, and with a disposition for, devotion to God.

An individual practitioner of Sufism can use this system to deepen his or her spirituality. Through the struggle with one's self, solitude or retreat, invocation, self-control and self-criticism, the veils covering the inner dimension of existence are torn away, enabling the individual to acquire a strong conviction concerning the truth of all of Islam's major and minor principles.

Sofi or Sufi

Sofi is used to designate the followers of Sufism, particularly by speakers of Persian and Turkish. Others use the term Sufi. I think the difference most likely arises from the different views of the word's origin. Those who claim that it is derived from the word *sof* (wool), *safa* (spiritual delight, exhilaration), *safwa* (purity), or *sophos* (a Greek word meaning wisdom), or who believe that it implies devotion, prefer Sufi. Those who hold that it is derived from *suffa* (chamber), and stress that it should not be confused with *sofu* (religious zealot), also use Sufi.

The word *sufi* has been defined in many ways, among them:

- A traveler on the way to God who has purified his or her self and thus acquired inner light or spiritual enlightenment.
- A humble soldier of God who has been chosen by the Almighty for Himself and thus freed from the influence of his or her carnal, evil-commanding self.
- A traveler on the way to the Muhammadan Truth who wears a coarse, woolen cloak as a sign of humility and nothingness, and who renounces the world as the source of vice and carnal desire. Following the example of the Prophets and their followers, as well as sincere devotees, they are called

mutasawwif to emphasize their spiritual states and belief, conduct, and life-style.

- A traveler to the peak of true humanity who has been freed from carnal turbidity and all kinds of human dirt to realize his or her essential, heavenly nature and identity.

- A spiritual person who tries to be like the people of the *Suf-fa*—the poor, scholarly Companions of the Prophet who lived in the chamber adjacent to the Prophet's Mosque— by dedicating his or her life to earning that name.

Some say that the word *sufi* is derived from *saf* (pure). Although their praiseworthy efforts to plase God by serving Him continually and keeping their hearts set on Him are enough for them to be called pure ones, such a derivation is grammatically incorrect. Some have argued that *sufi* is derived from *sophia* or *sophos*, Greek words meaning wisdom. I think this is a fabrication of foreign researchers who try to prove that Sufism has a foreign—and therefore non-Islamic—origin.

The first Muslim to be called a Sufi was the great ascetic Abu Hashim al-Kufi (d. 150 AH[9]). Thus, the word *sufi* was in use in the second Islamic century after the generation of the Companions and their blessed successors. At this point in time, Sufism was characterized by spiritual people seeking to follow the footsteps of our Prophet, upon him be peace and blessings, and his Companions by imitating their life-styles. This is why Sufism has always been known and remembered as the spiritual dimension of the Islamic way of life.

Sufism seeks to educate people so that they will set their hearts on God and burn with love for Him. It focuses on high morals and proper conduct, as shown by the Prophets. Although some slight deviations may have appeared in Sufism over time, these should not be used to condemn that way of spiritual purity.

---

[9] The Prophet's *hijra* (emigration to Madina) marks the beginning of the Muslim calendar. This event took place in July 16, 622 CE. As the Muslim calendar is lunar, it is shorter than its solar counterpart. (Trans.)

While describing Sufis who lead a purely spiritual life, Imam Qushayri writes:

> The greatest title in Islam is Companionship of the Prophet (pbuh). This honor or blessing is so great that it can only be acquired by an actual Companion of the Prophet. The second rank in greatness belongs to the Tabi'un, those fortunate ones who came after the Companions and saw them. This is followed by the Taba'i al-Tabi'in, those who came after the Tabi'un and saw them. Just after the closing years of this third generation and coinciding with the outbreak of internal conflict and deviation in belief, and along with the Traditionists, legal scholars, and theologians who rendered great services to Islam, Sufis had great success in reviving the spiritual aspect of Islam.

Early Sufis were distinguished, saintly people who led upright, honest, austere, simple and blemish-free lives. They did not seek bodily happiness or carnal gratification, and followed the example of the Prophet, upon him be peace and blessings. They were so balanced in their belief and thinking that they cannot be considered followers of ancient philosophers, Christian mystics, or Hindu holy men. Early Sufis considered Sufism as the science of humanity's inner world, the reality of things, and the mysteries of existence. A Sufi who studied this science was one determined to reach the final rank of a universal or perfect being.

Sufism is a long journey of unceasing effort leading to the Infinite One, a marathon to be run without stopping, with unyielding resolution, and without anticipating any worldly pleasure or reward. It has nothing to do with Western or Eastern mysticism, yoga, or philosophy, for a Sufi is a hero determined to reach the Infinite One, not a mystic, a yogi, or a philosopher.

Prior to Islam, some Hindu and Greek philosophers followed various ways leading to self-purification and struggled against their carnal desires and the attractions of the world. But Sufism is essentially different from these ways. For example, Sufis live their entire lives as a quest to purify their selves via invocation, regular worship, complete obedience to God, self-control, and humility, whereas ancient philosophers did not observe any of these rules or acts. Their self-purification—if it really deserves to be considered as such—was usually a source of creating conceit and arrogance in many of them, instead of humility and self-criticism.

Sufis can be divided into two categories: those who stress knowledge and seek to reach their destination through the knowledge of God (*ma'rifa*), and those who follow the path of yearning, spiritual ecstasy, and spiritual discovery.

Members of the first group spend their lives traveling toward God, progressing "in" and progressing "from" Him on the wings of knowledge and the knowledge of God. They seek to realize the meaning of: *There is no power and strength save with God*. Every change, alteration, transformation, and formation observed, and every event witnessed or experienced, is like a comprehensible message from the Holy Power and Will experienced in different tongues. Those in the second group also are serious in their journeying and asceticism. However, they may sometimes deviate from the main destination and fail to reach God Almighty, since they pursue hidden realities or truths, miracle-working, spiritual pleasure, and ecstasy. Although this path is grounded on the Qur'an and the Sunna, it may lead some initiates to cherish such desires and expectations as spiritual rank, the working of miracles, and sainthood. That is why the former path, which leads to the greatest sainthood under the guidance of the Qur'an, is safer.

Sufis divide people into three groups:

- *The perfect ones who have reached the destination.* This group is divided into two subgroups: the Prophets and the perfected ones who have reached the Truth by strictly following the prophetic examples. Not all perfected ones are guides; rather than guiding people to the Truth, some remain annihilated or drowned in the waves of the "ocean of meeting with God and amazement." As their relations with the visible, material world are completely severed, they cannot guide others.

- *The initiates.* This group also consists of two subgroups: those who completely renounce the world and, without considering the Hereafter, seek only God Almighty, and those who seek to enter Paradise, but do not give up tasting some of the world's permitted pleasures. Such people are known as ascetics, worshippers, the poor, or the helpless.

- *The settlers or clingers.* This group consists of people who only want to live an easy, comfortable life in this world. Thus, Sufis call them "settlers" or "clingers," for they "cling heavily to the earth." They are mainly people who do not believe, who indulge in sin and therefore cannot be pardoned. According to the Qur'an, they are unfortunate beings who belong to "the group on the left," or those who are "blind" and "deaf" and "without understanding."

Some have also referred to these three groups as the foremost (or those brought near to God), the people on the right, and the people on the left.[10]

---

[10] On the Day of Judgment, there will be two groups of people: those on the left side and those on the right side of God's Throne. The former did not believe in God and His Prophet, and led sinful lives. As they died without repenting, they will be judged worthy of entering Hell. The latter believed and sought to live according to the dictates and teachings of God, as revealed through His Prophets and Messengers. They repented and strove to obtain God's pleasure. They will be judged worthy of entering Paradise.

THE HEART AND SOME OF
ITS DYNAMICS

The heart is a spiritual resource with two aspects; through one it turns toward the world of spirits, through the other it connects with the world of physical bodies. If the body is under the command of the spirit according to all the rules of the Shari'a, then the heart carries into it the enlightening gifts it receives through the world of spirits, and causes breezes of peace and contentment to blow therein.

Just as the heart serves as an important bridge by which good and blessings reach a person, it can also be a means for all satanic and carnal impulses, temptations, and associations to occur in that person. As long as it is turned to the Truth, the heart functions as a source of light that radiates light to even the remotest, darkest corners of the person's inner world, but if it long remains oriented to the carnal appetites, the heart becomes the target of the poisonous arrows of Satan.

The heart is the seat of belief, worship, and perfect goodness or excellence (*ihsan*), and through it runs a mighty river flowing with radiance and inspirations that arise from relationships with God, humanity and the universe. But this extremely precious faculty has innumerable enemies that seek to dislodge it or divert it from its course. Among these are callousness (losing the ability to feel and believe), unbelief, conceit, arrogance, worldly ambition, greed, excessive lust, heedlessness, selfishness and attachment to rank and status—all these are on the alert to seek out the weak spots of the heart and to destroy it.

Belief is the life of the heart, worship is the blood that flows through its veins, and self-supervision and self-criticism are the foundations of its endurance. The heart of an unbeliever is dead; the heart of a believer who does not worship is in the throes of death; and the heart of a worshipping believer who does not reflect upon and control the self, nor face up to errors and sins, is exposed to all kinds of dangers and diseases. Although the first among these three classes of people have a "pump" in their chests, it cannot be said that they have a heart. Those belonging to the second class live in the cloudy or misty atmosphere of their surmises and doubts, they live imprisoned at a distance from God, without ever being able to reach their destination. As for the third class, although they have traversed some of the distance to the destination, they are at risk as they have not been able to reach the goal—they advance falteringly; defeat and success follow one upon another in their struggle on the way of God, and they spend their lives in a sisyphean attempt to reach the peak.

A sound heart is one of the means that leads a person right to God without deviation, and perfect goodness or excellence in worship (*ihsan*) is the greatest, most rewarding action of the heart. Excellence is the safest way to ascend the slopes of sincerity, the most secure means to reach the peaks of being approved by God, and the consciousness of self-possession before the Eternal Witness. Hundreds of thousands of people, equipped with belief and in deep fear and reverence of Him, have flown on the wings of good actions, have set out toward Him, but only a few have succeeded in reaching the peak. Let those who have not yet been able to reach it try their utmost to do so. The others who have been able to reach it, feel deeply the ugliness of whatever God dislikes and they close themselves off from this ugliness; at the same time they are willing to do what is pleasing to Him, to adopt that as their way until it has become a second nature for them.

RIYADA (AUSTERITY)

R*iyada* (austerity), which we can describe as disciplining life, appetite and thirst, and sleeping and waking only in order to develop the feelings of praise for and thankfulness to God and balancing these by keeping them within the limits of needs, has been used in the terminology of Sufis to mean the training of the carnal self and the acquiring of good, praiseworthy qualities. It has been accepted as a means of restraining the carnal desires, which include appetite, thirst and sleep, by resisting them.

From another perspective, austerity is described as holding back from carnal pleasures in order to acquire piety, righteousness, and nearness to God, and to discover the hidden realities of existence and the Divine truths. It combines the following of God's way without any deviation, making use of will power and conscience in the best way by taking refuge in the atmosphere of spiritual life against the pressures and excessive desires of the carnal self.

"State" and "station," regarded as crystal-like indicators of a person's spiritual life, are certain "pools" of indescribable spiritual pleasures mixed with the breezes from the worlds beyond that one can experience through austerity on the way to God. These are based on love of God and the attainment of His approval. Reaching these "pools" and feeling and living in the spacious world of the spirit within the love of God and His good pleasure is possible through austerity and through training the carnal self, and can be achieved by enhancing the spirit with virtues.

A person capable of sustaining an austere life is a person of tested faith or loyalty in relationships with the Creator, the Truth, and also in relationships with the created. This is the natural state for austerity—the ambition to become a person of truth by liberat-

ing oneself from worldly ambitions and carnal inclinations and becoming devoted to the Almighty Truth. Austerity is training the carnal self to realize true humanity and to make the love of God the
source of human feelings, thoughts and behavior. In other words,
the purpose of an austere life is to think for the sake of God, to
speak for the sake of God, to love for the sake of God, and to remain in the sphere of doing or not doing something only for the sake
of God, to obtain His approval and good pleasure—purely because
God wants us to do it or not to do it—and to always be with God.

Some see austerity as humiliating the carnal self, which we can
interpret as the annihilation of the evil-commanding self which always pursues evils, or as being freed from selfishness and self-con-
ceit or overcoming bodily desires in accordance with the maxim,
"Die before you die!" From this perspective, austerity can be regarded as plowing the carnal self, as one plows a field, in order to sow
the seeds of goodness and virtue, and bringing them into flower by
giving them the necessary water and heat in favorable weather.

The couplet,

> Be soil, such fertile soil, that roses can grow in you;
> For nothing other than soil can have the honor of growing roses.

describes this state of self which has acquired perfection, humility,
and self-annihilation.

Sufi scholars and thinkers have also taken another approach to
austerity. They distinguish two types of austerity. The first is "austerity in manners," which means being freed from weaknesses and
vices in order to acquire a second nature, while the other is "austerity in goals," which means having the best goal and pursuing it
in this world. This approach can also be summed up as disciplining
the carnal self and acquiring good, laudable virtues. The statement
found in the *Lujja*, "The wisdom in hurting the body is training the
reason and the soul" confirms this approach.

Some who have acquired austerity in the most approved manner have made another classification of austerity, as follows:

- The austerity followed by those who are at the beginning of the Sufi way to God consists of combining and adorning good morals or good nature with knowledge, and the practice of religion with sincerity and purity of intention, and to observe both the rights of the Creator and the rights of the created.

- The austerity followed by those who have advanced on the Sufi way to God is to become free of all considerations with respect to anything other than God and, by paying heed to the voice of the inner sense of reliance on God and of seeking help[1]—something that everyone feels in their conscience—to remain true to the direction to which their conscience points. Furthermore, this degree of austerity also demands being oblivious of even the way one is following, because of absorption in seeking God's good pleasure.

- The austerity followed by those who have reached the end of the way enables them to experience the Divine manifestations free from all differences and polarities. That is, it enables them to feel in the depths of their heart the unity and harmony of apparently opposed Divine Names and Attributes., with all their manifestations. It is, therefore, a way to see and experience God without seeing any difference between His being the All-Favoring and the All-Requiting or the All-Expanding and the All-Straitening or the All-Granting and the All-Preventing.

---

[1] Everyone has two important innate senses: Bediuzzaman Said Nursi, a famous Turkish scholar (d., 1960), describes them as the sense of reliance and the sense of seeking help. They can be viewed equally as two of humanity's essential needs. These verses urge or even compel one to find a point of reliance and a source of help, and therefore guide to God as the Infinite and All-Powerful One to rely upon, and as the All-Merciful and All-Helping to seek help from. (Trans.)

HURRIYA (FREEDOM)

The realization of every lawful desire without hindrance, freedom from any pressure, confinement, or subservience, the right to elect, to be elected, and to enjoy certain basic rights in political life—these are some of the definitions of "freedom," which has become one of the most widely concepts discussed in the recent history of thought and law.

The basic freedoms of humanity that range from personal rights to political and general ones—such as the freedom of belief, worship, thought, the freedom to have a family, to work, to own personal property, the right of freedom of expression and association, of electing, and being elected, etc.—are not among the subjects to be discussed in "Emerald Hills of the Heart." However, they have always been regarded as among the most important matters in human history.

Being the most fundamental and vital dimension and the most important human faculty, namely free-will, which is considered an important pillar of conscience, freedom (*hurriya*) is one of the most valuable gifts of God to humanity. This great gift has been defined in Islamic literature as an individual's assertion and enjoyment of his/her basic rights. However, in order to fully perceive freedom one must be able, to some extent, to perceive its opposite. This opposite is the individual's dependence on others for the enjoyment of those rights, which is a form of servanthood. It is God Almighty Who grants these rights to humanity, so a person has no right to change or sell them or transfer them to others. Those who commit such a sin, that is, change or sell their fundamental rights or transfer them to another, have lost their humanity to a certain extent and will be held accountable before God for that loss. Such an action shows, first of all, disrespect for human values, and those who commit such disrespect cannot be conscious of their existence, and those who are not conscious of one's existence have no relationship with the truth and no share in the love of and servanthood to God.

In short, it cannot be asserted that those who do not recognize God, Who is the Truth and the source of human rights, are free in the sense that they are conscious of human rights, nor can those who have not been able to free themselves from slavery to others than God be free in the real sense of the term.

What we have so far said about freedom is only by way of introduction to the freedom that is one of the emerald hills of the heart.

The freedom inherent in Islamic Sufism, being one of the most significant fruits of austerity, is that a person does not submit or bow to any power other than God, indicating thereby that the heart of that person has become a clear mirror receiving and reflecting the manifestations of God. The person who has reached this point on the way to God through austerity and by God's special help, severs inward relation with all things and beings other than God, and with emotions pulsing with freedom, heart beating joyfully with a yearning for freedom, and having broken all the restrictions around the selfhood, that person sets for him or herself this single goal and, in the philosophy of the respected saint Harith,[2] weaves the tissue of his or her thought with the threads of the hereafter.

True freedom is attainable only by freeing one's heart from worldly worries and anxieties about the things of this world, and so being able to turn to God with one's whole being. In order to express this reality, the leaders of the Sufi way say: "Child, undo the bonds of servanthood and be free; how much longer will you remain en-

---

[2] Abu 'Abdullah Harith al-Muhasibi (d. 858), was one of the leading Sufis. He was learned in the principal and derivative sciences, and his authority was rec-ognized by all the theologians of his day. He wrote a book, entitled *Ri'aya li-Hu-quqillah* ("The Observance of God's Rights") on the principles of Sufism, as well as many other works. In every branch of learning he was a man of lofty sen-timent and noble mind. He was the chief guide of Baghdad in his time. (Trans.)

slaved to gold and silver?" The answer of Junayd al-Baghdadi[3] to those who asked him what freedom was— "You can taste freedom when you are free from all bonds other than slavery to God"—also expresses the essence of freedom.

If freedom is directly proportional to sincere devotion and servanthood to God Almighty, and it is, then it is not possible to assert that those who live their lives under the direction of others are really free. In this respect, the following anonymous couplet speaks significantly:

> If you would like to beat the drum of honor,
> Go beyond the wheel of the stars;
> As this circle filled with rings is a drum of humiliation.

True freedom is necessary in order to be a perfect servant of God. The measure of a person's true freedom is servanthood to God. Those who cannot realize servanthood to God can neither be free nor attain human values in their full reach and meaning. Such people can never be saved from corporeality and sensuality so as to reach the achievable horizon of spiritual life with a "sound heart," nor can they feel the essence of human existence in the depths particular and special to it.

People who spend their life in the captivity of worldly considerations grow in arrogance in the face of the blessings granted to them. Instead of becoming more thankful to God, they attribute to themselves whatever achievement God has enabled them to realize, and are disappointed time after time when they fail, and shiver with the fear of losing whatever advantages they have accrued—such unfortunate people have no share in freedom, even if they are as kings in the world.

As long as the heart sets itself upon various goals, loved ones, and ambitions, it can never taste freedom. How can those be free who are constantly worrying about how to hold onto or pay back the

---

3   Junayd al-Baghdadi (d. 910): One of the most famous early Sufis. He enjoyed great respect and was known as "the prince of the knowers of God." (Trans.)

goods they expect from others, who have mortgaged most of their life's energy to others in return for worldly interests and bodily pleasures?

It is a great trial, one that leads to perdition if one wanders in the whirl of physical considerations and is confined to worldly aims with a heart attuned to worthless, fleeting objects. By contrast, it is a great favor from God upon those whose inner world He has sealed off from the many attributes of the ephemeral world that attract the carnal self; it is a great favor from God that He cuts away the relation of the heart with the world. For that relation is a form of bondage, and that cutting away is a bridge by which humanity is able to reach true freedom.

I'THAR (ALTRUISM)

I'thar (altruism), preferring others to oneself when doing a good deed, is, according to the moralists, giving precedence to the common interests of the community over one's own interests; according to Sufis, it is devoting oneself to the lives of others in complete forgetfulness of all concerns of one's own, it is self-annihilation in the interests of others.

The opposite of altruism is the stinginess and selfishness that arise from avarice and attachment to this world. Both stinginess and selfishness are regarded as reasons for becoming distanced from the Creator, the created, and Paradise.[4] While stinginess arises from avarice and attachment to the world, generosity, benevolence, and perfect goodness arise from altruism.

Generosity means that believers give some of their belongings to others without feeling any unease in the heart. Benevolence means considering one's own happiness as dependent on the happiness of others and, more than that, putting the welfare of others ahead of one's own happiness. As for perfect goodness or excellence (*ihsan*), it means preferring others, even when one is in need oneself. The Qur'an points to such excellence or the highest degree of altruism in this verse (59:9): *They feel in their hearts no displeasure because of whatever the others are given, but rather give them preference over themselves, even though poverty be their own lot.*

Altruism is valuable when one attains and follows it freely; it has no value if one is forced or if one performs such an act not out of one's own free will.

The generosity and benevolence that arise from and are dimensions of altruism have degrees, as follows:

---

4 *Sunan al-Tirmidhi*, "Birr," 40.

- Sacrificing one's soul in God's way (for God's cause), therefore for the sake of belief and for the good of the believers, is considered the highest degree of nobility.
- Being able, when it is necessary, to renounce a (rightful) claim to leadership or similar high position for the well-being and unity of society, is seen as altruism one step below the first degree.
- Preferring the (economic) welfare of others over one's own, is a third degree of nobility.
- Allowing others to benefit from one's knowledge and ideas without expecting anything in return, is a virtue not quite as noble as the previous ones.
- Giving to others out of one's income—this includes responsibilities for the giving of the prescribed and voluntary alms (*zakah* and *sadaqa*).
- Showing warmth, speaking soft and kind words, being of use to others, and being the means of various instances of good—these are examples of altruism that almost anyone can strive for in any situation.

The first of these degrees of generosity and benevolence is a profound and fundamental dimension of altruism that not everyone can achieve. Mawlana Jami',[5] the author of *Baharistan* ("The Land of Spring"), expresses it most memorably:

> It is easy to show generosity with gold and silver;
> Worthy of respect is he who shows generosity with his soul.

Among the characteristics and degrees of those who practice altruism are:

---

5   Mawlana Nur al-Din 'Abd al-Rahman ibn Ahmad al-Jami' (1414-1492), commonly called the last great classical poet of Persia, and saint, composed numerous lyrics and idylls, as well as many works in prose. His *Salaman and Absal* is an allegory of profane and sacred love. Some of his other works include *Haft Awrang, Tuhfat al-Ahrar, Layla wu Majnun, Fatihat al-Shabab, Lawa'ih, al-Durrah.* (Trans.)

- Offering food and feeding others at the cost of one's own hunger and thirst, and neglecting oneself in the provision of others. Provided that no one's rights are violated, this is a virtue characteristic of truly pious, saintly people.

- Despite all adversities, spending whatever one has as a favor from God in God's way and purely for His good pleasure, and in such a disinterested manner that one forgets what good one has done. This virtue is particular to those with considerable nearness to God, who take far greater pleasure in giving than receiving.

- Attributing to God exclusively all the accomplishments with which one is favored without seeing oneself as the agent of any good and, without expecting any return, even in the form of spiritual pleasures, for all that one does for God's sake, always fbeing aware of Him and experiencing oneself as the shadow of the light of His existence.

This last one is the attitude and practice of those nearest to God, including primarily the noblest of humankind and the greatest of all times and places, upon him be peace and blessings. His Ascension is a demonstration of his being accorded the highest honor and being sought after (by all the angels and many among human beings and jinn) as a reward for his incessant efforts for perfect knowledge of God. His return from the realms beyond the heavens to be among people in this world is such a great degree of altruism that nobody else has ever been able to achieve it. His emerging from Paradise and letting his profuse tears fall into the pits of Hell for the salvation of humankind expresses the greatest possible altruism.

> *O God! For the sake of your chosen Prophet, Muhammad, make us of those who do not begrudge what has been given to their brothers-in-religion, but prefer them to themselves, even though poverty be their lot, and may Your blessings and peace be on our master Muhammad and on His family and Companions.*

ADAB (MANNERLINESS)

Its meaning covers being sensible and reasonable, well- behaved, well-mannered, treating people kindly. *Adab* (mannerliness) is used in the terminology of Sufism to defend against errors and to distinguish the factors leading to errors. It is dealt with under the categories of "mannerliness in Shari'a," "mannerliness in serving God's cause," and "mannerliness before God, the Truth." Mannerliness in Shari'a is knowing the commandments of the religion and practicing them in daily life. Mannerliness in serving God's cause is being ahead of everyone in striving and making efforts but preferring others to oneself in obtaining the fruits, receiving the wages and being appreciated and rewarded for effort. It is also doing all the prerequisites for a desired result but attributing all good and comeliness and success to God. As for mannerliness before God, it consists in "refining" and "adorning" nearness to God, in collectedness and self-possession, avoiding excessive claims and reckless or casual speech or behaviour incompatible with the rules of Shari'a..

Another approach to mannerliness is dealing with it under the categories of "mannerliness in Sharia," "mannerliness in *tariqa* (the spiritual order)," "mannerliness in knowledge of God," and "mannerliness in attainment of truth." The first means practicing the Sunna (the way) of God's Messenger, upon him he peace and blessings, in all his acts, sayings, and approvals. The second means, together with utter submission to and perfect love of him, serving the spiritual guide, attending his discourses, and refraining from objection to him. The third consists in preserving the balance between nearness to God and self-possession, between fear and hope or expectation, and awareness of self-poverty and impotence in the lace of the Divine favours coming directly from God. As far the fourth, it is perfect attachment to God in complete detachment from ev-

erything other than Him, without any material or spiritual expectation and anxieties worldly or other-worldly.

In one respect, Sufism consists in "mannerliness;" it consists in
expressing the good manners proper to each occasion, each spiritual state, and each rank or station. However, only if believers have
been able to realize all of these good manners in their own inner
world, they can really be well-mannered in their attitudes and ways
of behaviour. Apparent and superficial manners, such as have not
been ingrained in their self and become an essential part of their nature, will mean no more than an outward show and cannot become
permanent as habits. Nor are they worth anything in the sight of
God, Who judges a person by his or her inner world. With his expressive style, Mawlana Jalal al-Din al-Rumi describes mannerliness
with its true and artificial aspects as follows:

> For the people of the heart,
> mannerliness originates in a person's inner world,
> For they are aware of secrets.
> As for the people of the flesh,
> They see mannerliness in the apparent behaviour of people;
> For God has hidden the secrets from them.
> We always ask God to enable us to be mannerly,
> Because one who is unmannerly is deprived of Divine favours.

According to Abu Nasr al-Tusi,[6] mannerliness could he summarized in the following three paragraphs.

- The mannerliness of literary men who seek beauty and virtue
  in writing and speech, which is regarded as "gossip" by the
  Sufis for it does not originate in the heart.

- The mannerliness of those who represent the religion of Islam at the level of a pure spiritual life, which is regarded as
  consisting in refining the selfhood through disciplines, and

---

[6] Sarraj, Abu Nasr 'Abdullah ibn 'Ali al-Tusi, (d. 959/60 or 988), was one of the famous Sufi scholars. His *al-Luma'* is a Sufi textbook written to prove the essential
conformity of Sufi claims within the framework of the Islamic creed. (Trans.)

the feelings through love and fear of God, and in meticulously following the religious commandments.

- The mannerliness of those who through continuous self-control and introspection maintain the purity of heart at the level of neither imagining or conceiving of anything contrary to the awareness of always being in the presence of God and overseen by Him.

Those who have been able to attain to the truth have attached much importance to all kinds of mannerliness and tried their hardest to make it an essential, ingrained part of their human nature. They have many wise sayings uttered in this respect, of which they have themselves striven to be the embodiments in utmost sincerity. To cite a few examples:

> Everything has an aspect of beauty and ornament,
> The beauty of people lies in mannerliness.
> There are those who, albeit of ignoble descent,
> Are most noble due to their mannerliness.

The following is a jewel-like saying quoted from Imam 'Ali, the cousin of the Prophet, upon him he peace and blessings:

> Nowadays misfortunes are common, which is not to be wondered at.
> What is to be wondered at is how one could remain upright
> and maintain one's integrity among so many misfortunes.
> Beauty is not that which the garment one wears adds to him.
> Rather, it is the beauty of knowledge and mannerliness.

The following is from *'Awarif al-Ma'arif* by Shihab al-Din al-Suhrawardi:[7]

> Belief requires absolute affirmation of Divine Unity, without which a person is not regarded as having a sound belief. This affirmation requires mannerliness without which one cannot be pious. Truly, one without good manners cannot be pious, for the

---

[7]   Shihab al-Din Abu Hafs 'Umar ibn 'Abdullah al-Suhrawardi (1145-1234) was a Sufi theologian. *'Awarif al-Ma'arif* is about the Sufi way. He also critized the philosophers following the ancient Greek Philosophy. (Trans.).

Prophets travelled their ways through mannerliness, and became each an elect in the Court of God.

In addition to what we have already said concerning the practical aspect of mannerliness or being well-mannered in behaviour, the following reflections are worth recalling:

It is mannerliness which a person should always wear:
Without good manners, one is as if naked.

....

Mannerliness is to be found in the people of knowledge.
A student without good manners cannot be a learned one.

....

The order of the world is through mannerliness;
Again, through mannerliness is human perfection.

Expressive of purity in thought, uprightness in the heart, and a deep relationship with God, mannerliness in speech has been stressed for centuries in all schools which concern themselves with moral and religious education or with spiritual training.

Wahbi says:

Do not open your mouth for idle talk,
be well-mannered in your speech.
Take care of what you may say so that afterwards
you do not become uneasy.

Another voices his thought about mannerliness as follows:

Mannerliness is a crown from the light of God:
Wear that crown and be safe from every misfortune.

The words of Mawlana Jalal al-Din al-Rumi in praise of mannerliness are beyond compare:

Know that the soul in a person's body is mannerliness; the light of a person's heart and eyes is mannerliness. Adam is from an elevated world, not from a low one. This dome (meaning the world) rotates on the axis of mannerliness, which is also its beauty and adornment. If you prepare your food on the head of Satan, know that it is mannerliness which will kill Satan. One who is deprived of good manners is not truly human, for the difference between humans and animals lies in mannerliness. Open your eyes and see that the Qur'an, the Word of God, consists in mannerliness. I asked the intellect what belief was. It whispered to the ear of the heart that it was mannerliness.

Mannerliness with respect to good morals described as words and behaviour approved by Islam, and as expressed in the words, actions, and acts of approval of the Holy Prophet, upon him he peace and blessings, is beyond the scope of the present answer.

O God! Lead us to what You like and approve of.

May God's blessings be on our master Muhammad and all of his family and his Companions.

'ILM (KNOWLEDGE)

'*Ilm* (knowledge) means information obtained through the human senses or through the Revelations or inspiration of God. It is also used to denote information that is in agreement with facts or realities, and to denote understanding something with its real, whole meaning and content. In addition, we come across usage of this term in the simple sense of thinking, understanding, comprehension, and conclusions drawn as a result of such mental processes. Sometimes the word knowledge can even mean familiarity.

Although it is well known which aspect of the term knowledge in Islamic Sufism is most relevant in the context of this book, we deem it useful to mention some secondary matters, such as the different types of knowledge and its sources.

Knowledge, first of all, is dealt with in two categories: knowledge without means or knowledge that is had without being acquired, and knowledge that is acquired through some means.

Every living being has its own peculiar characteristics and potentials. These characteristics and potentials are the sources of certain, innate knowledge, knowledge a creature has without having to acquire it. (The modern scientific term for this kind of knowledge is instinct.) A human being's being able to sense and perceive a lack of air, thirst, hunger, grief and joy, etc., a baby's knowledge of how to nurse, a bird's knowledge of how to fly and build nests, a fish's knowledge of how to swim, young animals' knowledge of how to avoid dangers, in short, these types of knowledge, knowledge of how to deal with the necessities of life, fall into the category of knowledge without means.

Knowledge acquired through the internal and external senses is included in the second category. Knowledge concerning the physical world is usually obtained through the five external senses—sight, hearing, smell, taste, and touch—while knowledge about the metaphysical or incorporeal realm of existence is acquired through internal senses—the mind and heart with their faculties of thought, reason, spiritual discovery and experience, intuition, etc.

As for the sources of knowledge or means of acquiring it, these consist of three, according to Islam:

- The five external senses, provided they are sound.
- True reports, of which there are two kinds: reports unanimously given by a group of truthful people of such a number that it is inconceivable that they have agreed to lie, and reports given by the Messengers of God, whom He has sent with special messages.
- The third source of knowledge is reason. Axiomatic knowledge and the knowledge reached by using the mental faculties are included in this kind of knowledge.

Knowledge is also divided into two groups: that which is acquired through the mental faculties, and that which is reported knowledge. The first can be divided up into three categories:

- Knowledge of such matters as health and education, which in Islam are regarded as incumbent upon every individual or a group of people in the community, according to the time and conditions.
- Another kind of knowledge acquired through the mental faculties is knowledge of which Islam disapproves. Sorcery, divination and occult sciences are of this kind.
- Sciences, such as geometry, mathematics, medicine, physics, chemistry, and history are included in the third category, the study of which Islam regards as obligatory on the community in order to discover God's laws of the creation and operation of the universe and for the well-being of the community.

Reported knowledge is of two kinds: knowledge based on spiritual discovery and inspiration and knowledge concerning Islam and Islamic life. The second kind has been separated under four heads:

- The knowledge of the fundamental principles, which include knowledge of the Qur'an, Sunna (the Prophet's way of life, sayings, and confirmations), the consensus of the scholars (*ijma'*) and analogy or deductive reasoning. These are the sources upon which the rules of the Shari'a are based.

- The knowledge of the subdivisions, which includes the knowledge of worship (the Prescribed Prayer, the Prescribed Alms-giving, Fasting, Pilgrimage and so on), the daily life of the believers, marriage and relevant matters, such as divorce and alimony (civil law), and legal penalties (criminal law), etc.

- Primary sciences, such as language, grammar, meaning, composition, and eloquence, which are ways to properly understand the religious sciences, such as Hadith (the sayings of the Prophet), the interpretation of the Qur'an, and jurisprudence.

- The complementary or secondary sciences, i.e. the sciences additional to the sciences of the Qur'an. They consist of sciences relating to the wording and composition of the Qur'an, such as phonetics and recitation; the sciences pertaining to its meaning, such as interpretation and exegesis, and those relating to its commandments, such as the abrogating and the abrogated, the general and particular, the explicit and implicit, the real or literal and the metaphorical or allusive, the succinct and the detailed, the clear and the ambiguous, the direct and firm and the allegorical.

As for reported knowledge based on spiritual discovery and inspiration, it has also been dealt with under two heads: the knowledge that occurs in one's heart as a gift from God, and the knowledge that arises in the conscience. What we will study among the topics of the "Emerald Hills of the Heart" is this kind of knowledge. Whether it is of the kind occurring in one's heart as a gift from God or of the kind arising in the conscience, this knowledge is and must be based on the Qur'an and the Sunna. Any knowledge one finds in one's heart or conscience which has not been filtered through these two pure sources is not reliable. It cannot be binding knowledge for either the individuals themselves or others, it cannot be considered as authentic, sound knowledge. This important point has been stressed by many great Sufi leaders. For example:

Junayd al-Baghdadi says: "All the ways that do not end in the Prophet are closed and do not lead to the truth." He also reminds us: "Anyone who does not know the Book and the Sunna is not to be followed as a guide."

Abu Hafs[8] explains: "Anyone who does not continually control him or herself in the light of the Book and the Sunna cannot be regarded as belonging to this way."

Abu Sulayman al-Darani[9] warns: "I admit the truth of what-ever occurs to the heart only provided it is confirmed by the Book and the Sunna."

Abu Yazid al-Bistami[10] admonishes: "I struggled against my carnal self for almost thirty years and did not find anything more difficult for it to accept than the objective criteria of the Book and the Sunna. You should not be misled by anyone, even if they work wonders like flying through the air, rather you should consider their care

---

[8] Abu Hafs 'Amr b. Salama al-Haddad of Nishabur (d. 879). A blacksmith of Nishabur, visited Baghdad and met al-Junayd who admired his devotion. He also encountered al-Shibli and other Sufis of the Baghdad school. Returning to Nishapur, he resumed his trade and died there in 879. (Trans.)

[9] Abu Sulayman al-Darani (d. 830). An ascetic known for his weeping in worship. He was held in honour by the Sufis and was (called) the sweet basil of hearts (rayhan-i dilha). He is distinguished by his severe austerities. He spoke in subtle terms concerning the practice of devotion. (Trans.)

[10] Abu Yazid al-Bistami (d. 873): One of the greatest Sufi masters. Junayd said: "Abu Yazid holds the same rank among us as Gabriel among the angels." His life was based on self-mortification and the practice of devotion. (Trans.)

in observing the limits set up by the Shari'a and following the commandments of the Book and the Sunna."

Abu Sa'id al-Kharraz[11] sums up the matter: "Any intuitive knowledge which is not compatible with the spirit of religion is false."

Abu al-Qasim Nasrabadi[12] teaches: "The essence of the Sufi way is strict adherence to the Book and the Sunna, holding back from the misleading inclinations of the carnal self and innovations in religion, being able to overlook the faults of others, not becoming negligent in one's daily recitations to glorify and praise the Almighty, being strict in fulfilling the religious commandments without applying special exceptions, and refraining from personal, insubstantial opinions regarding religion."

The Sufi leaders give knowledge precedence over the spiritual state of the Sufis, because that state depends on knowledge. Knowledge is the heritage of the Prophets, and the scholars are the heirs thereto. The Prophetic saying, "The scholars are the heirs of the Prophets,"[13] is the highest of the ranks recognized for scholars.

The knowledge of the truth or knowledge that leads to the truth is the life of the heart, the light of the eye, the cause of the expansion of the breast (with peace, exhilaration, and spiritual happiness), the stimulus to activate reason, the source of pleasure for the spirit, the guide of those bewildered as to which way to follow, the intimate friend of the lonely, and an invaluable table of heavenly foods offered on the earth and one to which the angels show great respect.

Knowledge is an important step toward belief, a standard to distinguish between guidance and error and between certainty and doubt, and a Divine mystery manifesting the truly human aspects of a person.

---

[11] Abu Sa'id Ahmad ibn 'Isa al-Kharraz of Baghdad, a cobbler by trade, met Dhu al-Nun al-Misri and associated with Bishr al-Khafi and Sari al-Saqati. Author of several books including some which have survived, the date of his death is uncertain but probably occurred between 892 and 899. (Trans.)

[12] Abu al-Qasim Ibrahim ibn Muhammad ibn Mahmud al-Nasrabadi: One of the famous Sufi masters and scholars. (Trans.)

[13] Al-Bukhari, *al-Jami' al-Sahih*, "'Ilm," 10.

There is no exaggeration in the following saying of a friend of God:

> A human being is truly human with knowledge;
> But without knowledge is entirely bestial.
> Action without knowledge is purely ignorance;
> So, O friend, you cannot find the Truth without knowledge.

By knowledge, the Sufis mean, rather than the familiarity that is reached with the mind, hearing and sight, the light and radiation that come from the realms beyond the material world and have their source in God's Knowledge. This light pervades the spirit and bursts like flowers in the meadows of the innermost faculties of the person, and swells and flows in the gifts of the All-Eternal One. In order to be able to receive this Divine gift, one should, first of all, turn with all one's inner world to the Eternal Sun and, freed from the influences of the body and carnal pleasures, lead a life at the level of heart and spirit, and open one's breast to God, the Truth, with belief, love, and attraction, and then one should be able to rise to a level where one can be taught by God through inspiration.

As declared in the Divine declaration (18:65), *We taught him knowledge of a special kind from Our Presence*, God-inspired knowledge is the rain of mercy that pours down into the depths of a person's inner world from the Realm of the Holy Presence—the Realm where those who are the nearest to God experience His Holy Presence—without any intermediary and veils. Deep devotion to God, sincere adherence and loyalty to Him as well as the Messenger, being sincerely well-pleased with whatever God decrees or causes to happen for one and trying to please Him, the sincerity and purity of intention in one's acts or doing whatever one does only to please Him and because He wants us to do it, and having a heart pursuing certainty in the matters of belief over and over again—all this is what is required to be rewarded with God-inspired knowledge, especially in abundance.

Since the Prophets received Divine Revelation and were taught by Him, their knowledge is a God-inspired knowledge that comes from Him without any intermediary. As for the knowledge of purified, saintly scholars and other saintly persons, this is also a God-inspired knowledge, the only difference being that the source is the rays of light of the Prophetic knowledge. Khadr[14] is regarded as the foremost one in receiving this knowledge. However, he can only be so regarded for a certain period of time and spiritual rank and for the state particular to him. In certain particular matters, some people may be superior to those who are superior to them in general terms. Similarly, in certain particularities of God-inspired knowledge, Khadr is superior to those who are greater than him. He is in no way superior to either the Prophet Moses, upon him be peace,[15] or the other great Messengers.

As a Messenger charged with teaching people God's commandments and guiding them in their lives so that they could attain happiness in both worlds, the Prophet Moses knew God's commandments concerning the human individual and social life and the sensitive relation between them and the outward and inward aspects or dimensions of things. But, Khadr's knowledge is restricted to the inward dimension of things. He points to this difference in his conversation with Moses: "Moses! I have a kind of knowledge which God has taught me and you do not possess, while you have another kind of knowledge which God has taught you and I do not possess."[16]

In conclusion, God-inspired knowledge is the kind of knowledge which one cannot acquire by studying or being taught by others. It is a special gift from God and a kind of illumination, from a

---

[14] Khadr is he with whom the Qur'an recounts (18: 60-82) the Prophet Moses made a travel to learn something of the spiritual realm of existence and the nature of God's acts in it. It is controversial whether he was a Prophet or a saint with special mission. It is believed that he enjoys the degree of life where one feels no need for the necessities of normal human life. (Trans.)

[15] The writer refers to the significant encounter and experience between Moses and Khadr that is recounted in the Qur'an, 18:60-82. (Trans.)

[16] Al-Bukhari, "Tafsir," 18:4.

sacred source, that one finds in one's heart. Rather than being the kind of knowledge about the Creator acquired by studying creation and which therefore leads from the created to the Creator, it is a kind that pours from the Maker to the conscious "works" of His art. It is even regarded as the emergence in the human spirit of the knowledge about some mysteries pertaining to God, the Truth, as special gifts from Him.

Anyway, it is always God Who knows best the truth in every matter.

HIKMA (WISDOM)

Hikma (wisdom), meaning knowledge, the understanding of Divine commandments, philosophy, the real reasons for the existence of events and of things, and grasping the goals and benefits in religion, has been interpreted by the exacting scholars of truth as being able to combine useful knowledge and righteous deeds in life. Righteous deeds are the willed outcome of knowledge applied, and the beginning of new Divine gifts.

Starting from the perspective of the description above, some scholars deal with wisdom in two categories, namely practical and theoretical, as they have done with reason. Theoretical wisdom is the effort that one makes along with a God-given ability to observe things and events as if they were an exhibition. It is also an attempt to penetrate the meaning behind and purpose for such events in order to study and read them like a book, to listen to them like a symphony, and to study and try to understand the mysterious relationship between the physical and metaphysical realms of existence.

As for practical wisdom, it is worshipping to discover and turning to the Owner of this exhibition, the Author of this book, the Composer of this symphony, running to Him in love and yearning, and deeply experiencing the awe and amazement of being in His Presence. So, to sum up, wisdom begins with reflection, curiosity, wonder, and the zeal to study and search, and continues with obedience and worship, ending in spiritual pleasures and eternal happiness.

Studying the Qur'anic verses where wisdom is mentioned, we can add to the above explanation the following points:

- Wisdom means the subtleties and mysteries of the Qur'an. Since the Qur'an is, in one respect, the correlative of the book of the universe and, in another, its interpretation and explanation, its subtleties and mysteries are also those of the book of the universe. The Qur'an indicates this in this verse (2:269): *He grants the wisdom to whomever He wills, and whoever is granted the wisdom, has indeed been granted much good.*

- Wisdom means Prophethood and the meaning of Messengership. The scholars of the Hadith have interpreted it as Sunna (the way of the Messenger). The verses, *God granted him (David) kingdom and wisdom* (2:251), and *We granted Luqman wisdom* (31:12), refer to this meaning.

- Wisdom, in both its theoretical and practical aspects, means goodwill, which is mentioned in: *Call to the way of your Lord with wisdom and fair exhortation and preaching* (16:125).

Some have defined wisdom as correct judgment, and acting as one should act and doing what is necessary to do at the right time and right place. We can elaborate on this meaning, which can be re-stated as being just, moderate, balanced, and straightforward as follows:

- Giving everything its due, or right judgment, without going to extremes, viewing and discharging our responsibilities in the framework of the Shari'a, fulfilling the necessary conditions and prerequisites for any desired result, avoiding extremes, even when doing good deeds, being careful to maintain the fact that religion can be practiced or lived under all circumstances, and leading a life in accordance with the Sunna of the Prophet.

- Always preferring God's decisions and judgments concerning us over our own choices, and leading our lives according to the rule, *Submit to God and be saved,*[17] i.e. being resigned to all of God's decrees and acts concerning our lives and nature, without ever forgetting that God has wisdom in whatever He does, and does nothing in vain.

---

[17] Al-Bukhari, "Bad'u'l-Wahy," 6.

- Being steadfast in following the Messenger strictly in our thoughts and actions in full perception of his way, and as stated in the verse (12:108), *Say: "This is my way: I call to God based on conscious insight and sure knowledge—I and those who follow me,"* serving our religion and humanity in his way with conscious insight and sure knowledge.

The principal sources of wisdom are Divine Revelation and inspiration.[18] This means that all the Prophets and all the spiritual guides, each according to his rank, are also sages or wise people whose special property is wisdom. Such people apply spiritual therapy to those diseased in mind and spirit (those who have followed wrong ways in thought and belief and who suffer from spiritual discontentment), and, by God's leave, cure them, trying to keep their spiritual lives cleansed of the viruses brought on by evil nature and sin.

In view of the missions (special tasks and occupations) of the Prophets and saints, we can add to the definition of wisdom the following:

- Wisdom is unity of thought, intention, and action. Right thinking, precision in expression, and acting in the right way are true signs of wisdom.
- Certainty in knowledge, soundness in action, and perfection in any performance, which we can paraphrase as supporting knowledge with action or practice, and doing any work of art with efficiency, which adds to the artist's zeal and ability, also demonstrate wisdom.
- Grasping the aims of religion and, in addition to representing it in individual life, trying to make it prevail in life or ordering life accordingly, is a dimension of wisdom.
- Perceiving the essence of existence together with its inner truth, as well as the peculiarities of each thing together with its relationship with all other things, and the Creator's pur-

---

[18] Revelation means God's special speech to the Prophets and mainly includes the Divine Scriptures, while inspiration is His putting guiding and uplifting thoughts, ideas and purposes into the hearts of saintly persons. (Trans.)

poses for the existence and life of things, is another, important dimension of wisdom.

- Approaching things in order to understand and analyze their uses and the benefits expected of them, and, as a vicegerent of God, to use them within the limits He has set, is an aspect of wisdom relating to art.

- Seeing everything in the light of the Divine way, which is responsible for the perfect accord, order, and balance in the universe, where everything is in its exact place, the observation of this same order and the balance in our lives, and the development of sciences that study the earth and the sky to maintain the balance in them, is another approach to wisdom.

- Pursuing the best goals in life, trying to make prevail what is good and preferable in the relationships between the rulers and the ruled, and, by adopting God's way of conduct and treatment of His servants in our individual and social life, making heavenly the systems of government on earth, realizing God's purposes for sending the Prophets, are other, excellent dimensions of wisdom.

In order to distinguish between reasoning and logic that are guided by the All-Merciful One, and those guided by the suggestions and misleading of Satan, one should submit one's intellect to the guidance of God's Messenger, upon him be peace and blessings, and always be on the alert. It is only by so doing that one can feel the Divine gifts of correct judgment, sound reasoning, and wise thinking appear within oneself; thereafter one begins to feel and think correctly and is saved from self- contradiction in one's behavior. In the end, wise, right thinking and behavior become second nature—this means the adoption of the Divine way of conduct. We can also describe this as the transformation of theoretical reason into practical reason, and theoretical wisdom into practical, or, according to some Sufi leaders, the angelic aspects of a human being surpassing their satanic ones.

Knowledge, combined with action is an important dimension of wisdom. Although action is not a part of belief or, in other words, neglecting to practice religion in daily life is not a sign of unbelief, it is certain that action is an important aspect of religion. Putting knowledge into practice or practicing the religious commandments in daily life after learning them is an essential of Islam. The verse (51:56), *I have not created the jinn and humankind but only to worship Me*, warns us of this. Mere information without action will not help. As pointed out before, existence is a book or an exhibition of wisdom, with the Qur'an being its voice or translator or description. What falls on humanity is to read and study the book of creation in the Qur'an. Those who are able to do so are, in the words of the Qur'an, rewarded with abundant good, and gain great value in proportion to the depth of their inner world and the sharpness of their faculties. Contrarily, those who see the realities on the face of existence but cannot discern the truths lying behind it and the purpose for it alongside the magnificent order it displays, are doomed to not receive its messages. This is manifestly a loss or failure.

> *O God! Show us the truth as the truth and enable us to live by it, and show us falsehood as falsehood and enable us to avoid it.*

FIRASA (DISCERNMENT)

F*irasa* (discernment) can be defined as profundity, productivity and coherence in thought and the forming of opinions, the ability to penetrate the meaning of existence, and acting on conscious insight. It is a light that God puts into a person when they have purified their heart of spiritual ailments such as vengeance, hatred, resentment, hypocrisy, and conceit and a light that adorns one with belief, knowledge and love of God, and zeal to serve His cause. Those who are favored with discernment become unique among people: their feelings and perceptions are deepened, they gain familiarity with the mysteries that others cherish in their hearts, and they can see the truths inscribed on their faces. In proportion to their discerning the truths and meanings that lie behind things, they can become a polished mirror in which the One Who has full knowledge of all that is beyond the reach of human perception manifests and reflects Himself. Pointing to such a degree of discernment, the master of creatures, the articulate voice of the visible and invisible worlds, upon him be peace and blessings, said: *Beware of the discernment of a believer, for he looks with the light of God.*[19] The close relationship between discernment and the light of belief is also expressed in the Qur'anic verse (8:29), *If you keep from disobedience to God in piety and reverence for Him to deserve His protection, He will make a criterion arise in your heart to distinguish between truth and falsehood, and right and wrong.*

However we approach the topic of discernment—whether from the viewpoint that it indicates that the heart is open to the knowledge and inspirations of the One Who has full knowledge of all that is beyond the reach of human senses and perception and that those

---

[19]   Al-Tirmidhi, "Tafsir al-Qur'an," (15) 6.

favored with it are usually right in their thinking, opinions, decisions and judgments, or from the viewpoint that discernment is the true conclusions that we draw based on our information, experiences, practices, the depth of our perception, and ability to read charac- ter—discernment is purely a gift of God. Those who have the great- est share in this gift are, each according to rank and capacity, the Prophets, saintly scholars, and saints. The one who is the first and foremost of all is the master of the Prophets, and the embodiment of the First Intellect.[20] While God refers to all people of discern- ment and high perception in the words (15:75), *Surely in this are manifest signs (of truth) for the people of discernment and acumen*, in the verse (47:30), *If We willed (that they should be known,) We would surely show them to you and you would surely know them by their faces and you would surely know them by the style of their speech*, He partic- ularly alludes to the superiority of the one who is the highest in dis- cernment.

Discernment gets sharper and stronger in proportion to the depth of belief and the greatness of certainty. Sometimes it even ris- es to such a degree that by virtue of certain special gifts from God, one can see with God's sight. The observations of some important Sufi leaders and their comments on discernment point to this fact.

Abu Sa'id al-Harraz says: "If you say that one looks with the light of discernment, it means that one looks with the sight of God."

Wasiti[21] comments: "Discernment is a God-given ray of light which appears in the heart like lightning and illuminates the incor- poreal worlds visible to some in certain circumstances, and causes one to rise to the rank of being able to see the whole existence as it is."

Darani defines discernment: "Discernment means discovering the depths of the human self and that the invisible worlds become visible and secrets obvious."

---

[20] The First Intellect is the archetypal being who receives the gifts of God first of all and then transfers them to others. (Trans.)

[21] Abu Bakr Muhammed ibn Musa al-Wasiti (d. 932). A Sufi who associated with al-Junayd and al-Nuri in Baghdad and who later moved to Merv where he died. He was also an authority on *fiqh*. (Trans.)

Shah Kirmani[22] reminds: "If a person blinds him or herself to religiously forbidden things, holds back from the influence of carnal desires and provocations, improves his or her inner world with self-supervision and outer world with adherence to the Sunna, and is able to always keep within the limits of the religiously lawful, he or she is always infallible in discernment."

All those aspects of discernment develop through belief and do not lead one who is favored with them to err. What reason is there for them to err while it is He Who causes one to see and the eyes that see are from Him?

As it was due to God's gift of discernment to His Messenger that he was able to know people very well and to employ every-one in a suitable position, it was also the same Divine gift which we are able to observe in many of the wonderful summations, evaluations, decisions, and judgments of Abu Bakr, 'Umar, 'Uthman, and 'Ali.[23] It would take many volumes to explain their discernment.

In addition, there are wise purposes for the creation of reason and spirit. So, God may favor some spiritually ordinary people with instances of discernment, either because of the value He attaches to the reason and spirit that He has granted to humanity, or as a reward in advance for the good things that they will do in the future. Such instances of wisdom may be regarded as a special gift from the Creator of causes, granted before these people have deserved them. Now, based on 'Abdullah ibn Mas'ud's[24] exposition, let us mention some examples:

- The vizier who bought Joseph to Egypt said of him to his wife: "Give him honorable, goodly lodging. It may be that

---

[22] Sayyid Ahmad Shah Kirmani was a Sufi syahkh who followed the way of Shihab al-Din al-Suhrawardi. He lived in Kashmir in the 16th century. (Trans.)

[23] Abu Bakr, 'Umar, 'Uthman, and 'Ali were the four foremost among the Companions of God's Messenger (Muhammad) and his first four successors called "The Rightly Guided Caliphs." (Trans.)

[24] 'Abdullah ibn Mas'ud was one of the early Muslims who was well-versed in the Qur'an and Islamic sciences. He was also very close to the Messenger. He died during the Caliphate of 'Uthman. (Trans.)

he will prove useful to us or we may adopt him as a son."
(12:21)

- One of Prophet Shu'ayb's daughters said to her father concerning Moses: "O father! Hire him! For the best man that you can hire is that strong, trustworthy one." (28:26)

- The wife of the Pharaoh expressed to him her opinion about Moses, whom they found in the river: "He will be a consolation for me and for you. Kill him not. He may be of use to us, or we may choose him for a son." (28:9)

There is another kind of discernment which is obtained through austerity. If that discernment is not based on accurate belief and righteous deeds, it can be a means of gradual perdition for the one who possesses it. Whether the one who has it is a believer or unbeliever, a Muslim or a Christian, or a saint or layman, everyone can achieve certain (spiritual) discoveries or wonders through austerity.

Some regard reading someone's character from their physical traits as another kind of discernment, and this kind has been included among the concepts in the practice of Islamic Sufism. However, it obviously has nothing to do with the discernment that we are dealing with here.

> *O God! Guide my carnal self to the piety necessary for it, and purify it. You are the best to purify it, and You are its guardian and master.*
>
> *May Your blessings and peace be on our master Muhammad and on His family and Companions.*

WAJD AND TAWAJUD
(ECSTASY AND WILLFUL RAPTURE)

W*ajd* (ecstasy) is overflowing with spiritual joy and enthusiasm, and rather than using reason, logic, or will, one follows the spiritual state in which one is. It consists of God's surprising visit to the heart of one of His servants with special favor. When this favor originates in God's Grace, breezes of nearness to Him begin to blow; when it originates in His Majesty,[25] self-possession accompanied by sorrow, fear, and awe, appear.

Some have explained ecstasy as the spirit's being unable to bear the turmoil caused by love during reflection on God, invocations to Him, and recitations of His Names. It has also been interpreted as being the amazement, excitement, and trembling that the heart undergoes when it receives special favors from God that originate in His Grace and Majesty.

Although derived from the same root word, *wajd* (ecstasy) and *wujud* (finding) are different from one another. While finding, as will be explained later, means passing beyond the sphere of the influence of the carnal self and the limits of corporeality and finding the Desired One as He is, free from all qualitative and quantitative considerations and restrictions, ecstasy is the overflowing of the heart with feelings of love, yearning, zeal, respect, and exaltation. Ecstasy is a surprising and unexpected emotion. The next step is the state of being

---

[25] The Attributes of God can be understood as, broadly, of two kinds, with two kinds of manifestations. One kind are the Attributes of Grace—such as Mercy, Compassion, Love, Forgiving, etc. The other kind are Attributes of Majesty— such as being overwhelming, compelling, punishing, etc. (Trans.)

in constant ecstasy as the fruit of a continuous recitation of God's Names and His praise, glorification, and exaltation.

Ecstasy generally manifests itself in two ways:

- Some Divine gifts and manifestations of His Glory emerge in the heart, without the person's willing or intending it. We also call this "disclosure" (*mukashafa*), which cannot be related to any cause originating in human beings them-selves.
- Ecstasy manifests itself also in the form of spiritual pleasures and zeal, or amazement and astonishment. These feelings pervade the whole being and arouse in the person feelings of awe, tearfulness, and crying. This kind of ecstasy is mainly witnessed in circles where people recite God's Names together. These feelings arise unintentionally in the hearts of people. Enraptured by the sounds of the hammer used by Zarkubi in Konya, Mawlana Jalal al-Din al-Rumi[26] said:

> The souls that have clung to water and clay,
> Are pleased on being freed from them,
> And begin to dance in the air and breezes of love,
> Becoming perfected like the full moon.

If ecstasy appears as the result of willful concentration and by being forced, it is called willful rapture (*tawajud*). This can be seen in initiates, especially at the beginning of the way. Our master, upon him be peace and blessings, advises: "Weep when you are reciting the Qur'an. If you cannot, force yourself to."[27]

If we add willful rapture and the finding (*wujud*) to the two kinds of ecstasy mentioned above, we can divide the subject into four titles:

- Willful rapture resembles ecstasy, the difference being that it emerges as a result of forcing the self and spiritual con-

---

[26] Jalal al-Din al-Rumi (1207-1273): One of the most famous Sufi masters of the Islamic history; founder of the Mawlawi Order of the whirling dervishes, famous for his *Mathnawi*, an epic of the religious life in six volumes. (Trans.)

[27] *Sunan Ibn Maja*, "'Iqama al-Salah," 9.

centration. It is witnessed in initiates who are still on the way and is the lowest degree of the actions of the heart.

- Ecstasy is the unexpected overflowing of a heart which has been equipped with belief, knowledge and love of God, and with spiritual pleasures, with yearning, zeal, spiritual joy and the Divine gifts. It is the main topic being discussed here, and is the state which is based on the hadith: "There are three things which show that one who has them has tasted the pleasure of belief: loving God and His Messenger more than anything else, loving for God's sake, and being careful with the things that lead to Paradise and Hell."[28]

- Constant ecstasy is the state in which the heart is favored with a continuous spiritual tension, with spiritual experiences, and varying, uninterrupted Divine gifts by virtue of the depth of its relationship with the Necessarily Existent Being and the Giver of Life, and the heart's committed search for the ways of nearness to Him. The verse (18:14), *We made firm their hearts and they rose, proclaiming: "Our Lord is the Lord of the heavens and the earth. We will never call anyone apart from Him God!"* expresses this sort of love and excitement.

- Finding is the highest point of excellence; it is mentioned in a Prophetic Tradition as worshipping God as if one were seeing Him,[29] and the effusive feelings of excitement and astonishment result from being favored with the burning manifestations of Divine Existence.

In itself, ecstasy has also degrees:

- The lowest degree is that which arises from reflection on God's signs and using the other senses and faculties to have a sound and deep relationship with God. A heart with this

---

[28] Al-Bukhari, "Iman," 9; Al-Muslim, *al-Jami' al-Sahih*, "Iman," 67.

[29] The hadith is: "*Ihsan* (Perfect goodness or excellence) is that you worship as if seeing God. Even if you do not see Him, He certainly sees you." The hadith mentions two degrees of excellence: worshipping God as if seeing Him, which is the greater one, and worshipping Him in the consciousness that God sees His servants. Al-Bukhari, "Iman," 37; al-Muslim, "Iman," 1. (Trans.)

degree of ecstasy experiences the pleasure of belief in and
knowledge of God, closing itself to all others than the Almighty.

- The second degree is that, in proportion to the profundity
  of the heart, and owing to the gifts that stream into it, the
  conscience or conscious human nature is awakened to the
  illumination and inspirations far beyond the receptive capacity of the ears, eyes, and mind.

- The highest degree is the inconceivable state of seeing, knowing, and thinking of Him alone in everything and always
  feeling His company without considering any other being,
  by virtue of the fact that all human faculties having taken on
  His color (with which He has colored the whole universe).
  One who has attained this degree can achieve amazement
  (*dahsha*) if able to take half a step further, and will fall into a stupor (*hayman*) if proceeding the full step. It is difficult to understand and interpret these two states with our
  normal human capacity of perception and reason.

> *O God! All praise be to You for Your Light by which You have
> guided us. And all praise be to You for Your mighty Clem-
> ency by reason of which You forgive us.*
>
> *And may Your blessings and peace be upon him whom You
> sent with the mission of Messengership as a mercy for the whole
> creation, and on His family and all of His Companions!*

DAHSHA AND HAYMAN
(AMAZEMENT AND STUPOR)

While discussing ecstasy and willful rapture, we have mentioned the states of *dahsha* (amazement) and *hayman* (stupor). Although amazement and astonishment were written about in the first volume of this book, a few more words will be said here concerning amazement alongside stupor; this is not a lasting station for a traveler on the way to God, but only a transitional halt.

Meaning fear and dismay in the face of a frightening event or situation, amazement is the feeling of shock which travelers to God experience during their spiritual journey on coming face to face with the manifestations of the Beauty and Grace of the Beloved. Although there is no explicit statement touching on it in the Book or in the Sunna, a relation with the verse (12:31), whose meaning is, *When they saw him, they so admired him that they cut their hands*, can be established.

Some have described amazement as the shock when encountering an incident beyond one's understanding and endurance, and power to explain. This can also be described as experiencing the truth that the Divine manifestations exceed the limits of reason, and that our love for Him goes beyond the limits of patience; amazement also means getting into a state beyond one's capacity of perception.

We add here some further explanations about this state:

- Travelers on the way to God feels amazement when the state in which they find themselves exceeds the limits of their knowledge and perception, and then they go into a state of ecstasy beyond their endurance, where God will favor them with spiritual discoveries disproportionate to their efforts. One can go into ecstasies unintentionally, when reciting the Qur'an or performing prayers, although self-possession and a feeling of awe are essential to both; the heart can go into spiritual arrhythmia as a result of excessive rapture, destroying the balance and self-control in an initiate; a traveler on the way to God behaves hastily and sometimes in an uncontrolled manner, under the enrapturing influence of witnessing God's signs, although seeking God always demands loyalty and faithfulness. All of these are causes of amazement.

- When, under the influence of the state that the initiates have entered upon, or because of the spiritual pleasure they feel, they see the whole creation annihilated in God's Existence and all time ending in eternity, and the spirit witnessing God's signs, then they are swept up in amazement. That is the spiritual station where travelers on the way to God can hear through God's own hearing and see through God's own sight.[30]

- When the slopes of the heart are unexpectedly exposed to the shower of gifts from the All-Glorified One and the Divine favors, when the lights of nearness to God envelop one, and when secrets are disclosed to the extent that they result in reaching the horizon of worshipping God as if actually seeing Him, amazement pervades the whole being of the lover of God. The person is then lost in the depths of self-annihilation and the considerations of amazement. The following verses of Gedai,[31] expressing this spiritual station, are truly beautiful:

---

[30] Hakim al-Tirmidhi, *Nawadir al-'Usul*, 3:81; Ibn Kathir, *Tafsir al-Qur'an*, 2:580; Ibn Hajar, *Fath al-Bari*, 1:13.

[31] Ahmed Gedai (1826-1901). A Turkish mystic poet. Born in Tokat and died in Istanbul. Famous for his poems in the type of Turkish folk music. (Trans.)

> I did not know myself as I see me now,
> I wonder whether He is me or I am Him?
> This is the point where lovers lose themselves;
> I have burnt away, so give me water!

This feeling experienced by those still on the journey may sometimes cause confusion. For this reason, those who do not lead their lives in strict accordance with the Qur'an and the Sunna and who do not feed their subconscious with the lights that emanate from the sun of Prophethood, upon him be peace and blessings, may be deceived through the influence of these feelings and experiences. Such deception may lead them to utter words of pride incompatible with the rules of Shari'a, words that are irreconcilable with self-possession.

Stupor (*Hayman*) is used to denote one whose thirst is deepened by drinking, not quenched or satisfied, and also one who is mad with passionate love.

In Islamic Sufism, stupor means that an initiate is deeply in love with God, and therefore loses self-control in great ecstasy, drowning in wonder, appreciation, and spiritual pleasures under the influence of the surprising Divine gifts and manifestations that pervade the heart during the journey to God. Since there are no explicit statements in the Qur'an and the Sunna concerning stupor, many exacting scholars have tended to see it, like amazement, as a spiritual state rather than a station, something transient rather than lasting. Although some have attempted to relate it to the verse (7:143), *Moses fell down in a swoon (as if struck by lightning)*, it is evident that the situation of a Messenger receiving Divine Revelation cannot be reconciled with a swoon. So, I feel that we should approach Moses' falling down in a swoon on Mount Sinai as his conscious amazement and shock, an attitude that he felt was fitting for him in the face of God's partial manifestation of His Majesty in all Its transcendence and above all corporeality.

Like amazement, stupor can also be analyzed in three categories:

- When initiates, aware of helplessness, poverty and worthlessness before God, are favored with Divine gifts far beyond their capacity during the first stages of their journey, then they—like Prophet Job, who entreated God, saying, "I cannot be indifferent to any of Your favors,"[32]—joyfully desire more and more gifts. Such an attitude, when observed in those who are on the way, is characteristic of those in the first stages.

- In the face of abundant gifts granted in advance in response to the sincerity and the virtue that God knows that individual will acquire in the future, the initiate renews him or herself in perception, spirit, and will, and observes with deep pleasure the wonders and marvels, whose doors have been half opened. In the mood expressed in the verse (66:8), *Our Lord, perfect our light for us!*, the person, with great determination and spiritual tension, longs for and expects what lies beyond the favors already granted. The couplet of Gedai,

> I have dipped my finger into the honey of love;
> Give me some water!

very beautifully expresses this degree of stupor.

- Initiates attain a state where they feel they are standing on the same point as their sight reaches, and they begin to observe the universe from the horizon of annihilation and disappearance. That is, nothing other than God exists any more for them and they feel their existence annihilated in God's Existence, which they experience every moment with a new manifestation of Him. They acquire an unshakable certainty that God always sees them, that certainty being a gift of recompense for reaching the highest point of excellence, and they overflow with the yearning and zeal to see Him.

We should mention here that all these favors come in proportion to the strength of belief, and as long as the initiates can main-

---

[32] Al-Bukhari, "Ghusl," 20; Sunan al-Nasa'i, "Ghusl," 7.

tain their relation with God from the heart and continue to lead their life in utmost loyalty to Him. This depends on strictly following the master of the creatures, upon him be peace and blessings. Any extraordinary state that arises and one does not feel perfect attachment and devotion to him, is likely in most cases to be deceptive. Those seeking the gifts of the Almighty must certainly enter the circle of Muhammad, upon him be peace and blessings, and the lovers of the Almighty's light must conform to the rhythm of that circle.

> *O God! I ask You for useful knowledge, and seek refuge with You from any knowledge of no use; and ask You for acceptable action.*

> *May Your blessings and peace be on our master Muhammad, and on his family and all of His Companions.*

BARQ (LIGHTNING)

Barq (lightning) is a light that flashes in an initiate during the first steps of the journey toward sainthood. This is the first invitation to those seeking nearness to God. The scholars of truth have related the emergence of lightning to the verse (20:9-10), *Has there come to you the tiding of Moses' experience? He saw a fire and said to his family: "Wait here! I see a fire afar off"*, and have concluded that such a flash of light means the beginning of Prophethood for Prophets and of sainthood for saints.

The first steps to be taken on the way of truth are belief, righteous deeds and wakefulness. For this reason, lightning can be regarded as the first step of, not this journey, but rather the spiritual states (of sainthood) that one steps through during the journey.

The difference between lightning and ecstasy is that ecstasy emerges in the home of meeting with the Beloved, while lightning flashes when permission to enter the further sanctuary of the Beloved is given. For this reason, ecstasy sends zeal into the heart, awakening in it a burning desire to meet the Beloved from among the lights of state, urging the petitioning of more and more of His gifts and to rise to higher ranks. As for lightning, it hits the eye like a dazzling light and reminds one that the door of the Beloved is ajar. For those who are to cross the threshold of sainthood, we recall the following couplet of Ibn Farid,[33] a couplet full of excitement:

---

[33] 'Umar ibn al-Farid (1181-1235) is one of the most venerated poets in Arabic, whose expression of Sufi experiences is regarded as the finest in the Arabic language. He studied for a legal career but abandoned law for a solitary religious life in the Muqattam hills near Cairo. He spent some years in or near Makka, where he met the renowned Sufi al-Suhrawardi. (Trans.)

Has a dazzling lightning flashed from the direction of Mount Sinai,
Or have the veils over the face of Layla[34] been opened part way?

So it is that while living in the dark night of corporeality and bodily desires, Layla began to show herself step by step and to send the hope of union into the hearts, and in the end the nights changed into days in the hearts of those who had been burning for union with her.

Because it signifies permission to enter the way to union, lightning is considered as the start of the journey for the travelers on the way to the Truth. At this setting out, God Almighty makes His servants, who are candidates for sainthood, aware of His offerings and grandeur and of the servants' own helplessness and poverty, enabling them to awaken to the love of God and to form a sincere relationship with Him, abandoning attachment however slight to transient, decaying, earth-bound things. These are the first gifts of God. In addition, like the favors offered to Moses on Mount Sinai, initiates need to feel some things and change their solitude into company (with the True, Eternal Friend) to better endure the difficulties of the journey and the loneliness. So lightning can be considered as the pleasure of feeling God's friendliness, and a favor given to counter the difficulties that a traveler is bound to face during the journey.

Lightning has another face, by which an initiate is reminded of God's omnipresence and given the signal of self-possession. Initiates are warned that entering the Realm of the Holy Presence requires self-possession. Fear and alarm are aroused in their inner world by this warning. So, with its two aspects—one bringing deep pleasure and desire, the other causing fear and alarm—lightning serves to prevent the traveler both from falling into despair and from uttering words of pride incompatible with the rules of Shari'a.

The gifts coming on the wavelength of lightning are the Lord's favors to the traveler; they are provision for the journey. These favors are the means of innocent delight for the traveler, because of Him

---

[34] In Oriental literature, Layla symbolizes the beloved one, and in Sufi literature, the True Beloved One, Who is God Almighty. (Trans.)

Who sent them, and as a result of the recognition of poverty on the part of the one receiving. The traveler acknowledges this favor, as indicated in the verse (10:58), *Say: "In the grace and bounty of God and in His mercy—in this, then, let them rejoice."* Reflecting on the Divine favors received, the person confesses that everything is from Him and proclaims: "All praise be to Him," expressing the feeling of unworthiness for such favors, as Gedai did:

> That which I have—I am not worthy of it;
> This favor and grace—why are they bestowed on me?

Thereupon the traveler journeying to God bows in humility and thankfulness.

The saying of the pride of humankind, upon him be peace and God's blessings, *I am the master of the children of Adam, yet I am not proud at all,*[35] is the crystal in which this reality is reflected, from whichever side it is looked at.

> *O God! I ask you for good in its entirety, with all its beginning and end and with its visible and invisible, and high ranks in Paradise.*
>
> *And may Your blessings and peace be on our master Muhammad, the intercessor whose intercession is acceptable to God, and on his family and Companions, all of whom are of great merit and loyalty.*

---

[35] Al-Tirmidhi, "Manaqib," 1; Ibn Maja, "Zuhd," 37.

ZAWQ AND 'ATASH
(PLEASURE AND THIRST)

Meaning the feeling of happiness and satisfaction, and enjoyment and amusement, *zawq* (pleasure) in Sufi terminology is one of the first breezes of Divine manifestation and one of the first gifts that appear from time to time on the horizon of witnessing the signs of God. It is also the invasion of the heart by which the "hidden treasury" of God is uncovered so that one can know Him by the rays of the Divine light, which we can call succeeding flashes of lightning. Furthermore, it is the first mansion where one can distinguish right from wrong. Yearning for lofty, elevated goals, for virtue, for sincerity and purity of intention in one's actions, can be regarded as the passport for entering this mansion.

As long as one maintains relationship with God faithfully and from the heart, one begins to feel in the depths of the heart the spiritual pleasure that we can also call "imbibing," but an "imbibing" without need for a cup or cup-bearer. This pleasure makes the travelers on the way to God intoxicated, according to their rank. As they feel the pleasure, they grow thirstier and desire more and more pleasure, with the result that thirst and satiation follow one upon another in the spirit. They express this state as Gedai did, who says:

O cup-bearer, in the fire of love,
I have burnt away, so give me some water!

This comes to the point where the travelers on the way to the Truth, their desire and yearning for Him ever growing, feel pleasure embedded in longing and satisfaction embedded in hunger. They burn with passion for the door that is ajar to be opened completely. The interruption of these favors is impressed on them like a fast, while the resumption of the favors is like a feast, and they murmur in expectation as Muhammed Lutfi Effendi[36] does:

> Offer the wine of union: it is time to break fast;
> Improve this ruin: it is time to display favors.

Another approach to thirst is to see it as such a longing and passion for the Truly Beloved and Desired One that the initiate aches intensely for satisfaction saying, "My liver has become roasted: will there not come help in answer to my sighs?"; the heart of the initiate overflows with love, burns away in flames, and his/her eyes scan the horizon in expectation of Their Lord *Who offers them pure drink* (76:21). However, so long as a loving initiate remains imprisoned in the lampshade of corporeality, the Truly Beloved One does not manifest Himself to him/her in His perfection. This is why the thirst of the yearning lover who still lingers between corporeality and spirituality increases more and more to the point of being consumed in the flames. The following couplets by Saʿdi al-Shirazi[37] are truly beautiful in expressing such a degree of spiritual pleasure and thirst:

> You show Your Face, then avoid showing Yourself,
> Increasing thereby both demand for You and our heat.
> Whenever I see the Beloved Who has seduced me into His love,
> I am confused how to act, and bewildered on the straight path.
> First He burns me in flames, then extinguishes with sprinkles of water,
> This is why you sometimes see me in flames,
> And sometimes drowned in water.

Just as ordinary pleasure with its painful and pleasant aspects impresses itself on other organs and parts of the body, so also this pleasure impresses itself on the heart and the conscience or on con-

---

[36] Muhammed Lutfi Effendi (1868-1956) is one of the Sufi masters who lived in Erzurum. He has a *Divan* containing many beautiful, lyrical poems.

[37] Saʿdi el-Shirazi (1215?-1292), the greatest didactic poet of Persia, author of the *Gulistan* ("Rose-Garden") and the *Bostan* ("Orchard"), who also wrote many fine odes and lyrics.

scious human nature. God's Messenger declared: "One who is pleased with God as their Lord (The One Who sustains, administers, and brings up), who is pleased with Islam as their religion, and with Muhammad as their Messenger has tasted the pleasure of belief."[38] He sometimes expressed this pleasure with the words used to denote bodily pleasures, as in the hadith where he prohibited his Companions from fasting every other day: "I am not like you; my hunger and thirst are satisfied (by God in ways unknown to you)."[39] Whereas, the pleasure tasted by the heart and spirit as a result of spiritual life is purely spiritual, it is more constant when compared with ecstasy and feeds the heart and spirit with ever new radiations. As for ecstasy and stupor, they are gifts that come in certain states of the initiate's journeying and, despite their being dazzling, they emerge in proportion to the seeker's spiritual depth.

Pleasure also differs according to its sources. God's promise of Paradise, eternity, and a vision of Him, one moment of each being superior to thousands of years of worldly life spent in happiness, in return for belief, confirmation, and obedience, is one of those sources of pleasure. Without considering any of the material and spiritual or worldly and other worldly joys, the conscious human nature's pursuit of nearness to God and always feeling His company and Presence give another kind of pleasure. Completely freed from conceit and egoism, being favored with absolute nearness to God and feeling the uninterrupted pleasures of subsistence with God at the summit of seeing, hearing, and knowing Him alone, is another summit of taste. In short, everyone has their share in the spiritual pleasures in proportion to the degree of their belief, confirmation, and knowledge of the Almighty God.

It is when initiates feel indifference to bodily pleasures, when they are satisfied with them, it is then that they begin to feel constant thirst for spiritual pleasures. We can describe this as an unquenchable thirst. Initiates yearn more and more for the Divine gifts that

---

[38] Al-Muslim, "Iman," 56; Al-Tirmidhi, "Iman," 10.
[39] Al-Bukhari, "Sawm," 48; Al-Muslim, "Siyam," 55-56.

an excellent guide will pour into their hearts through words and be-havior, and feel their conscious nature open to an infinite degree to the knowledge and love of God and spiritual pleasures. Such a con-scious nature or, rather, heart, which is its primary pillar, continu-ously yearns for God until it attains absolute nearness to Him. In time it is completely freed from the prison of corporeality and the density of bodily life and, favored with transcendence of time and space and flying in the heavens of the heart and the spirit, it con-stantly moves between thirst and satiation, expecting the doors that are slightly ajar to be opened wide.

When at last the disciple willing the Beloved and in love with Him becomes willed and loved by the Beloved, when illumined with His light, colored by His color, and, when, as a result of the burning manifestations of the Divine Existence, all things other than Him have been burned up, the true nature of existence shows itself. Be-yond all states and appearances, the One, Unique Being is felt free from all qualitative and quantitative considerations and restrictions; He is the One Who creates all states and makes His servants go from one state to another, He is the one Who gives abundant favors, and the Creator of all acts and deeds. In the following verses, Jalal al-Din al-Rumi illustrates this highest degree of pleasure:

> Drink such wine that the jar containing it should
> be the face of the Beloved,
> And the cup in which it is offered be intoxicated
> with the wine itself.
> Drink such wine from the cup of the Everlasting Face that
> its bearer should be the One alluded to in
> Their Lord offers them pure drink.
> When that wine is brought forth, it leads you to a purification
> of the filth of corporeality at the time of intoxication.
> How strange a drink, how exceptional a taste,
> how unusual a pleasure,
> How nice a fortune, how great an astonishment,
> how peculiar a zeal!

Another Sufi, as if leading our hearts to taste the pure wine of pleasure, voices his feelings as follows,

> See, all have been intoxicated when Their Lord
> offers them pure drink,
> Four, five and seven; are all intoxicated by the
> Unending Majesty.

O God! Offer us of the wine of Your love and include us among those loved by You!

Let Your blessings and peace be on our master Muhammad, the master of all loved by You, and on his family and Companions, who are approved by You.

QALAQ (PASSION)

Literally meaning boredom with the place where one is and with the surrounding conditions, feeling discomfort as if in imprisonment or captivity, *qalaq* (passion) is intense love, deeper than the desire for Paradise that the ordinary worshipper feels, more profound than the feelings aroused by a Sufi leader's knowledge concerning God, and more intense than the lover's love for the beloved, and which exhausts his/her power to endure such love. The initiate falling in love to such an intense degree finds on the horizons of his or her innermost world glimmers of a meeting with the Beloved and feels his or her heart beating with the idea that above all is God's being pleased with them (9:72).

The Prophet Moses, upon him be peace, expresses this degree of passion that burns endurance to ashes with the desire of union in the words (20:84), *I have hastened to You, my Lord, so that You may be well-pleased (with me)*. He manifests his extraordinary yearning and excitement to meet with his Lord.

There is another kind of passion manifesting itself in the form of distress in figurative love—the love felt by a person for one of the opposite sex—and that arises from the worry that the beloved may be loved by others. Jami' expresses such passion as follows:

> When one says that he is a lover, this casts
> me into worry and distress,
> For I am afraid that he is in love with my beloved.

Such passion should not be confused with the passion an initiate feels on the way to God. All sorrows and joys felt on this way are because of Him and from Him. For this reason, any pain or sorrow a traveler to God feels is sweet in itself, and the pleasures are as pleasant as the water of Paradise.

When the zeal and yearning felt to meet with the Beloved come to an unendurable point, whatever there is in the heart other than the desire for union vanishes. It even happens that love is, to a certain extent, not considered any more, and seekers progress to the following states according to the intensity of their passion:

- All things, each according to its own "wavelength," begin to tire the seeker; the result is that at times the heart feels a desire for union with Him, while at other times it burns with the yearning to die to meet with Him. The fire is so great that the seeker sees none other than Him.

- Despite corporeality and bodily desires, the seeker begins to be so immersed in profound spiritual life that neither reason nor will-power retain the capacity to control or give direction. As a result, the person cannot help falling into confusion in matters that require the ordinary operations of common sense and discernment:

> I did not know myself as I see me now,
> I wonder whether He is me or I am Him?

Not only in the performance of duties of worship and obedience to God, but also in worldly affairs the seeker now travels on the horizons of witnessing God's signs distinctly.

- When the veil between a hero of passion and the Beloved is partly lifted so that the way to union shows itself to some degree, the initiate goes into a spiritual state of being seized by a fire from which there is no longer any possibility of rescue or escape. The initiate thinks of nothing more than meeting with the Truly Beloved One. The lover is at the same time as being a lover also a beloved, a willed one at the same time as being one who wills, and one sought for at the same time as one who is seeking.

It can be said that in the state in which he was before he began to receive the Revelation, God's Messenger experienced the first two kinds of passion mentioned above. The following verses that we quote from a long poem of Yazicizade Mehmed Effendi[40] express this in a chaste language:

> Why is it that you stay in such a sorrowful mood?
> Why is it that there is sadness in your blessed inner world?
> ....
> Without answering them, he turned back again
> to where he stayed and unburdened himself to the Almighty.
> ....
> He said: "My heart is in love and desire; my soul is on fire;
> Why are these tears coming from my eyes, O Never-ending All-Ruling?
> I have lost my patience, having come to the end of my endurance;
> What can I say to my Beloved? I have no strength to bear all that
> takes place.
> ....
> Climbing the mountain, he prostrated, putting his face on the earth;
> He wept and entreated God, saying: "O One never-ending!"
> The angels saw him and pitied him,
> And the maidens in Paradise shed their tears:
> "O God! Your beloved one has made his upright body doubled over."

Many Companions of the Messenger, upon him be peace and blessings, made similar utterances on this same point. "Tomorrow, I will join the friends—Muhammad and his Companions," is only one example of these.[41]

The one who feels the greatest passion is also the master of the creatures, upon him be peace and God's blessings. At a time when the world offered itself to him with all its pomp and splendor, as the greatest of all creation, as one who had completed his duty and had come to the point where he could express his yearning for union with the Truly Beloved One, he said, "O my God! (Now it is time to go)

---

[40] Yazicizade, Mehmed ibn Salih (d. 1451) Author of *Muhammadiya*. Buried in Canakkale, Turkey. (Trans.)

[41] Ahmad ibn Hanbal, *al-Musnad*, 3:223, 262.

to the Highest Friend!"[42] and turned with all his being to the Absolutely Beloved One with the desire of fulfilling what was required of him by the rank of being beloved by Him. He put a full stop to the lines of ascent and descent[43] by proving that he uniquely enjoyed the rank of being His beloved one. He was no longer Muhammad but was transformed into being Ahmad,[44] and fully perceived that whatever he had and accomplished was all from God.

> *On him and his family be the most perfect of blessings to the fill of the heavens and the earth.*

---

[42] Al-Bukhari, "Marda'," 19; Al-Muslim, "Salam," 46.

[43] A human being's coming to the world from the world of spirits is that person's descent, and the life in this world ending in death with the subsequent chain of events until he or she enters Paradise, which is his or her return to God, is the ascent. (Trans.)

[44] The Messenger's name before his coming to the world was Ahmad. Prophet Jesus promised his coming with this name (61:6). He was Muhammad during his life-time in the world and during his mission of Messengership. He is also called Ahmad in the other world after his death. With its own peculiarities, his being Ahmad is called the reality of his being Ahmad (*Haqiqat al-Ahmadiya*) in the Sufi terminology, and his being Muhammad with its own characteristics, the reality of his being Muhammad (*Haqiqat al-Muhammadiya*). (Trans.)

GHAYRA (ENDEAVOR)

E ndeavor (*ghayra*) literally means making every effort of concern, and being alert in striving, for chastity, honor, and esteem. It signifies being on the alert in respect of religious prohibitions. God is limitless in His concern for the purity of His servants and is infinitely pleased with the care they show and the endeavors they make in preserving it. For this reason, He has made some things, including indecencies and evil acts in particular, unlawful. So His servants, at least, must respond to His concern by being as careful as possible not to commit such acts. This is endeavor (*ghayra*); in this lies a person's honor.

In order to remind us of this point, God's Messenger, upon him be peace and blessings, said: "Do you wonder at the degree of Sa'd's concern? I am more concerned than Sa'd, and God is more concerned than me." Concern requires fulfilling with great zeal whatever God likes and orders and being as determined as possible not to commit whatever He dislikes and forbids. It also requires loving from the bottom of one's heart the Essence, Attributes and Names of the Necessarily Existent Being, and doing one's utmost so that He may be loved also by others, and preferring relationship with one's Lord to everything in the world and the Hereafter. In expressing these last two points in particular, the following verse of a saint is highly significant:

> I wish all the people of the world love Him Whom I love,
> And all that we speak about would be the Beloved.

If the endeavor required is the assumption of a determined attitude not to commit evil and therefore related to God's absolute dislike of such acts, then this would mean that one must adopt a manner that belongs to God. He who was the voice of truth, upon him be peace and blessings, said: *There is no one more concerned than God. It is because of His concern that He has prohibited all indecencies to be committed, whether in public or secretly.*[45] This draws attention to the Divine source of concern and endeavor. By saying, *God displays concern, and a believer also displays concern. God's concern is for the prohibited acts that His servant may commit,*[46] he reminds us of the mutuality of concern and the ardent endeavor that is required by it.

The scholars of truth have interpreted concern and endeavor in two ways:

- Recognizing no alternative or rival to the Beloved.
- Fixing all of one's attention on the Beloved and trying to outdo all else in loving Him.

However we want to understand endeavor, whether it be resisting corporeal desires and trying to lead our lives on the horizon of the heart and the spirit, or waging war against evil morals and establishing a way of life formed of good morals or virtues, or feeling in our hearts that we belong to Him exclusively—all these are among the principal elements which will bring us up to the level of true humanity. They are a response to God Almighty's infinite concern for His servants. God's concern is that He does not leave His servants forever vulnerable to others' sense of what is fair, just and right, and He honors them with exclusive loyalty and servanthood to Him, He does not throw them into the humiliation of subjection to false, imaginary deities. In response to this, the required concern of His servants is, in the words of Mawlana Jami', the craving for One, the invoking of One, the seeking of One, the seeing and following of One, the knowing of One, and the mentioning of One.

Some view endeavor as the initiates' making Him their unique concern, their sole hope of contentment, and excluding all else other than Him from the sphere of their efforts which must be directed toward Him alone and exclusively. It has been regarded as the manifestation of the state in which that some wander sighing for the

---

[45] Al-Bukhari, "Nikah," 107; Al-Muslim, "Tawba," 32-34.
[46] Al-Muslim, "Tawba," 36.

Beloved from whom they are separated, are. The initial verses of the *Mathnawi* by Jalal al-Din al-Rumi sound like melodies of such endeavor and longing:

> Listen to the flute, how it recounts;
> It complains of separation.
> ....
> I seek a bosom split in parts by separation,
> So that I can explain to it my painful yearning!
> Whoever has fallen far from his origin,
> Longs for the day when he will be reunited with the Beloved.

Those who have made serious endeavor with utmost concern have treated the subject of endeavor in three degrees:

The first consists of the endeavor that is practiced and known by regular, profound worship of God, by those who embroider their lives with the threads of piety and righteous deeds. In order to become perfected, they exert such endeavor that even a single, slight error is enough for them to suffer pangs of conscience for a life-time.

The second degree of endeavor is practiced by those who have set their hearts on God, the Truth, exclusively, who go from state to state, who travel from love to pleasure and thereon into deeper and deeper yearning. They make every endeavor to please Him and, as stated in the verse, *To whatever direction you turn, there is the "Face" of God* (2:115), they always turn to Him with all their faculties and under all circumstances, and are on the alert against letting their eyes slide to another beloved. They always try to find Him in any corner of their hearts for special meetings, as mentioned in a hadith, *I have a special time with God.*[47] They regard it as the greatest disrespect for time to fail to spend even a moment in knowing and pleasing Him. They tremble with the threat, *This is because you exulted on earth without right, and you behaved insolently!* (40:75), and they hear with eagerness the Divine call, *Eat and drink at ease as reward for your deprivations and sacrifices in past days!* (69:24) resounding all the time at different pitches.

---

[47] al-Ajluni, *Kashf al-Khafa'*, 2:173.

The endeavor of those endowed with true knowledge of God, which is the third degree, is always to pursue deeper and deeper knowledge of Him, saying, *We have not been able to know You as Your knowledge requires*. They glimpse unbelievable beauties and sometimes keep what they have witnessed concealed, even from their own eyes, in jealousy. Sometimes they bemoan this world as being a place where He cannot be seen and complain of their eyes, in that they are unable to see Him and belittle their own being as they cannot keep concealed their special relationship with the Beloved and His special favors to them. Like a compass, they are always sensitively poised and agitated until they reach the day of final, eternal reunion with the Beloved, a day when they will acquire steadiness.

> *O God, I want (Your) forgiveness and endeavor (to please You)! O God, lead me to what You love and are pleased with!*

> *And may Your blessings and peace be on our master Muhammad Mustafa.*

WALAYA (SAINTHOOD)

L iterally meaning a person, a community, or a country that is under the direction and rule of another, *walaya* (sainthood) denotes annihilation with respect to carnal selfhood and egoism in favor of awareness of being under the dominion of the All-Living, Self-Subsistent One and of the need to acquire nearness to the Necessarily Existent Being. Travelers on the way to God who has attained this level, having given themselves up to the direction of God, are favored with self-possession, and live in nearness to God. The first step in sainthood is indicated in the verse (2:257): *God is He Who loves, guards and directs those who believe; He has led them out of all kinds of (intellectual, spiritual, social, economic and political) darkness into the light, and keeps them firm therein*; and also in *Know well that the confidants (saintly servants) of God—there will be no reason for them to fear (both in this world and the next, for they shall always find My help and support with them), nor shall they grieve* (10:62).

One who has been favored with sainthood is called a *waliyy* (saint). *Waliyy* is one of the Names of God Almighty. A saint on whom this Name is placed and who has become a polished mirror in which this Name is reflected is considered as having been favored with "self-annihilation in God" and "subsistence with Him." Nevertheless, this favor can never make a saint indifferent to the master of the creatures, upon him be peace and the blessings of God. On the contrary, whatever rank a person has attained on the way to God, one of the most blessed and illuminating sources for the confidants of God, the Truth, is the person of Muhammad, upon him be peace and blessings, who is the sun of Prophethood and the pure source of truth; he is the one they should follow strictly. Moreover, he is the first among those sources that are the means of guidance attainment of sainthood for people. In several verses, the Qur'an stresses exactly this point, bringing our attention to that source of enlightenment and that mine of truth. For example (3:31): *(O Messenger,) say (to them): "If you indeed love God, then follow me, so that God may love you and forgive you your sins."*

This truth is expressed in a colorful language in *Gulshan al-Raz* by Mahmud Shabstari:[48]

> The Prophet is like the sun, and the saint is like the moon
> facing the sun, which says: "I have a special time with God."
> A saint can only find a way to *so that God may love you,*
> which is the meeting room with Him,
> Through *If you indeed love God, follow me.*

As the moon receives its light entirely from the sun, so a saint is enlightened by following the Prophet, by becoming like him a polished mirror in which the Divine light is reflected. It can even be said that not only the saints that came after Prophet Muhammad, but also all the previous Prophets received their light from him, who is the sun of Prophethood, upon him be peace and blessings:

> He is the sun of virtues and the others are
> the stars that diffuse light for people at night.
> All the miracles the blessed Messengers worked
> were because his light reached them.
>
> (Busiri)

The word *waliyy* (saint) is used as an agent or as a past participle. It denotes, in the first case, one who resists sins and regularly fulfills the duties of worship and obedience with patience, while in

---

48 Sa'd al-Din Mahmud Shabistari (1250-1320) is one of the most celebrated authors of Persian Sufism. Because of his gift for expressing the Sufi spiritual vision with extraordinary clarity, his *Gulshan-i Raz* ("Secret Rose Garden") rapidly became one of the most popular works of Persian Sufi poetry. (Trans.)

the second case, it denotes one who has been favored with God's help and protection. Both of these meanings are in accord with the covenant made between God and His servants, which is mentioned in the following *hadith qudsi*:[49]

> God Almighty declares: "Whoever shows hostility to My saintly servant, I will surely wage war on him. My servant cannot get near to Me with something more lovable to Me than fulfilling the things I have made incumbent on him. Then, My servant gets nearer and nearer to Me until I love him by fulfilling the supererogatory acts of worship. When I love him, I become his ears with which he hears, his eyes with which he sees, his hands with which he grasps, and his feet on which he walks. (His hearing, seeing, grasping, and walking take place in accordance with My will and commandments.) If he asks Me for something, I surely grant it to him, and if he seeks refuge from (something), I surely take him under My protection.[50]

The saintly scholars have always dwelt upon two important dimensions of sainthood and consider them as two parts of a single unit:

- An initiate's scrupulous observance of God's commandments, and in return,
- God's taking him/her under His special care and protection.

Such care and protection manifest themselves as sinlessness in a Prophet, and protection against sins in a saint. Sinlessness and protection from sins are different from one another, but that is not our subject matter here.

A saint is surely a noble, blessed one, and can be favored with working of wonders.[51] However, the working of wonders is not a con-

---

[49] A *hadith qudsi* is a saying of the Messenger, the meaning of which is inspired directly by God. (Trans.)

[50] Al-Bukhari, "Riqaq," 38.

[51] Any extraordinary act or achievement with which a Prophet is favored outside the known "laws of nature" is called a miracle, while a wonder is an action performed by a saint. A saint's wonder worked by following the Prophet can only be an imitation or copy of a Prophet's miracle. (Trans.)

dition of sainthood. It is a disputed matter whether a saint knows or should know of being a saint. After all, a saint is surely an object or recipient of some special favors of God.

Ibrahim Adham[52] defines sainthood with its dimensions and the favors it receives as renunciation of the world (not in respect to earning a living, but rather with respect to loving it from the heart), turning to God with all one's being, and continuously expecting His turning to oneself.

According to Yahya ibn Mu'adh,[53] sainthood is enduring every hardship and difficulty on the way to attaining friendship with God.

Sainthood, in the words of Bayazid al-Bistami, is not to allow any desire to be known by others, despite one's deep and continuous worship and obedience to God and one's extraordinary care in fulfilling other duties of servanthood. According to Abu Sa'id al-Kharraz, God opens the door slightly to one qualified for sainthood by enabling regular mention of Him and recitation of His Names. When the initiate begins to take pleasure in mentioning Him or in the recitation of His Names, the One Mentioned leads him or her by the hand to the summit of nearness to Him. Then, He clothes him or her in the bejeweled robe of His close friendship according to the degree of the person's loyalty and faithfulness. In this position, the initiate feels Him only, thinks of Him only, keeps His company only, and holds back from everybody else other than Him, because of his or her duties to Him. Whomever God especially favors, they tremble with fear lest it lead to their perdition. While it is a requirement of a Prophet's mission that he publicizes his Prophethood and the miracles associated with it as a manifestation of this special, sacred favor, it required among the courtesies of sainthood that

---

52 Abu Ishaq Ibrahim ibn Adham, born in Balkh of pure Arab descent. He renounced his kingdom in Balkh and wandered westwards to live a life of complete asceticism, earning his bread in Syria by honest manual toil until his death in 782. (Trans.)

53 Abu Zakariya' Yahya ibn Mu'adh al-Razi, a disciple of Ibn Karram, left his native town of Rayy and lived for a time in Balkh, afterwards proceeding to Nishapur where he died in 871. A certain number of poems are attributed to him. (Trans.)

a saint keeps both himself and God's special favors towards him concealed. Concerning this, Muhy al-Din ibn al-ʿArabi[54] writes:

> It is compulsory for God's friends to conceal the wonders they work;
> So do not ridicule yourself, nor become disgraced, by publicizing them.
> However, the Messengers are obliged to publicize their miracles,
> For they are connected with the coming of the Revelation.

The wonders we mention are those that can be witnessed by others or worked through the agency of the external senses and organs, such as mind-reading, giving information about things that are hidden or invisible, and crossing great distances or achieving many things in a relatively short time. Far from desiring them, saints of great stature have felt seriously uncomfortable even with the wonders that have proceeded from them unintentionally.

There is another kind of wonder related to the religious life which is not visible. Comprehension of the spirit of religion, attainment of good morals, strict observance of both the rights of God and the rights of the creatures, practicing what one has learned of religion and being blessed with its consequences, certainty in knowledge of God, sincerity and purity of intention in religious deeds and services, reaching the degree of acting as if seeing God when worshipping God in daily life, and similar attainments are wonders of this kind. Such Divine favors, which the common people cannot see and therefore attach no value to are the greatest values of the things that the distinguished servants of God should always pursue. Even if we should avoid publicizing such actions, seeking them out is tantamount to seeking out the Truth. The heirs to the greater sainthood—the sainthood of the Prophet's Companions, which is marked by meticulous observance of religion and self-dedication to

---

[54] Muhiy al-Din ibn al-ʿArabi (1165-1240): One of the great and most famous Sufi masters. His doctrine of the Transcendental Unity of Being, which most have mistaken for monism and pantheism, made him the target of unending polemics. He wrote many books, the most famous of which are *Fusus al-Hikam* and *Al-Futuhat al-Makkiyya*. (Trans.)

serving it—have long been counted among the heroes of this attainment.

> *O God! Make us of those of Your servants who pursue sincerity, and whom You have favored with sincerity and purity of intention, and who have achieved piety and abstinence from all forbidden things big or small, and whom You have made near to You, and who love and are loved by You. Amen.*

SIR (SECRET)

Meaning something kept hidden from the knowledge or view of others, *sir* (secret) is a spiritual faculty deposited in the heart as a Divine trust. As a Divine trust, it has the same significance for the heart as spirit has for the body. Will-power, the mind, feelings, and the heart are the four pillars of the conscience and human conscious nature—these are called "the heavenly faculties"—that are given by the Lord in the same way that a secret is a faculty and dimension of the heart. Each of the pillars of conscience has a function and goal particular to it with respect to the relationship between the Lord and His servants. Will-power is charged with submission and devotion to the Lord, the mind with acquiring the necessary information to know God, the feelings with love of God, and the heart with a vision of God's "Face." As for secret, it is open to and innately charged with discovering Divine secrets.

All creation has been brought into existence by the Power of the Necessarily Existent One. This gives rise to a relationship between the Creator as Lord (One Who sustains, brings up, and protects the creation and administers life) and the creation, the things and beings, of which He is Lord. This relation contains secrets that are concerned with God's Lordship and which are called the "secrets of Lordship." Lordship manifests Itself, first of all, in the heart: the seekers feel this manifestation developing as they learn more about Him and in a deeper manner, until the point where they experience the concentrated manifestation of the Divine Names in themselves and see the whole of creation, including themselves, as consisting only in the manifestation of those Names. Finally, they obtain the pleasure of witnessing the Lord in everything with all His Names.

This witnessing opens to them the door of some Divine secrets called the "secrets of manifestation."

Some have interpreted secret as meaning a heart that is purified of all carnal vices and stains caused by attachment to anything else other than the Lord, and which has a clear relationship with the world of spirit.

Based on the verse (11:31), *God knows the best whatever is in their inner worlds,* we can describe a secret as being a pure bosom full of loyalty and faithfulness, open to Prophetic messages, and preferring God and the other world to all else. We can regard secret in this sense as being the heart at the level of secret.

Some have viewed the qualities mentioned here as the reasons or means of a secret's rising in the heart. When God prepares a heart to have these qualities, endowing it with the possibility and opportunity of accepting religion, the acceptance of God's Existence and Oneness, the confirmation of the afterlife, and the affirmation of the Prophets, the heart immediately uses this possibility and opportunity and tries to achieve the goals that can be achieved through secret. In other words, since God knows that such a heart will use this Divine trust—secret—in the best way possible, out of His special grace, He causes it to flourish. For it is He Himself Who declares (6:53): *Does God not know best who are the thankful?*

Such a pure, elevated heart or its owner are indicated sometimes by, Surely *God loves a servant who is pious, indifferent to all save Him, and has unknown depths,*[55] and sometimes by, *How many servants there are, whose hair is untidy, and who are repulsed from doors, and denied respect and attention, but if they swear by God for something, God does not prove them to be untrue.*[56]

In view of the above explanations, the people of secret can be divided into three classes:

- The people of truth whose eyes do not see any save God, and who always pursue His good pleasure and know how

---

[55] Al-Muslim, "Zuhd," 11.
[56] Al-Muslim, "Birr," 138; Al-Tirmidhi, "Manaqib," 54.

to resist the carnal self. Their aims, for which they make every effort, are so sublime that they cannot be prevented by any worldly desire, and are so pure that they are in accord with the Divine commandments, and their lives are ordered to gain eternal happiness. The ways they follow are free of any doubt, and they are always aware of God's purpose in any of their acts, even for a millisecond. They avoid fame and any distinction, knowing that servanthood to God is the aim of their existence; they value it above all worldly and other worldly considerations. Their daily lives are described in the following verse (24:36-37):

> In houses which God has allowed to be exalted and in which His Name is mentioned: therein are men who glorify Him in the morning and evening and whom neither trade nor buying prevents from mention of God and establishing the Prayer and paying the prescribed Alms; who fear a day when hearts and eyes will be over-turned.

- The faithful souls who try to hide from others their degree of relationship with God and their rank with Him: they keep the Divine gifts granted to them concealed from others, as if they were guarding their chastity, and although each is a star in the heaven of sainthood, they all try to appear as if they were but fireflies. Though each is a dove striving on God's way, they prefer to appear like magpies, knowing themselves to be nothing, even when they are declared in the heavens to be so holy as to be among the worthiest in the sight of God. In serving on God's way, they are extra-ordinarily active, dynamic and humble, although they outstrip all others; they are altruistic and disinterested when it is their turn to receive wages; they have no expectations in this world. They are described in the following verse (5:54):

> A people whom He loves, and who love Him, and who are most humble towards the believers, and dignified and commanding in the face of the unbelievers, continuous-

ly striving in God's way in solidarity, and fearing not the censure of anyone to censure them.

When they are alone with God in devotion, they are extraordinarily profound, while being exceptionally wise and successful in worldly affairs. They are remarkably careful and determined when guarding the honor of their community, and they hold themselves as aloof as possible from mean acts which may bring disgrace upon them or may cause others to feel suspicious.

- The heroes have reached the summit of perfection under the care and protection of the All-Preserving and with the help of the All-Helping: they do not spend even a moment without Him, and use every event, thought and consideration as a means to mention Him. Self-annihilated in His company, they live unaware of themselves. Whatever good they do for others and whatever service they render on God's way, they conceal it, not only from others, but also from themselves. Even if they sometimes feel some pride in themselves, they regard this as if it were a terrible affliction and immediately try to escape. They spend their lives amidst ecstasy and exhilaration, and rejoice in the Divine compliments, and in His special help and perfect care.

These heroes are unknown among people and remain hidden, enveloped by secrets, although they are God's favorites and among the most vital elements of existence. God, the Truth, looks at things with their eyes and the universe is fed with the pure water of their secrets.

> *O God! Help us with mentioning You, and being thankful to You, and worshipping You properly.*

> *And may Your blessings and peace be on our master Muhammad, the master of those who regularly worship God in the best way possible and with sincerity, and on his family and all of His Companions.*

GHURBA (SEPARATION)

Literally meaning the state of being a foreigner, homelessness, loneliness, separation, and being a stranger in one's own land, *ghurba* (separation) has been defined in the Sufi language as renouncing the world with the charms to which one feels attachment on the way to the True, Desired One, or living a life dedicated to the other world though surrounded by this world and its charms. Separation can be viewed as the states in which those who improve the world spiritually find themselves. Some of these states, which we can also consider as kinds of separation, are moving from one state to another, turning one's face from the created to the Creator, and descending from the limitless, heavenly realm to that of the created to guide the created to ascend to the heavenly one.

The following words were reported to have been said by the Messenger, the greatest hero in ascension to God and descent amongst the people in order to guide them to God after the completion of his ascension: *The most lovable to God Almighty among His servants are those who are separate.* When asked who such people were, he replied: *Those who are able to keep themselves separate from people for the sake of their religion and live a true, religious life. They will be resurrected together with Jesus, the son of Mary.*[57] The idea of taking the first step toward the eternal life of the hereafter alongside our master Jesus is a meaningful way of expressing and understanding the depth of his feeling of separation.

There are Prophetic reports that a person who dies away from home dies a martyr.[58] The separation mentioned in these reports al-

---

57 Ibn Qayyim al-Jawziya, *Madaric as-Salikin*, 3: 195.
58 Abu Ya'la, Musnad, 4:269; Ibn Maja, "Jana'iz," 61.

so includes the separation in which God's saintly servants find themselves. They have attained to certain spiritual states, yet they suffer among those unaware of spirituality and these spiritual states. Also included in this separation is the separation that the righteous suffer among wicked transgressors, the separation that people of belief and conviction suffer among the unbelievers and heretics, the separation that people of knowledge and discernment suffer among the rude and ignorant, and the separation that people of spirituality and truth suffer among the bigots, who restrict themselves only to the outward wording of the religious rules.

In other reports concerning homelessness, separation and being an outsider in one's own land, the Messenger points to the holy ones of every age who strive to make God's Word the most elevated in the world. For example: *Islam began helpless and with the helpless and outlandish, and will return to the same condition of helplessness and being represented by the outsiders. Glad tiding to the outsiders who try to improve in a time when all else are engaged in destruction and corruption* (or, according to another narration, *who increase in faith and righteousness when all else weaken in them*).[59] Despite the fact that the people of truth feel and know separation in their consciences, despite the fact that they feel and love this separation and that they breathe the breezes of being in God's company, in one respect they see separation as living in the realm of bodily existence, the realm between pure materialism and spirituality, and a requirement of being on the way to God. They not only endure separation, no matter how difficult it becomes, but they are always ready and desirous to fly to the realm where the souls fly. They always suffer separation from the higher realm of spiritual beings, the realm which those who have a true knowledge of God accept as their native land, and they long for reunion in the intermediate realm of the worldly life. The following verses in the *Mathnawi* by Jalal al-Din al-Rumi express this separation:

---

[59] Al-Muslim, "Iman," 232; Al-Tirmidhi, "Iman," 13.

> Listen to the flute, how it recounts;
> It complains of separation.

When the horizon of the Realm of Permanence manifested itself to him, Bilal al-Habashi[60] expressed the same feeling of separation and longing for reunion: "I am returning to mynative land from the land of separation."

Everyone comes alone into this world, which is a caravan-serai where the caravans come and leave after staying a short while, and everyone is seen off alone, without finding the opportunity to be freed from the feeling of separation. For this reason, those who suffer longing for the realms beyond feel separation peculiar to themselves, while the others who have set their hearts upon the world whose properties, dominion, and happiness are all transitory, suffer pangs of another kind of separation. In this world, every person is a Khusraw Dahlawi, who said: "My heart has become tired with separation and desires the native land," and everyone is weary of the narrow framework of this world, they are in pursuit of new horizons, and they crave their native land.

In the light of what we have so far explained, we can deal with separation in the following three categories—useful, harmful and neutral:

The separation that is useful and praised by him who brought the Divine Law is that felt by God's saintly servants. When we mention separation, what comes to mind is this form of separation. This separation is that which is crowned with friendship with God, which has the depth of knowing Him, and the dimensions of loving and yearning for Him. Those who feel this separation rise to friendship with God, without ever feeling themselves completely alone. They consider the transitory moments of loneliness as signs that they are ascending toward Him and see themselves as being supported by

---

60   Bilal al-Habashi: The first muazzin of the Holy Prophet. He was a slave from Ethiopia and was one of the earliest believers in Islam. During his slavery, he was tortured inhumanely because of his faith. The Prophet liked Bilal very much and in the 2nd year AH, when Prayer and Adhan (the call to the prayers) was prescribed, Bilal was given the honor to call the Adhan. (Trans.)

God's protection, His Messenger's leadership, and the company of the believers. They continue their relationship with the world in proportion to its essential value. They are ascetics whose every moment is spent in devotion to Him, ascetics who are always at war with feelings of pride and fame. As stated in a Prophetic Tradition, they are the royalty in the Gardens of Paradise, but they live life in such a way that they attach no importance to other things. With all their manners and in their appearance and their actuality, in their manner of dressing and acting, they are normal mortal beings among other mortals. They regard all worldly and other worldly favors as a means of mentioning their true Owner, of being in constant thankfulness to Him and they are zealous to strive in His way. Whatever gift God bestows on them, they see it as a garment to be worn temporarily, a garment that must not be spoiled by them and one about which they must feel no loss when it is gone.

From another perspective, those outsiders who are admired even by the saintly persons of higher ranks, such as the pure, godly ones and those made near to God by God Himself, hold tight to the way of the Prophet, as if they were clinging to it by their teeth, as stated in a Prophetic Tradition.[61] When other people turn away from it, they wage war on the innovations in religion, fix their thoughts and feelings on God's absolute Oneness, spend their lives in the pleasure and enthusiasm that come from adherence to God, regard following the master of the creatures, upon him be peace and the blessings of God, as submission to the captain of a ship that is taking its passengers to the Almighty, and view following a guide in their time as following him in essence.

This kind of separation, which is regarded as the most important and blessed source of sainthood belonging to those who lived in the Age of Happiness—the time of the Messenger—and those who will come toward the end of time and follow them in adherence to God's religion and serving it, is a way to perfection. It is extremely difficult to advance on this way, and does not seem greatly attract-

---

[61] Abu Dawud, "Sunna," 5; Al-Tirmidhi, "'Ilm," 5.

ive to people, but it is very valuable and immune to claims of self-assertion and words of pride that are incompatible with the rules of Shari'a and irreconcilable with self-possession. In every age, a handful of pure souls have gathered together around this source, breasted the adversities surrounding their community, fought against the dangers that lie waiting in ambush for the spirits, embraced human beings with love, helped them realize their worldly and other worldly expectations, and then said farewell to this world without tasting its pleasures to go to the other. This they had to do, as an easy life and bodily pleasures are deadly poison for them and to imbibe these would mean that they had contradicted themselves. Instead of living contradictions and controversies, which is the bitterest of separation, something that is worse than death for those who order their lives, not for their own but for others' happiness, they prefer to receive their documents of discharge from worldly responsibilities and emigrate to the realm where the friends are.

The second kind of separation is that which is of no use and impresses the one who suffers it as a calamity. It arises from denial of God, from heresies, and misguidance. It continues in the intermediate world of the grave and even in the other world, bringing no reward to those who suffer it. This kind of separation is the most pitiable.

The third separation is neither useful nor useless, it is a separation that begins in the womb of the mother and continues until the grave. This is a separation which every mortal human being is destined to suffer. Although it sometimes brings reward to those who suffer it because of the purity of intention in their acts, it usually causes pangs for souls that have fallen away from the Almighty and that have not been able to maintain righteousness in their inner worlds. The meaning of the following couplets of a poet are truly helpful when trying to understand the states of those who suffer such separation:

> If a person stays in separation from his home even for a moment,
> He is not as powerful as even a piece of straw,
> be he as firm as a mountain.
> That helpless, poor one may seem still to be where he is,

But he always sighs when he recollects his home.
I have many complaints of separation from friends;
Nevertheless, this is neither the time nor the place to tell of it.

O God! Make me one who often mentions You, often thanks You, one often turning to You in repentance, submitting to You deeply, and often appealing to You in contrition!

May Your blessings and peace be upon our master Muhammad, the master of those who often turn to You in contrition, and on his family and Companions, who wept much in Your way and often appealed to You.

IGHTIRAB (DOUBLED SEPARATION)

Ightirab (doubled separation) is a feeling resembling that which arises from falling into error after reform, or night following day, or the darkness of distress that surrounds the heart after exhilaration. Those whom the Messenger praised in His saying, *Glad tidings to the outsiders*, have always had a dread of such a feeling.

Resembling the separation described above in many ways, doubled separation may arise either from a physical condition or from one's spiritual state, or from one's spiritual profundity and knowledge of God. In the third case, it is felt more deeply.

Doubled separation which arises from a physical condition is homesickness, separation from one's family, relatives, and friends. Particularly when all the means for reunion no longer remain, the spirit sinks into an unbearable feeling of separation. If such a separation is not balanced with a belief in God and the Resurrection, it becomes very difficult to endure. If one bears it with belief, one will die a martyr, as stated in the Prophetic Tradition, *The death of one away from his home is martyrdom*. If it is not accompanied by heresy and unbelief, according to *Every misfortune brings a reward*, then it is a gift from God that is beneficial, as it leads to God. According to some, such separation, the pain of which has been softened by belief, is such a sweet suffering that it brings as great a reward as one has the strength to bear. Even though a person may sigh and moan when faced with this pain, the human conscience welcomes it. The following couplets of a poet express this well:

> Those away from home and who see me in this state,
> Let them sit by my grave when the time is due.
> For only those suffering separation know each other's state;
> They are keepsakes entrusted to one another.

O my Lord! You are One Who provides means
for those without means;
It is only You Who will provide means for both me and others.
As out of night You bring forth day, You are also able
To bring forth joy and happiness out of my sorrows.

The feeling of separation arising from one's spiritual state is appreciated and honored in the Prophetic saying, *Glad tidings to the outsiders.* Such people are righteous people struggling with what a corrupt age brings; a scholar devoted to truth lost in a community drowned in ignorance; a faithful one dedicated to truth in a world permeated by hypocrisy—all those suffer separation within separation. When such people witness the great waves of corruption spreading over the land, the ruination of the ignorant masses, and the regard paid to hypocrisy and hypocrites they find themselves in increasing loneliness and become possessed of a great desire to tell the truth to others in order to guide them.

As for the separation that arises from spiritual profundity and a knowledge of God, those suffering from this feel and expect that which exists in the purely Divine Realm, and find themselves in the depths of spiritual pleasures. Nevertheless, until they meet with the Almighty, they feel in their souls the separation of those who are closed to the Truth around them, never being able to free themselves from feelings of separation that arise while journeying toward God. Although they always yearn for nearness to God and to meet with Him in the warmth of His friendship, they are sometimes under the influence of the fear, worry, and sensitivity that they feel during the journey; sometimes the eyes of their hearts are veiled by some evil thoughts and imaginations occurring to them unintentionally. Such people suffer separation, each according to their particular degree. Though the separation of some may be substantial, the separation that most suffer is only imagined or of the kind that arises from worry and excessive sensitivity. They tremble with the fear that this separation, which arises during their relations with the Almighty in different wavelengths, may affect their faithfulness, loyalty and nearness to God, and wound them spiritually. Since initiates view such separation as a sign of loss while they are striving and advancing toward gain, they feel helpless. In the worries or thought of being abandoned or left alone, they sigh in great pain and may cry out: "I wish my mother had not given birth to me."

While those who suffer separation from home console themselves with the thought of the eternal union in the hereafter, and those whose separation arises from their spiritual states can find comfort in their renewed pursuit and in glimpses of knowledge and love of God, the separation felt by those who have reached contentment in the knowledge of God is absolutely unbearable. The worldly people, who neither see nor know what is beyond the material world, are unaware of what state such people are in. Nor can those known for their regular worship of God or those renowned for their asceticism recognize them or understand their condition, because they cannot get beyond their worship and asceticism. But the horizons and aims of those endowed with the knowledge of God and the efforts that such make to reach their horizons and realize their aims, are as deep and high as the greatness of their relationship with the One Whom they adore.

O God! Show us the truth as the truth and enable us to abide by it, and show us falsehood as falsehood and enable us to avoid it.

May God's blessings and peace be upon our master Muhammad and his family and Companions. Amen, O All-Aiding One!

ISTIGHRAQ (IMMERSION)

Literally meaning absorption, diving into, becoming deeply involved in, *istighraq* (immersion) denotes transportation by joy, oblivion of the world, the cleansing of the heart from worldly worries enabling one to turn to God wholeheartedly, and, in consequence, going into such deep ecstasies that one becomes un-aware of even oneself and one is filled with wonder. Those who have acquired love and friendship of God and who have been honored with His special nearness and compliments, travel between love and witnessing the truths that pertain to Him. They throw away whatever exists in their hearts other than Him, fixing their eyes on Him only, becoming absorbed in the observation of His beauties.

Initiates in this state, with the inner perceptions and feelings that come from self-annihilation in God, see everything annihilated in God also. Those who are enraptured with the pleasure arising from such a state cannot help but utter sayings such as "I am the true one" or "Glory be to me, how exalted my being is!" Although such sayings issue from mouths under the influence of the spiritual state and pleasure that pervades the being, they have sometimes been taken to be true. It sometimes occurs that initiates cannot distinguish between what is substantial and what is apparent and, confusing their drop-like being with the infinite ocean of Divine Existence, utter unbecoming words of pride that are incompatible with the rules of Shari'a and irreconcilable with the self-possession that one must have before God. Even if every initiate cannot experience such a depth of self-annihilation and the pleasure that issues from it, most of them feel and experience this state. Some of them are regarded as being directly taught by God or the Prophet, without needing another teacher or guide; this is called "the way of Uways al-Qarani."[62] Muallim Naji[63] refers to this way as follows:

> See, what kind of immersion you have caused me to experience;
> My eyes see you as if you were the tears which they shed.

Immersion has three degrees:

The first degree is that in the beginning, an initiate acquires knowledge of some truths, but not being able to experience what is known, he/she is not perfectly conscious of the truth of it. Knowledge is different from experience. Any knowledge concerning the Divine truths is usually theoretical until belief, love and spiritual pleasure become second nature for the initiate. When an initiate feels and experiences these in the very center of the conscience, then knowledge has been absorbed in the spiritual state. This knowledge absorbed and lost in the conscience is the knowledge of a Prophet. We call it knowledge only because at the beginning it is knowledge. At the end of the journey, where this knowledge is completely absorbed and lost in the conscience inciting the initiates to and guiding them in action, it becomes the spiritual state and a station in which the initiates finds peace. With respect to Prophethood, the best description of the initial degree of immersion is in the verse (37:103): *When both (Abraham and Ishmael) submitted (to God) wholly, Abraham laid Ishmael down on his face (to sacrifice)*. The last, perfect degree of this Prophetic knowledge, which has become the Prophetic state, is impossible for us to perceive.

Those whose knowledge has become their state have always been examples to be followed by people. It is difficult to describe such people, even with comparisons and parables. On the other hand, there are others who are described in the Qur'an as, like an ass carrying books (62:5). A scholar unaware of the knowledge he or she has and

---

[62] Uways al-Qarani (d. 656) is regarded by some as the greatest Muslim saint of the first Islamic century. (Trans.)

[63] Muallim Naji (1850-1893). A famous Turkish poet whose views of literature and education has affected many. He defended the classical Turkish poetry. *Istilahat-i Adabiya* ("The Terms of Literature") is his most famous work. (Trans.)

whose knowledge has not become his or her state is no different from an ass who merely carries the books. Any state which is not based on knowledge is tantamount to heresy, while knowledge which has not become a state is ignorance and heedlessness. Straightforwardness through knowledge means rising to a heavenly point on the wings of the state based on knowledge.

Initiates who have attained the second degree in immersion and in whose spirit the truth concerning the Essence of the Divine Being has developed, rise to the rank in which the One Who freely bestows gifts favors them with special gifts. At this rank the spirit severs its relation with all other than the Almighty and turns to the horizon that the appreciative heart has indicated. In the eyes of initiates honored with such a favor, the variations between the manifestations of the Divine Names disappear and everything seems to them immersed in the light of the Divine Essence and veiled by His Attributes. Seekers after the Truth who, until they have attained to this rank, mention the Eternal One Who freely bestows gifts with His Names, such as the All-Beautiful, the All-Majestic, the All-Subtle, and the All-Over-whelming, take themselves into a life intoxicated with gifts that come directly from the Divine Being Himself, Who is the All-Light. They do not think to make any distinction between the Essence of the Divine Being and His manifestations.

To describe this state, Jalal al-Din al-Rumi, the most advanced one in intoxication, says:

O Muslims! I am unaware of myself: what means do you offer?
I am neither of the world, nor of the other world, nor of Paradise nor of Hell;
Neither am I of Adam nor of Eve, nor of the highest abode of Paradise.
I am from nowhere and nowhere has no signs with which to make me known.
I am divested of both body and soul, being in the royal tent of the Beloved.
I have thrown away both my eyes, seeing the two worlds together, and
I know Him Who is the One, mention the One, search for the One, read the One.
O Shams al-Tabrizi! I am so intoxicated in this world that
Nothing but intoxication can be a cure for me in this abode.

The third degree is that an initiate may attain to the point beyond the sphere of the manifestations of the Divine Attributes and become immersed in the most sacred manifestation of the Essence of the Divine Being, Who is known as the First and the Last, the Outward and the Inward. This state is also viewed as a return to the station where the initiate's heart recognizes the Almighty as a Hidden Treasure, or as a return to the unconditioned realm where everything pertaining to the created realm vanishes. A spirit which gets into this state usually expresses itself by saying: "There was God without there being anything that existed with Him. Now He is as He was before."[64] It addresses itself to its confidants:

> The place where I am has developed into no-space;
> This body of mine has wholly become a soul;
> God's Sight has manifested Itself to me; and
> I have seen myself intoxicated with His meeting.

> (Nasimi)

It is very difficult to express more beautifully than in that stanza the relationship and difference between the Existence of the Self-Existent One and the portion of all other beings, whose existence is totally dependent on Him. However, the following verses of 'Abd al-Rahman Khalis are also truly beautiful:

> O Muslims! What is this state in which I am and which bewilders me?
> Sometimes I am a crazy lover, sometimes a wretched, insane one.
> Sometimes I am a poor one having no place, and sometimes the king of time.
> For I am intoxicated with the wine of love, knowing nothing else.
> I am one who pays no attention to the cap of austerity.
> All praise and gratitude be to God that I have drunk the wine of love;
> I am speaking in the land of Oneness the words of Him Who is One,
> Not worried that the King of Time may do anything to me,
> And having no fear of those who wear coarse robes.

I have omitted the words that were uttered in the state of total intoxication as against the Book and the Sunna of the Messen-

---

[64] Al-Bukhari, "Tawhid," 1; Ibn Hanbal, *al-Musnad*, 4:431.

ger. Even though not to utter such words is a self-contradiction for the friends of God who are under the overwhelming influence of the spiritual state, the same action would mean straying from the path for those who are sober and can make a distinction between the Creator in His Transcendence and the created. It is especially heresy for common people to utter such words in mere imitation of those who have been overwhelmed by the spiritual state.

> *O God! O One Who guides the astray, guide us to the Right Path, and peace and blessings be on him who is the most honorable of God's creation—Muhammad—and his family and Companions, who are the rightly guided. Amen, O All-Aiding!*

GHAYBA (ABSENCE)

L iterally meaning disappearance and no longer being existent, *ghayba* (absence) denotes that the heart has cut its relationship with the corporeal world in order to give itself to exclusive devotion to God. Although derived from the word *ghayb*, which means being not present, *ghayba* (absence) signifies self-annihilation and no longer having a relationship with the surrounding world, despite being present.

Travelers to the Truth experiencing absence no longer have any interest in the laws that are in force in the life of existent beings and the conditions in which they find themselves. They have completely freed themselves from the states that belong to the carnal self under the dazzling shower of the Divine gifts which have come uninterrupted to invade their hearts. In this state they are unaware of how and where they are or even of their own existence. Because of the intensity of the Divine manifestations that they experience, they no longer can see although they look, they can no longer hear although they listen, and they are lost in feelings of wonder while thinking. For them, there is no difference between presence and absence. This can be partly explained by the analogy of the women who, when they saw the Prophet Joseph, were so struck by his beauty that they cut their hands. Joseph's beauty could only be a shadow of the shadow of His Beauty, reflected from beyond many veils. If seeing Joseph's face caused presence to change into some degree of absence, it does not require much explanation how the burning manifestations of the Divine Beauty can dazzle the eyes and bewilder minds.

Presence and absence change places, one turning into the other, only when initiates separate themselves from everything else other than the lights of His Essence. In this state, they feel and think of Him only and restricts their eyes to observing His manifestations exclusively. By so doing, they feel enveloped in His Presence completely and no longer see or hear whatever takes place and whatever is said. If, under the influence of some attributes of human nature, initiates come to see and hear things and happenings—which is called a "return"—all things other than God come into view and their hearts suffer an eclipse, without receiving light from the real Owner of light. They can free themselves from this eclipse by perfect love of and yearning for Him and by perfect resolution.

Like contraction and expansion, there can be long or short tides between feeling enveloped by God's Holy Presence and feeling eclipsed from Him. Feeling enveloped by His Presence is sometimes understood as being synonymous with witnessing Him in His manifestations, sometimes as witnessing His signs, and sometimes as self-supervision. This station may cause an initiate to slip from the straight path because of the intensity of God's manifestation of Himself with all His Names throughout the universe and with some of His Names on an individual thing or being in particular. So, both this station and the manifestations received in it must be viewed in the light of the Prophetic way. Otherwise, initiates who feel pervaded by these manifestations may go so far as to claim that they have seen the Divine Being Himself. Provided that one does not confuse the Essence of the Divine Being with His invading manifestations and utter words of pride that are incompatible with the rules of Shari'a, feeling enveloped by the Presence of the Divine Being means living in the shadow of the Realm of the Holy Presence, and is pure spirituality that has almost nothing to do anymore with the physical or animal dimension of our existence. Hafiz al-Shirazi[65] says:

> If you, O Hafiz, desire to always feel
> enveloped by His Holy Presence;
> Never be heedless or unmindful of Him.

---

[65] Hafiz al-Shirazi (1230-1291) is the greatest lyric poet of Persia, who took the poetic form of the *ghazal* to unparalleled heights of subtlety and beauty. (Trans.)

> If you desire meeting with your Beloved,
> Renounce the world and the worldly people.

These words of Hafiz are also important in expressing our understanding of austerity. Shaykh al-Akbar Muhyiddin ibn al-'Arabi shares the same consideration: "A heart's feeling enveloped by God's Presence depends on its distance from people."

The state which is called absence in respect to ourselves and presence in respect to God, the Truth, has degrees according to the level of an initiate:

- A lover of God leaves no room in the heart for anybody other than Him; fixes the gaze on Him only and continues normal relations with other things or beings only because of Him; feels, sees, and hears something of Him in whatever is encountered during the spiritual journeying.

- An initiate mindful of the rules of the way combines knowledge and this state in the depths of the spirit. In other words, at the horizon reached, knowledge has become for the person second nature or a state. Having been saved from the error of entanglement in knowledge that is mere information (i.e. has not yet become a state), and from the heedlessness arising from a state not based on knowledge, the initiate is favored with absence from the created and with the Presence of the Creator.

- A friend of God who has risen to the station in which everything is seen as annihilated in the Divine Being, not only feels the state and station attained, but is also so immersed in the manifestations of the Essence of the Divine Being that even His Names and Attributes are no longer discerned as such. The person may unburden him or herself with words that sometimes suggest the transcendent Unity of Being, sometimes the Unity of the Witnessed. Sometimes it may even occur that the uttered words imply a sort of pantheism or monism. It should not be forgotten that this arises from a confusion of the truth with something that is a total experience and that is tasted by the spirit. ʿAbd al-Nafiʿ expresses his feelings belonging to the station where one can easily fall into wonder and amazement, as follows:

> Look on, what is this amazing state!
> I wonder whether it is absence.
> Reason cannot perceive this ocean-like state;
> It is not possible to resist its waves.

This station is also that in which one knows the Divine Being with Himself, beyond knowing Him with His Names and Attributes. In this station, one knows the Divine Being with Himself, infers His Existence from Himself, and reaches Himself by Himself. One considers Him as the First and the Last, the Outward and the Inward; not as a spirit or a body, not as an essence or an accident, but rather as being absolutely free from occupying a place, from eating and drinking, being contained by time, changing and transforming, having form and color. In this station, which is one of the highest stations and where one is at risk of lapsing and falling, one considers the All-Holy Being beyond all concepts of modality and hopes to view Him with the wonderstricken eyes of the heart.

> *Our Lord, do not let our hearts swerve after You have guided us, and bestow upon us mercy from Your Presence. Surely You, only You, are the (Munificent) Bestower.*
>
> *And give peace and blessings to our master Muhammad, who is one ever turning to God in contrition, and on his family and Companions, who are all honored and righteous.*

WAQT (TIME)

In the language of Islamic Sufism, *waqt* (time) denotes the time when the Divine gifts pour on a traveler to the Truth in accordance with one's nearness to Him. These gifts invade the inner world with their Divine quality according to one's capacity to receive them in the frequencies particular to them. If the gifts come with an air of fear and sorrow, the traveler becomes as an embodiment of fear and sorrow; if they come with the air of rejoicing and exhilaration, then breezes of peace and joy begin to blow in one's world of feelings, without causing loss of self-possession.

One who is conscious of the Divine origin of the gifts may express resignation with such words as "Your favor is welcome, and so is Your resentment." One acts in peace and contentment and tries to attain confidence in the valleys of reliance, surrender and commitment. Negligence of what is necessary for a traveler to do in order to hunt these gifts that come from the Truth—for example, neglecting to do what falls to the free will in order to obtain a desired result—is a fault on the part of the saintly ones, who have reached the ranks of perfect godliness and nearness to God. Since this means that the heart has lost some degrees in its relation with God, the Truth, the traveler is punished according to his or her rank. Those who have risen to a certain rank are expected to use all their time in the most profitable way possible, and to try to strengthen their relation with the Almighty and multiply their rewards. It is because of this that a Sufi is called "a child of time."

Being "a child of time" means that initiates always consider what they must do at all times and, doing what is best in God's sight, use all times and opportunities given by God as if each were a seed capable of producing seven or seventy or seven hundred grains. This also means fixing one's eyes exclusively on God and always turning expectantly and hopefully to the source from which the Divine gifts come. Also, one makes one's will dependent on God's Will. The beginning of this rank, marked by an initiate's spiritual state and pleasure, is time and its end is the intersecting point of being contained and not contained in time and place. We can also view it as the projection onto an initiate's heart of the Messenger's rank—he reached the highest point predestined for him, a point at which he became so close to God that there was left only the *distance between the strings of two bows adjacent to each other or even less* (53:9). Mawlana Jalal al-Din al-Rumi indicates this as follows:

> A Sufi is an example of how one can be a child of time;
> But as for a purified saintly scholar, he is free from both time and state.

The periods of time when the Prophets, purified saintly scholars, and saints, are sent to the world, charged with special duties, and honored with the reward of their efforts, are the periods when the doors to the Divine gifts are wide open and the world is enlightened and honored by the Divine Light. Those periods, and every part of the Age of Happiness, that is, the Time of the Messenger, in particular, are regarded as the Days of God in proportion to the density and extent of radiation of the lights those holy people diffuse. On the other hand, time gets darker in proportion to the fading of the enlightening thought that they diffuse and in proportion to the world's being deprived of this thought.

If the Almighty wills that His servants who are traveling on His way be favored and embraced with mercy, He strengthens them with time, making it a ladder for them to climb beyond time, or enabling them to do many useful things in a short time, things that would be impossible in a normal timeframe. If, by contrast, He wills to throw those who stray from His way into loneliness and boredom, He wraps time in evil for them and allows them to wander on the slopes of time in a dark, barren land that is closed to the Truth. We call this barren part of time "time" only in order to make a comparison. Otherwise, time is a gurgling stream that continuously flows into the observatories where God's acts are observed.

The true heroes of time have always taken the present day into consideration and tried to use it in the best way possible. They take the previous and the following days into account, but only from the viewpoint of their being the beginning and end of the present day; they regard the previous day as the basic element of the fabric of our lives and the following one as the weft. As for those foremost in nearness to God who live as if beyond the limits of time, they make use of all of time, they have assigned time to God in such a mysterious way that according to the famous adage *One who does not taste, does not know*, we cannot perceive it. Those people who do not live on the same horizon can neither grasp the showers of gifts with which they have been favored nor understand the profundity of their knowledge of God and the depth of the spiritual pleasures they taste. As time serves like rain pouring down from the heavens and a fertile field bursting with vegetation, they sometimes think of the past favors of God and increase their devotion to Him, saying, "Should I not become a thankful servant?"; sometimes they speak to themselves of such feelings of gratitude and are immersed in waves of gratitude. Their responsibilities always bring them good and blessings, and the good and blessings they receive lead them to more gratitude.

By virtue of being conscious of the source of the favors and understanding the main reason lying behind the compliments, an initiate experiences pleasures beyond all understanding and begins to perceive punishments as if they were favors. Though such a degree of favor may open the door for some people of certain disposition and temperament to free and easy behavior and the utterance of proud words that are incompatible with the rules of Shari'a, those who travel on the way to God guided by the Sunna of the Prophet always behave with self-possession. In obedience to the Divine commandments, they adorn their nearness to God with utmost respect for and awe of Him; they fly in the depths of the heaven of sainthood on the wings of knowledge and the knowledge of God. Attributing to God alone whatever favors they may receive and whatever achievement they may realize, their lofty ranks will never prevent them from the utmost humility. Traveling from state to state, they drink gifts sip by sip from the bowl of self-possession.

For others who can take one more step forward, things and events no longer become visible, the past and future are confused, and time melts away in the infinity of the absolute Owner of Time and completely disappears from their view. Traveling in such a mysterious valley, they taste the pleasures of seeing everything annihilated in God and, in the face of the scene which things and beings display under the overall manifestations of God's Names, they feel wonder, absorbed in turning to God and amazement at His signs and acts. They even take the manifestations of His Names and Attributes for His manifesting Himself in visible forms or in nature or other things. This mood is the point where an initiate may become confused in the world of his or her feelings, thoughts and pleasures. Some people of different temperaments may, as mentioned above, confuse God's manifestations of His Names and Attributes with His manifesting Himself in different forms, and see a drop as if it were an ocean, a particle of light as if it were the sun, nothing as if it were everything, and utter such words as: "I am the true One; How exalted my being is!"; "There is nothing that exists save God;" and "There is nothing that truly exists save God."

We should point out that the fact that everything is from Him and is sustained by Him does not mean that nothing else exists, or that everything is not different from Him, or that everything is identical with Him. If things and events are not viewed and analyzed in the light of the Prophetic Message and with an insight and consciousness based on it, and if the spiritual journey is not based on self-possession and discernment (between truth and untruth, origin and shadow, God and His acts and works), it will be difficult for people of certain disposition and temperament to be freed from such confusions.

O God! Guide us to the Straight Path, the path of those whom You have favored.

May God's peace and blessings be upon our master Muhammad and on his family and all of his Companions!

SAFA' (PURITY)

Safa', in the language of Islamic Sufism, signifies the state of a heart at peace because it has been purified of all kinds of things that contaminate it, such as sin, feelings of vengeance, jealousy, and hatred, and suspicion of others. The verse (38:47), *They were, in Our sight, among the most purified, chosen, truly godly ones*, which expresses the holiness and greatness of some Prophets, stresses purity in the greatest degree. The word *mustafa*, derived from *safa*, and which means pure essence, extract or the cream of something, is the special title used to express in particular the rank of our Prophet, due to his being the essence and cream of existence and the master of both worlds—this and the next. So, having a special distinction among all ranks and being a symbol of transcendence among the Prophets, it has always been a goal toward which the Prophets and the purified, saintly scholars have tried to rise.

Purity originates from the purest and most blessed of sources and reaches the pool of the human heart, from which it issues and flows into other hearts to enlighten them on new wavelengths according to the capacity and disposition of each and the requirements of time and conditions. It sheds light on the ways of the travelers to the Truth so that they can follow them easily. It purifies their hearts and equips them with sincerity, guiding them to the truth of Divinity, causing their spirits to move in ecstasy with the infinite pleasures of supplication and their hearts to move with love, zeal, and yearning for meeting the Beloved. It is usually dealt with in three categories:

The first is purity of knowledge. It occurs when a traveler continues the journey under the guidance and in the light of the knowledge taught by the Messenger, upon him be peace and blessings. The Book and the Prophetic Sunna are followed strictly and with utmost care during the journey, the requirements of doing so being never neglected. With the good pleasure of God as the sole aim of the journey, the traveler faces all hardships and difficulties, without ever losing the resolve to continue on the way.

In other words, purity of knowledge occurs when an initiate who is traveling under the guidance of the sun of Prophethood, puts heart, spirit, and reason under the command of this sun. Following him to the utmost possible in all thoughts, actions, and attitudes, the traveler is annihilated and revived in him, and appeals to his judgment to solve all the problems encountered. The traveler is honored with various favors to the extent of love and knowledge of the supreme goal—God—and zeal and yearning to meet with Him in the footsteps of the pride of Messengers, upon him be peace and blessings. The author of the *Gulshan al-Tawhid* ("The Rose-Garden of Divine Oneness"), talks about this rank as follows:

> Go and pursue such knowledge that
> It can open your heart and solve all your problems.

By contrast, any knowledge that does not inspire in people the true aim of life and, in order to realize that aim, does not equip their sight with the necessary light, their will with strength, their spirits with love and zeal, and their hearts with the desire to reach the realms beyond the heavens, is not promising, even though it may not be a delusion or mere illusion.

The second rank in purity is purity of state. It occurs when the heart opens and closes with the awe of God and love of the truth. It expresses its excitement and anxiety in supplications and entreaties to the Almighty, removing feelings of loneliness and gloom that come between it and the truth, becoming a hill where the breezes of peace blow. Setting itself solely on God alongside all the other faculties, such as the emotions, consciousness, and perception, the heart flings all else except the Almighty into the abyss of nothingness, like a stone, in order that nothing should veil God from it.

When seekers after Truth attain the state of purity and refinement, their hearts overflow with the manifestations of the truth of Divinity, their spirits are flooded with the love of truth, and enraptured with the real beauty of existence which they observe through the windows that have been opened in them. In this state, they turn to the Realm of the Holy Presence with the most enchanting of supplications voiced with the full force of their sincere feelings, feelings that have begun to speak instead of themselves. They unburden themselves, feel that God is turning to them, and taste the deepest of pleasures. It even happens that in this state they invoke the Divine Being Himself as *Allah*—the Proper Name of the Supreme Being encompassing all other Names —and as the All-Merciful (*al-Rahman*)—the primary Title of the Supreme Being which, like the Name *Allah*, can be used for Him exclusively—among the Attributes with which they qualify Him. In the rising waves of their feelings, they sense the pleasure that the angels have in worshipping the Almighty, witness the self-possession of other spiritual beings, are enchanted with the mysteries of the higher, incorporeal realms of existence and the beings that inhabit them, and feels as if they have transcended the limits of humanity. In the following couplet, the author of *al-Minhaj* points to this spiritual state, which one who does not experience it cannot grasp:

> Sometimes a person is dumbfounded in this state,
> without being able to utter a word,
> And sometimes only one who experiences it can know what state this is.

Purity of meeting with God, which is the third rank in purity, occurs when the worshipping servants become as nothing or, to put it in other words, feel and know annihilation of their own being, attributes, and actions in the Being, Attributes and acts of the Necessarily Existent Being, and live immersed in observation of the blazing manifestations of God's Existence and Knowledge. In other words, the pleasure that the worshipping servant feels in God's service is combined with, and melts away in, the duties of servanthood due to His being the Lord (One Who creates, sustains, brings up, and protects), and the mysteries of existence become unveiled and come into view on all sides. The manifestations of God's Existence and Knowledge that pour in completely pervade the conscience, and the shadow of the truth, which will become visible in the other world, begins to be seen with the eye of the heart. To paraphrase the state, God declares to His servants whom He has made near to Him: *He hears by Me, and sees by Me, and holds by Me, and walks by Me.*[66] So, such servants observe from their observatories of heart and inner-most faculties, such as the Secret, the Private and the More Private, the pure spiritual realm with some of its mysteries, and the pure realm of the Divine Dominion with some of its particularities, and the spiritual realm of the Divine Power with some of its aspects, and the truths originating from the Divine Being. They know the sub-stantial truth behind realities that are evident to everybody, and ac-quires certainty in their knowledge, and their certainty rises to the degree of certainty that comes from direct experience (*haqq al-ya-qin*) according to their capacity. Peculiarities vanish and particular natures melt away in the burning rays of the manifestations of His Face, and only His Self-Subsistence is felt. In this rank, initiates, who have reached a state of pleasure that pervades the whole being, feel as if a drop has become an ocean, a particle the sun, and everything has turned into nothingness. They feel and know Him only, and be-gin and end with Him, and work by Him. They may go so far as to confuse His Being with His manifestations. Those who are not able to enlighten their feelings, consciousness, and faculties of per-ception with the light brought by God's Messenger, may make mis-takes or be confused in their comments. Many people have uttered words showing this confusion:

> When you have seen the lights of the sun,
> You no longer exist, (burnt away by the lights of His Face).
> A drop is lost in the waves of the ocean, and you, being a drop,
> Have been lost in the ocean of mysteries.

---

[66] Al-Hakim al-Tirmidhi, *Nawadir al-Usul*, 3:81; Ibn Kathir, *Tafsir al-Qur'an*, 2:580; Ibn Hajar, *Fath al-Bari*, 11:374.

> You will no longer be able to find the drop.
> Though it is not in the capacity of everyone to be lost,
> Those who are annihilated like you are not few.

If those who try to explain purity of meeting with God use words that suggest incarnation and union in order to convey their states and pleasures, they are apt to be confused in their interpretations. Therefore, they must immediately appeal to the light of Muhammad, upon him be peace and blessings, and correct their confusion. On the other hand, those who adopt an interpretation and attitude that arise from a spiritual state and pleasure simply as a thought system and philosophy, are clearly misguided and are regarded as being in rebellion against God until they enter the way of the Messenger and his Companions.

> *O God! Show us the truth as the truth and enable us to observe it; show us falsehood as falsehood and enable us to avoid it.*

> *O God! We ask You for forgiveness, health, and approval. O God! Guide us to what You like and are pleased with; and may Your peace and blessings be upon our master Muhammad, the sun of guidance, and means of happiness, and on his family and all of his Companions.*

SURUR (REJOICING)

Meaning joy and delight, *surur* (rejoicing) is a kind of contentment that embraces a person from both within and without. Even though every conscience feels it differently, what is common in the rejoicing felt by everyone of those who rejoice is that breezes of intimacy come from the true Friend at different wave-lengths, invading the human inner world.

Lovers of God are made aware of rejoicing with the fragrance of meeting Him, the loyal with the faithfulness in their hearts, and the heroes of nearness to Him with sentiments of certainty. According to their capacity of perception and feeling, each type of person exclaims, *In the grace and bounty of God and in His mercy—in this, then, let them rejoice. This is what is best for them, not all (the worldly riches) that they may amass* (10:58). When they consider the origin of rejoicing that has arisen in them, they breathe peace and feel exhilaration with the joy of the Divine gifts that come to them.

Belief and all the results it promises, *islam* (being a Muslim) and all the exalted goals it directs people to, the Qur'an and the fruits with which it is laden pertaining to this and the other worlds, excellence (*ihsan*) and the vision of God in the hereafter which it promises—each is a mercy and bounty of God given to persons according to their rank, and the joy and contentment that these gifts rouse in their hearts are the flowers of rejoicing that open in the emerald hills of the heart.

Belief, *islam*, the Qur'an and *ihsan* (excellence) are the greatest gifts of God and the rejoicing that arises from being honored with them, with its inherent suggestion of gratitude and praise, is the greatest of all favors. Such rejoicing exceeds all worldly joys and pleasures and it is worth sacrificing the world and whatever is in it for its sake. It is because of this excellence that the Qur'an proclaims: *This is what is best for them, not all (the worldly riches) that they may amass.*

While the Qur'an condemns any joy which does not arise from some Divinely approved thing and it is not certain what it will bring, it praises the rejoicing that comes from the knowledge of God and Divinity, obedience to the Messenger and the fruit of such behavior, and being a Muslim and the fruit of this. In many verses, the Qur'an states: *Let them rejoice* (10:58); *Rejoicing in what God has granted them* (3:170); *Feeling exhilaration in what is sent down to you* (13:36); *For them is the glad tiding (of happiness and triumph) in the present, worldly life and in the hereafter* (10:64); *God will give beauty and cheer to their faces and rejoicing in their hearts* (76:11), and *They will return to their family in rejoicing* (84:9). While those feeling a joy which does not arise from anything that has been Divinely approved are threatened with an evil end, the others are offered the pleasure of happiness and exhilaration.

According to the source of the rejoicing and the way in which it is felt, rejoicing can be dealt with in three categories:

The first type of rejoicing is that which is embedded in spiritual pleasure. Such rejoicing is a Divine screen against the fear of falling far from the Truth, and of being defeated by the darkness of ignorance of Him, and of the worry of being exposed to loneliness.

The worry of the common believers about remaining distant from the lights of the Truth and breaking away from Him shows itself along with the fear of being unable to surmount the difficulties that surround access to Paradise, and the fear of becoming entangled in the bodily appetites that lead to Hell. The fear that the distinguished ones among believers feel about being exposed to loneliness is accompanied by the fear that one may feel no desire for the good, Divinely approved things, and no aversion to sins or immoral behavior. As for those foremost in nearness to God, they fear and worry that their feelings about separation and isolation are accompanied by a hesitation or slowness in choosing between remaining in this world and going to the hereafter. All of these things cause everybody grief and anxiety to varying degrees. The rejoicing that appears on the horizon of the heart when its arguments have gained precedence becomes a means of exhilaration against this grief.

Whether it is caused by a lack of knowledge of God or is the basis of wrong behavior and rebellion, ignorance causes grief and anxiety to the spirit. To prevent this, the absolute Friend removes the darkness of heresy, misguidance, and denial that sometimes infiltrates into the spirit; with the breezes of rejoicing which He causes to blow in the breasts and illuminate the hearts of His friends with His own Light, making them sources of light as indicated in the Verse of Light (24:35). We can interpret this as the Almighty's bringing forth those whom He loves into light from the darkness, reviving their hearts with the light of His Knowledge, and making them candidates for eternity. The light-diffusing Divine declarations in the Qur'an point to certain dimensions of this Divine favor. For example: (2:257) *God is the Owner and Confidant of the believers, bringing them forth from the darkness (of unbelief, heresy, and misguidance) into the light (of belief, islam, and perfect goodness)*; and (6:122) *Is, then, he who was dead (in spirit), and We raised him to life, and set for him a light by which he moves among people without any deviation— is he like the one who is lost in depths of darkness, out of which he cannot emerge?*

When the spirit falls far off from the pure spiritual realm, which is the true source of the Divine gifts that flow into it, it becomes wretched, feels lonely and isolated, and is dragged towards other paths with different expectations and feels discontent. Yet, as declared in the verse (13:28), *Know well that in the remembrance and mention of God do hearts find rest and contentment*, a heart which is fed on remembrance and the mention of God can overcome all adversities with the pleasure it has in the rejoicing that God has caused to arise in it.

The second type of rejoicing is that which comes from witnessing God in everything with all His Names and Attributes. Seekers who progress from knowledge to knowledge of God wholly submit their

bodily life and free will to the Divine Will by virtue of their obedience, devotion and spiritual connection to God, and their relation
with Him from the bottom of their hearts. They rise to a new life
by the Lord's will; the result of this is that rejoicing appears and the
spiritual dimension of their spiritual existence that looks to the other world gains predominance. Even though they fulfil what they
should do to obtain a result, their belief in, submission to and reliance on God are a much more powerful resource in their decisions
and actions, and they feel events with their peculiarities at wavelengths
that belong to the realms beyond. This may be viewed as self-annihilation in God. The author of *al-Minhaj* pictures the deep rejoicing that arises from such rejoicing as follows:

> A state which proceeds from knowledge of the Unseen;
> It is not possible to perceive that knowledge except through pleasure.
> Always make efforts so that you can be freed from your own self,
> (For acquiring this knowledge is only possible
> by becoming free from one's own self.)
> It is incumbent on you to acquire it, if you can pay its price.
> Knowledge of the outer dimension of existence
> is mixed with clay and muddy water,
> While knowledge of its inner dimension (nourished with Divine gifts)
> guides the soul and heart.
> (Spiritual) knowledge is a hidden treasure which comes to you,
> In proportion to how much you can be freed from your own self.

The rejoicing that arises from acceptance of the heavenly realm,
which is the third type of rejoicing, removes the feeling of loneliness and isolation from every part of the spirit. It prompts travelers to the Truth to witness the Divine Being in His signs and causes them to overflow with the hope of knocking on the door that
witnesses the manifestation of His Names and Attributes, and in
the hope that their spirit will drown in the joys that pertain to the
other world.

At this level of rejoicing, the heart, the spirit, and the other faculties, all turn to the One Who eternally speaks, with a most sincere desire and—as indicated in the saying, *If He did not want to*

give, He would not have given the desire to ask—they are honored with acceptance by the One Who answers and bestows freely. Seekers who rise to this level are enraptured with the streams of rejoicing in their spirits and begin to feel the breezes of His intimacy blowing from the Realm of the Holy Presence. They feel as if at the threshold of the pure spiritual realm of Divine Mercy and become aware of the pure realm of the Divine Dominion with an overflowing desire and excited readiness to knock on the door that witnesses Him in His signs and the manifestations of His Being. It is as if they have been turned into pure spirits, becoming quite intoxicated with what they see and hear beyond all concepts of modality, and smiling at all those favors by the Grace of God.

> *O God! Include us among those whose faces are bright (with the vision of You), and who are looking towards Your Holy Face.*

> *May God's peace and blessings be upon Muhammad, upon him be the most perfect of blessings and salutations, on his brothers among the Prophets and Messengers, and on all the members of his family.*

TALWIN AND TAMKIN
(COLORING AND SELF-POSSESSION)

Meaning coloring, taking on a color, painting, and presenting different views, *talwin* (coloring) in the Sufi language is an important degree belonging to those who continuously seek to change their states for higher ones and to gain stability in the ranks they reach during their journey through actions in pursuit of God's good pleasure.

If coloring is, as asserted by some, the presentation of ever-different views by continuously changing states, then those who are in this state are still in the initial stages of the journey, without having yet reached the horizon they are aiming for and without having attained peace or rest in their hearts. If, on the other hand, they can feel or sometimes find themselves in the final stage of the journey, and their changing of states and the lags in time occur as stated in the verse (18:19), *"We have stayed a day, or part of a day,"* then, by means of their intention, will-power and resolution, they will fly from one rank to another. As they never avert their eyes from the goal on which they have set their hearts, and since they always keep company with Him in their souls and emotions, they are not even aware of the fact that they advance, though sometimes they linger. By removing the short-comings that are caused by instances of indecision or changes that arise from being in a state with intention and far-sightedness, they will be safe from displaying their changes of colors, especially in moments when they are satisfied with the charm and magnificence of the goal. In addition, if the superb performance they display during their journey is favored with gifts, granted in advance, bearing the colors of the goal, even their temporary halts will serve as a means of gaining stability. The different colors they take on, or the different views they present may be regarded as self-possession, by virtue of the goal for which they are heading. For this reason, we can say that the travelers to truth at this degree breathe self-possession in their coloring; coloring in this sense is a Divine imprint. Any Divine work or imprint cannot be defective, for the Almighty is perfect in all His Attributes, Names, acts, and works. The verse (55:29), "In every moment He is in a different, new manifestation (beyond all conceptions of modality)" refers to this truth.

Leading scholars in Islamic Sufism have dealt with coloring in two categories:

The first is the coloring which is witnessed at the beginning of the spiritual journey and which is still not free from the influence of the carnal self and desires, which may be risky and deceptive for the initiates, leading them to make groundless claims like, for example, being the Mahdi[67] or the Messiah.

The second is the coloring which is praised by God, and comes from the Truth on the wavelength of guidance, and in response to acknowledgment of helplessness and poverty before God and thankfulness and reflection. It is accompanied by contentment, and there is a potential for the traveler to reach the desired goal. In addition, it opens the way to further colorings, which can function as ladders of self-possession. Such coloring rarely deceives and does not cause the traveler to make groundless claims nor to utter words that are incompatible with the rules of Shari'a and self-possession. Although it is apparently as charming and splendid as the former, this coloring is free from the influence of the carnal self and desires, because *A wind may blow away a piece of straw but how can it blow away a mountain?* (That is, an initiate who has reached this degree of coloring is like a mountain deeply established in the ground of religion and cannot be blown away by the wind of carnal desires and groundless claims.)

---

[67] Al-Mahdi is the Muslim Messiah promised to come toward the end of time to revive the Islamic life. (Trans.)

The author of *Mizan al-'Irfan* expresses the same truth in a beautiful style:

> He feels constant worries on a slippery ground,
> While crossing distances without stopping at all.
> He advances forward from one attribute to another,
> Being promoted from one rank to the other.
>
> ....
>
> Every moment he changes states,
> With his feet in a different realm every day.
> He always takes steps toward higher stations,
> Presenting a new view, taking on a new color.
> This is how one advances to perfection,
> This is the state of one who experiences coloring.

Self-possession is the opposite of wavering and instability, and denotes steadfastness, dignity, solemnity, and contentment. The leading scholars of Sufism see self-possession as deepening in straightforwardness and gaining stability to attain contentment and peacefulness. Whether at the beginning or the end of the journey, seekers with self-possession who aim at the horizon of resignation always feel the beauty of their end—dying a believer—and the joy to come at meeting with the Beloved. They are even unaware of being elevated from one state and station to another.

Travelers to the Truth takes on colors at the beginning of their journey as an indispensable characteristic of state. For they always see, hear and feel different things while crossing the long distances from the Names to Him Who is called by the Names and the Attributes and Him Who is qualified by the Attributes, and from state to station. Since what they see, hear and feel has a certain kind and degree of influence on their being, their manners display coloring; this is bound to continue until the travelers reach their goal. When finally the truth of "subsistence or permanence with God" manifests itself on the horizon of "self-annihilation in God," the coloring gives up its place to self-possession. The author of *Mizan al-'Irfan* describes this occurrence:

> When a man of God attains his goal,
> God announces to him, "Return to your Lord...!"
> When he has reached the Ka'ba of the goal,
> And the way ended in the Highest, Most Desired One;
> This is the self-possession gained on the Sufi way,
> In which the excellent have attained excellence.

Self-possession is a few steps above contentment and denotes stability and composure which requires the greatest patience and resolution; these attributes are found in the great Messengers, something that the Qur'an refers to (30:60): *Let not those who have not attained certainty lead you to unsteadiness.*

Those at the beginning of the journey can attain self-possession through sincere intention, extremely strong will-power, and true knowledge that comes from its true source and the guidance of a perfect guide. They must make the attainment of the good pleasure of God their goal on the journey, they must be equipped with a strict religious life according to the *Ahl al-Sunna wa'l-Jama'a*[68] (or the way of the Messenger and his Companions), and travel guided by the master of the creatures, upon him be peace and God's blessings. In other words, the goal must be God, the equipment, a careful life in strict accordance with His commandments, and the way, the Straight Path which is free from all kinds of excessiveness.

The self-possession of those who have dedicated themselves to God wholly should assign their hearts to God exclusively and keep them free from attachment to all else save Him in order to receive His gifts. Ibrahim Haqqi of Erzurum[69] stresses this, saying:

> The heart is the home of God; purify it from whatever is there other than Him.
> So that the All-Merciful may descend into His palace at night.

---

[68] *Ahl al-Sunna wa'l-Jama'a* is the overwhelming majority of the Muslims who follow the way of the Prophet and his Companions in belief and actions. (Trans.)

[69] Ibrahim Haqqi of Erzurum (1703-1780) was one of the most outstanding figures in the Ottoman Turkey of the 18th century. He lived in Erzurum and Siirt in the Eastern Turkey. He was a prolific, encylopedic Sufi guide and writer, who wrote in many subjects such as Theology, Morality, Mathematics, Astronomy, and Medicine. His *Ma'rifatname* ("The Book of Knowledge and Skills") is very famous and still being widely read. (Trans.)

The self-possession of those favored with the knowledge of God is that whatever they do they do it as if they were seeing God, and in whatever state they are they are in it is as if they were seeing God; this is the highest point of excellence from where they see everything annihilated in God. They have reached this point where they are in constant self-supervision by realizing their "self-annihilation in God" and "permanence or subsistence with Him." At this point, they are perfectly aware of the Source from which they receive gifts and always turn to that Source with deep yearning and wonder. They feel that they exist by His Existence and subsist by His Self-Subsistence. Following the lights diffused by the perfect guide of humanity, upon him be peace and blessings, they claim neither the Unity of Being nor the Unity of the Witnessed, and keep within the sphere of the truth described in: *It is incumbent upon you to follow my way (Sunna) and the way of my rightly guided and guiding successors.*[70] With the conviction that their existence is solely from Him and they subsist because of His being the All-Subsisting One, they feel well-established in existence and securely maintained, and acknowledge that permanent existence is possible by self-annihilation in His Existence. They submit to Him with all their being and say:

> I have given up all existence for the sake of Your love,
> And orphaned my family so that I could see You.

O God! I ask You to equip me with being well-pleased with You after any misfortune comes upon me, and for a peaceful life after death, and for the pleasure of Your vision, and for zeal to meet with You. And may God's peace and blessings be upon our master Muhammad, who guides us to the way of peace, and upon his family and honored Companions. Amen, O All-Aiding One.

---

[70] Al-Tirmidhi, "'Ilm," 16: Abu Dawud, *Sunan*, 6.

MUKASHAFA (DISCLOSURE)

Mukashafa (derived from *kashf*, meaning uncovering or discovering) denotes that the Divine mysteries will be disclosed to those well-versed in the Divine truths when, by rising through a spiritual struggle, they are able to perceive and come to know the truths about the Divine Names and Attributes. Travelers to the Truth who have attained this rank are regarded as having completed their journey in the Divine Names and Attributes, each according to individual capacity, with the result that the Divine mysteries begin to pour into the heavenly faculties—that is, all of the spiritual faculties, such as the heart and the spirit—that have been entrusted to humanity and which are the projection in humanity of the Divine Throne of Mercy. The veils before the pure spiritual realms are opened slightly to these people, and the truths that stand in front of and behind things are disclosed to them. This is called *disclosure* because one gains familiarity with the things unseen behind the veils. Disclosure is used to define familiarity with abstract truths and meanings which are by nature invisible, while the terms "witnessing" or "observation" is used to deal with beings.

Disclosure (whose Arabic origin—*mukashafa*—is in the form that suggests mutuality) implies that intimate friends disclose secrets to one another. The best example of this is that of the Messenger, honored with God's praise to the greatest degree, who attained the rank at which God revealed to him almost all the secrets of His Speech (53:10).

God discloses some of His secrets to His friends who unburden themselves to Him. His friends talk to Him from their hearts and the One Who knows all the things hidden in creation showers the gems of His knowledge into their hearts. They rise to the horizon of recognizing their Lord with His All-Beautiful Names and All-Pure Attributes in proportion to this disclosure in order to be immersed in the lights of this recognition. The Absolute Hidden One removes the veil slightly from before the seeing of their hearts so that they can perceive the truth of light and He raises them to the peak of excellence. Until reaching this horizon, every initiate can make a connection with the pure spiritual realms from behind the veils. Whatever they see during their journey to that horizon, they see it as if from behind a smoky piece of glass and cannot clearly discern the manifestations of the Divine Names, Attributes and Essential Qualities. Even if they feel that they have discerned some things, it is but a mere illusion.

The veils between the travelers and the ultimate truth differ according to their relations with the Truth. Just as being closed to the truth of the Names and Attributes is a veil, the heart's turning to some object other than God is another veil. The interpretation of existence according to mere human philosophy is yet another veil. To search for source of light other than the light of Muhammad, upon him be peace and blessings, is another, dangerous veil. Moral deviations, such as jealousy, arrogance, conceit, ostentation and selfishness, are veils that lead to misguidance and unbelief in proportion to how great an obstacle they are to discerning the truth. The traps laid by these veils are those arranged by the carnal self, Satan, the world which looks on our desires, our weak spots, and our human shortcomings. Each of these traps is deadly. When a person becomes entangled in these, all of his or her endeavors to rise in rank on the way to God are in vain and it is inevitable that he or she will suffer separation on the way to meet with God.

The first step of disclosure for those who fulfill the requirements to travel on the way to God is a manifestation of the knowledge of God, which the One eternally witnessed in His signs produces in their hearts. If they are steadfast on the way, they can advance as far as the final point, where they will be able to witness or observe Him in His signs. Nevertheless, such manifestations may not be constant and the way may sometimes be obscured, with the result that travelers may suffer setbacks. However, the desire to advance in their hearts never ceases; even if sometimes they feel dizzy and waver, they constantly endeavor to reach the goal with a desire that is insurmountable. It is heroism to follow the rules and requirements of the journey without falling into despair, and those who continue on the way heroically are favored with constant disclosure and advancement. They rise from the certainty that comes from knowledge to the certainty that comes from observation. If they are able to take two steps more forward, they are favored with the clearest disclosure supported by self-possession and wakefulness. If they are able to advance further, their journey ends in observation—seeing the All-Holy One, Who is called by the Most Sacred Names with the eye of the heart or insight—this will be explained later.

The clearest disclosure is when the Divine lights pervade the heart and all other faculties so as to enlighten and to be felt by all the emotions. In other words, an initiate feels the Source of these lights beyond what is demonstrated by His signs and proofs. This was the beginning of the spiritual journey of the master of the creatures, upon him be peace and blessings. Throughout his life, all of which he spent at the highest of all ranks and at the summit of all virtues, he continuously traveled from closure to observation and always felt and experienced the mysteries of belief deeply. Especially during his ascension, he acquired certified familiarity with all the mysteries that belong to the realm beyond, including Paradise, Hell, the angels, and even the sounds of the Pens of Destiny. Then he returned to the world in order to keep the way open for others to travel along, each according to individual capacity. Furthermore, he secured this way with reflector-like lights that he installed along it. In the ranks in which he traveled and made observations, he progressed without his eyes swerving and without his mind becoming perplexed, as declared in the verse (53:17), *His eye did not swerve nor did it stray*. When it came to the point where he was too great for this world of formation and deformation to bear and when he entrusted the way and journey to those who would come after him, he proceeded to his Lord, saying: *O my God! (Now it is the time to go) to the Highest Friend*! His faithful followers have made the same journey in spirit which he made in the universal dimensions and which he has bequeathed to them with its means and results so that each can realize in part his journey, according to their capacity. Some have expressed their feelings, observations, and insights in the following words, "O Sariya! (Withdraw) to the mountain, to the mountain!";[71] some with words which reveal their special relationship with God: "Even if the veil of the Unseen were removed, my certainty (of belief in the pillars and truths of belief) will not increase;"[72] and some with the glad tidings, "Be hopeful! The highest voice which will be heard worldwide among the revolutions of the future will be that of Islam."[73]

> *O God! You are the First without any preceding You; You are the Last, there are none to succeed You. I seek refuge in You from the evil of all moving creatures whom You hold by the forelock, and I also seek refuge in You from committing sins and going into debt. And may God's blessings and peace be upon our master Muhammad and his family and honored Companions.*

---

[71] During the wars with the Sassanids, 'Umar, the second Caliph, saw Sariya, the Muslim commander, surrounded by the enemy at the front while he was himself on the pulpit in the Prophet's Mosque in Madina thousands of miles away, and gave him the instruction, "(Withdraw) to the mountain, to the mountain!" Al-Tabari, *Tarikh al-Umam wa'l-Muluk*, 3:42. (Trans.)

[72] This quote belongs to 'Ali, the fourth Caliph. 'Ali al-Qari, *al-Asrar al-Marfu'a*, 193.

[73] Bediuzzaman Said Nursi, *Sunuhat-Tuluat-Isharat*, 44.

MUSHAHADA (OBSERVATION)

Mushahada (observation) means using insight to see in Divine acts the Divine Names that give existence to them, and to become aware, in the manifestation of the Names, of the All-Holy One Who is called by those Names. In other words, observation denotes that those favored with Divine nearness reach the horizon where they leave the corporeal realm behind and observe like bright mirrors reflecting God's absolute Oneness.

Observation is seeing with insight or with the eye of the heart, and is therefore different from seeing. In his *Sharh-i Muhammadiya* ("The Exposition of Muhammadiya"), Ismail Haqqi Bursawi[74] stresses this difference: Observation, a great Divine gift, is seeing with insight, not with the eyes. What is seen with the eyes is the shadow and manifestation of the Divine Light. As for what is seen with insight or observed, it is the truth of the Divine Light and the observation of the Truth Himself, seen with the eye of the heart, beyond all concepts of modality.

Observation is also different from disclosure. Disclosure is that an initiate acquires familiarity with certain meanings and abstract truths; the object of observation is beings, though not, of course, the Divine Being that absolutely cannot be comprehended. In other words, when the term "observation" is used with respect to the Divine Being as the object of observation, it means turning to Him with one's illumined and with illumining insight in such a way that one attracts Divine attention to oneself, while disclosure is the state in which one feels the Divine Names and Attributes.

---

[74] Ismail Haqqi Bursawi (1653-1725) is one of the great Sufi guides and writers. He spent much of his life in Bursa, Turkey. His *Ruh al-Bayan* (a 4-volume commentary on the Qur'an) is very famous. *Kitab al-Natica* is his last work. (Trans.)

Observation is made possible by a vigorous heart with keen sight and hearing. These senses are highly sensitive and receptive, completely connected to the realms beyond, and conducive to perfect concentration. The verse (50:37), *Surely in this is a reminder for one who has heart or give ears having a full capacity of seeing*, can be interpreted as referring to this fact.

Like disclosure, there are degrees of observation. One can think of these degrees as being assigned to different capacities in order to observe the truth. Everyone is favored and honored with observation according to the depth of their belief, the strength of their certainty, and the capacity of their heart.

The lowest of these degrees is observation through knowledge of God supported by knowledge and belief. Initiates who have reached this point feel that by virtue of their strong certainty, they feel in their conscience that the lights of Divine Existence pour on the horizon of their perceptions in the form of Divine knowledge. Such persons begin to walk with a deep yearning to the point where they will see everything annihilated in God.

The second degree of observation is so clear that it is as if one were seeing with one's eyes. One favored with knowledge of God who has reached this point transcends His signs and the pieces of evidence provided by creation and, melting away in the originality of the Divine Names and Attributes, attains the observation of God's Oneness beyond His acts, Names and Attributes, which provide His signs and evidence in existence. Conscious of the fact that one's existence is only shadowy, the seeker fixes his or her eyes on Him exclusively. Concerning this station, the author of *Mizan al-'Irfan* says:

> Discovering the (Divine) Being is an elevated station,
> Where the currency of speech is not valid nor in demand.
> Whoever attempts to knock on the door at that station,
> Always receives the answer, "You will never be able to see Me!"
> If he is shown a sign like that resembling the one shown to Moses,
> It will be only a single manifestation of His Majesty.

The third degree is observing everything as being annihilated in God. Those perfected ones favored with knowledge of the Truth and who have attained this highest degree annihilate their material being and feel attracted by the All-Existent One with the All-Beautiful Names and All-Sacred Attributes by virtue of belief and a certainty that has been transformed into observation. With sight that has gained the keenness that it will have in the hereafter where the veils over the eyes will be removed, they know fully Who their Creator, Lord, Originator is, and the One Who has endowed them with the light of existence and Whom they worship. They are freed from any connection with all else save Him.

Junayd al-Baghdadi describes this station as the manifestation of the Unseen, which is perceived by means of the Divine lights in the time when hearts overflow with rejoicing. The author of *Mizan al-'Irfan* says concerning the same point:

> If the absolutely Sovereign Being manifests Himself,
> The existence of the universe is no longer felt.
> If the Truly Beloved One manifests Himself,
> Will any trace be left of the shadow of darkness?
> However, this point leads some to confusion;
> They take His lightning-like manifestation for the Being Himself.

What the author of *Mizan al-'Irfan* is reminding us of is not to confuse the original with the shadow, and to take an observation from the conscience and the heart in a state of pleasure for the observation of the True Being Himself. The following verses are only a few drops from the essence of such confusion:

> If you have been given two eyes to know the Truth,
> Then see the two worlds-this and the next-filled with the Friend!
> Though we are each a drop, we are drowned in the ocean;
> Though we are each an atom, in fact we are the sun.

> *O God! Show us the truth as the truth and enable us to observe it, and show us falsehood as falsehood and enable us to avoid it. And give peace and blessings to Your Messenger, the chosen one, and to his family and Companions, esteemed and faithful.*

TAJALLI (MANIFESTATION)

T ajalli (manifestation), which has almost the same meaning as showing itself, display, and appearance, in the language of Sufism means being favored with God's special gifts. It also denotes that the Divine mysteries have become apparent in the heart of the seeker by means of the light of knowledge of God Almighty. Every traveler to the Truth can feel this favor in the conscience according to capacity and station.

The manifestation which is felt and perceived in every realm, be it low or high or simple or composed of parts, especially those included in humanity, which has the potential to attain perfection in all fields and is the most polished mirror to God, is called the manifestation of (Divine) works. A step forward is the manifestation of (Divine) acts, which means that the Divine acts are perceived with their meanings and purposes in the heart of the servants who are favored with glimpses of the manifestation of the Names as a result of their having a true view of God and His acts with God's help, but without falling into naturalism. The manifestation of the (Divine) Names is when they take on the color of the Divine Names as their feelings have become mirrors to them. After this is the manifestation of the Divine Compassionateness or the particular manifestation and the manifestation of the Divine Mercifulness or the universal manifestation. The former is the manifestation with which the believers, including in particular the most loyal ones, are favored and by which they are embraced from all sides, while the latter denotes the manifestation with which God favors the whole of creation by giving it existence and by maintaining it. Believers come to perceive in their hearts one or some of the Divine Attributes with their true nature, meanings and actions. This is the manifestation of the Divine Attributes. God elevates His servants whom He has favored with this manifestation to such a rank that, under the guidance of the Attribute or Attributes manifested, He makes them hear sounds others cannot hear and see things others cannot hear. There is another kind of manifestation that is connected with the Divine Attributes and this is called the manifestation pertaining to the Attributes; that is, it is purely a manifestation of an Attribute in a way that does not bring to mind the Divine Being Who is possessed of this Attribute. If, in particular, the Existence and Knowledge of God manifest themselves in the heart of a perfected believer in all their nature, meaning and actions, in the company of other Names and Attributes, this is called the manifestation pertaining to the Divine Being Himself. Although the manifestations of the Divine Names and Attributes are usually ignored with regard to this greatest and most intense manifestation, what is true in respect of this is that the Necessarily Existent One cannot be viewed and considered without the veil of the Names and the imaginary outlines that are drawn by the Attributes so that people may have knowledge of Him.

The first and universal manifestation that pertains to the Divine Being Himself occurred as the special manifestation of His Divinity and Lordship on the Prophet Muhammad, who was also known as Ahmad and Mahmud, and who was regarded as the ultimate cause for the whole creation being transferred from existence in the (Divine) Knowledge to the external, sensed existence. The community of Muhammad, upon him be peace and blessings, has a particular share, albeit shadowy in this manifestation. What the Prophet Moses experienced on Mount Sinai was a particular manifestation of the Divine Lordship by means of the mountain, which was only an aspect of the greatest manifestation mentioned with respect to the Prophet Muhammad—albeit such comparison is of matters beyond all human concepts of modality.

We can approach this last point from the viewpoint of Sufism as follows:

Like the desire of Prophet Adam for the forbidden tree, which resulted in all of his descendants coming to this world, including, in particular, the greatest of them all, Prophet Muhammad, upon him be peace and blessings, Prophet Moses had an intense love for the Truly Existent One and an irresistible desire to speak to Him. At a time when the evident signs of his Prophethood and Messengership came one after the other, he sighed from the bottom of his heart with an overflowing yearning: "Show me Yourself, that I may look upon You!" (7:143). The Voice of the Power, Which always speaks with wisdom, answered: "Never can you see Me (with your eyes in the world)." The Almighty meant: How can you see Me, seeing that you are still behind the veil of seeing Me and prevented by separation, being in the corporeal world. You are a shadow of the light of My Existence. If You rise to the horizon of seeing Me by Me, then you can see Me, but not with your eyes as I declared, *Eyes comprehend Him not* (6:103). When you desire to look, you must look at the mountain of existence with the eyes of non-existence so that the mountain of existence may remain as it is and you will be able to see what you desire to.

Nevertheless, none except Prophet Muhammad would be favored with this manifestation. So, for an answer to Moses' over-flowing yearning to see the Divine Being and refusal to the appeal to see Him with his eyes in the world, the Almighty Lord displayed a manifestation of His Lordship on Mount Sinai or the nature of Moses, and either the Mount or both it and Moses shook violently and fell down as if struck by lightning. When the teaching for guidance had finished, Moses woke up from his faint that had been caused by the might of a manifestation of the Divine Lordship, and said: "My God! I proclaim that You are free from all kinds of defect, and that You alone are All-Holy (to be worshipped as God, and the Lord). From now on I turn to You with the consideration of annihilation in You and subsistence with You. We can observe You in Your signs, not with the darkness of our egos, but with the light of Your Being. I am among the first to believe in this truth."

The gist of the matter is:

> Love functioned as if the soul of Sinai, and
> When it was intoxicated with love, Moses fell down in swoon.

The manifestation of the Lordship has different categories:

The first is the manifestation of the Being Himself. Although this is a manifestation beyond the Names and Attributes, it has uniqueness of its own. Yazicizade Mehmed Effendi, the author of *Muhammadiya,* implicitly criticizes the Mu'tazilites who deny a vision of God in the Hereafter and expresses this spiritual perception as follows:

> Since His image shows itself wholly within my soul,
> My heart wipes away both name and form from this imaginary picture.
> As it is possible to view Your Face and I desire to view It,
> For I keep my ears free from the words of the Mu'tazilites.

The manifestation of the Divine Attributes, which is the second category or degree, is the manifestation of one or more of the Attributes within certain restrictions. This has been dealt with in two sub-categories:

The first is the manifestation of the Divine Majesty, with which people of self-possession are favored, and the other is the manifestation of the Divine Grace, of which people of coloring feel in need.

If those who have not attained self-possession and wakefulness receive the manifestation of the Attribute of Existence, they may say, as Junayd al-Baghdadi said: "There is but He under my robe." When those who are not people of self-possession are visited by the overall manifestation of Divine Oneness with His Names and Attributes throughout the universe, they can express the state they fall into with pleasure, like Bayazid al-Bistami, who said: "Glory be to me, how exalted my being is!" If they are invaded by the manifestation of the Attribute of Permanence, they can utter the sentence that is irreconcilable with the rules of Shari'a, that Hallaj al-Mansur[75] did: "I am the Truth!"

When this manifestation occurs as the manifestation of the Divine Power and Will and is received in its true nature in wake-ful-

---

[75] Husayn ibn Mansur al-Hallaj (857-309) is famous for his utterance "I am the Truth." He mostly lived is Basra. He is also famous for his austerities. (Trans.)

ness, and not in a state of pleasure, it will be as expressed: *When you threw, it was not you who threw, but God threw* (8:17). It is only the master of creatures, upon him be peace and blessings, who could receive this manifestation in its originality and true nature. If it is the manifestation of the Divine Creativity, it is the Prophet Jesus who became a polished mirror to it in an extraordinary manner, as stated in the verse (3:49): *I fashion for you out of clay something in the shape of a bird, then I will breathe into it, and it will become a bird by God's leave.*

The third is the manifestation of Divine acts. This manifestation is an aspect of the Divine Attributes and means that temporary acts have been annihilated in everlasting acts. The author of *Muhammadiya* expresses this also in a vivid style as follows:

> The All-Beautiful Beloved One has displayed His Light
> again from the palace of Majesty;
> This is why I am once more enraptured and crazy
> because of the inexhaustible wine.
> My eyes and heart have removed from themselves the veil of ignorance,
> And a call has been made to my soul from the One All-Exalted.
> I have given up attachment to love as I have found His love.
> Those who have found His love have abandoned grief-laden love.

Initiates lying in wait for a manifestation sometimes become so intoxicated that they feel Him in whatever they see. It even occurs that as they are so immersed in their present state, they see themselves in whatever they look at and cannot help but utter words that are irreconcilable with the rules of the Shari'a, such as "I am the Truth," or "Is there anybody else save me in both worlds?"

So far many have made such confusions and uttered such words. We can cite here only a single example:

> I am not myself, if I am myself, then he is You;
> If I am wearing a shirt, it is also You.
> Full of suffering in Your way, I am left without body and soul;
> If I still have a body and soul, they are but You.

The manifestations that cause those receiving them to utter such words are manifestations connected with the Attributes. Those deceived by their reason or the illusions which they take for the truth, have fallen away from the sphere illuminated by the master of the creatures, upon him be peace and blessings. They have both ruined themselves and deceived others. Let us listen to what the author of *Mizan al-'Irfan* says about the state of such people:

> If an intense manifestation comes from the Divine Being,
> Some initiates lose balance in this state.
> This is a hard trial and great trouble for the initiate.
> If he is not a perfected guide or
> under the guidance of such a perfected one,
> He may be hanged like Hallaj al-Mansur.
> This is truly a difficult state for an initiate:
> Whoever utters, "I am the Truth," without being like Mansur,
> He will become an unbeliever (with his) body and soul.
> In short, this state is a slippery place,
> Where the perfected ones among the saints do not long remain.

O God! Make us of Your servants who pursue sincerity and whom You have favored with sincerity and purity of intention, and who have achieved piety and abstinence from all forbidden things great or small, and whom You have made near to You. And may God's peace and blessings be upon our master Muhammad and his family and all of his Companions.

HAYAH (LIFE)

Hayah, which can be translated as liveliness and being alive, means that a heart which is already dead because of ignorance, misguidance and disbelief, comes to life through belief, and knowledge and love of God. The verse (6:122), *He who was dead (in spirit), and We raised him to life, and set for him a light by which he moves among people without any deviation*, makes this point clear.

The scholars of truth regard life as being when one is freed from the imprisonment of the body and corporeality and rises to the level of the life of the heart and spirit. The aspect of this favor which is represented by the master of the creatures, upon him be peace and blessings, who, although an individual, gained universality, can be seen in the verse (42:52), *Thus, We have revealed to you from Our (world of) Command (the Qur'an as) a spirit (promising life to the hearts)*. The aspect which concerns all others who promise life is indicated in the verse (8:24): *O you who believe! Respond to God and to the Messenger when the Messenger calls you (in the name of God) to that which gives you life.*

The life of the earth, with all its revival and instances of growth and flourishing, is essentially related to the soil and its content, water with its vitality, air and the gases contained in the air. Similarly, true human life is dependent on the knowledge of truth, a strong willpower and endeavor, a sound character and good morals, a deep desire for God's company, and rejoicing at the awareness of such a great favor. All these together serve as a runway or ramp from which to rise up to the realm where souls fly and reach the eternal life.

The earth derives all its riches from the source described in (16:65): *God sends down from (the direction of) the sky a kind of water and therewith revives the earth after its death*; in (50:11): *We have re-*

vived with that water a dead land, and so is coming forth (from the graves); and in (21:30): *We have made every living thing from water.* Likewise, dead souls exposed to a dearth of faith, and lack of knowledge and of love of God, are revived through belief; they begin to feel what life really means through their knowledge of God, they dive into its depths through love, and attain a full life through resolution, will-power and determination. Then, as long as initiates realize the goal of *Follow God's way of acting*[76] under the guidance of the supreme exemplar of good morals, the one who is praised in the verse (68:4), *Surely you are of the best morals*, they attain God's company in the infinite air in which they beat their wings, and feel constant gratitude and enthusiasm. When the time is due, they feel so expanded with the rapture of being in God's Presence that it is as if they transcended the limits of time and space and been favored with the rank, *When I love My servant, I become his hearing with which He sees and his sight with which he hears and his hand with which he holds and his feet with which he walks.*[77] Their spirits continue, by the Power of the All-Powerful Sovereign, flying toward eternity in the Gardens of Paradise, the Presence of the Lord of the Worlds, and the company of the Most Compassionate of the Compassionate.

In this rank, which is the essence of true life, there is neither death nor decay. Death and decay only occur with respect to the carnal self and corporeality, and there is permanence with respect to the heart, spirit and other spiritual faculties. This permanence is also viewed as "self-annihilation in God" and "subsistence by Him."

There are three breaths in the life of an initiate who has reached this degree: the breath of fear, the breath of expectation, and the breath of love. As the carnal self fulfils an important mission on behalf of corporeality and the body, fear, expectation, and love are each an important dynamic for the life of the spirit and heart. Always feeling fear and love of Him causes the conscience of the initiate to feel an overflowing pleasure by far greater than what a child feels upon seek-

---

[76] Al-Jurjani, *al-Ta'rifat*, 1:216.
[77] Al-Bukhari, "Riqaq," 38.

ing refuge in the arms of the mother who has just chided him. Thinking of Him as the All-Compassionate, All-Loving Lord, and considering the depth of His Mercy, is such a spiritual pleasure that if it were to take on a physical form, it would appear like a Garden of Paradise. Finding or reading His Names on the face of His works, breathing His Attributes on the climate produced by the manifestations of His Attributes, and feeling the pleasure embedded in wonder at the consideration of the relation between His works, Names and Attributes, gives such an indescribable pleasure that only those who have been able to realize this degree of spiritual ascension can feel it.

Those who can most swiftly reach this most precious goal, even though they are unable to feel the grace of this sacred journey at every step, are those who set off by being able to acknowledge their poverty and helplessness before God, and their gratitude and enthusiasm. They know how to become an ocean while each of them is still a drop; they know how to travel among galaxies while each is still a particle, and although they see themselves as nothing, they are able to live in the wheel of existence in accordance with its ultimate goal. They always travel saying, as Ibrahim Haqqi said:

> I have attained pride through poverty,
> And supplicating to the Truth,
> I always utter, O All-Living, O Self-Subsistent!

They overflow with enthusiasm and gratitude, and are enraptured with the lights of the true life and existence, which are found a step beyond this horizon. Without considering the assertions of some, such as the Unity of Being and the Unity of the Witnessed, they feel the truth of life and existence beyond all conceptions of modality, and say: This life is not sufficient for such an expanse of pleasure.

> *O God! Guide us to the Straight Path, the path of those whom You have favored. And may God's peace and blessings be upon the master of the creatures, the means of the life of the two worlds, and upon his family and all of his Companions.*

SAKR AND SAHW
(INTOXICATION AND SOBRIETY)

In the language of Sufism, *sakr* (intoxication) means that an initiate is enraptured by the rays of the manifestations of God's "Face." His/her returning to his/her former, normal state is *sahw* (sobriety). These two terms are usually used together as *sahw u sakr*.

There is a relation between intoxication and absence. If the inner world of seekers after the Truth who feel intoxication is not satisfied with the Divine gifts, then they lack something in intoxication, and suffer irregular tides with respect to the state of absence. It is coloring, rather than self-possession, which is witnessed in their actions. For this reason, such seekers should be regarded as those who have perhaps feigned intoxication rather than being actually intoxicated. However, it sometimes occurs that the gifts come in showers and invade the whole being, with the result that then they do become fully intoxicated.

Intoxication sometimes arises from a strong belief, a considerable knowledge of God, and is balanced by fear and awe, making itself felt in a broader sense. As for the degree of intoxication which is felt by those who have advanced further on the way and who have approached nearer to God, whenever such travelers are honored with the light of the manifestation of the "Face" or with the vision of the "Face" beyond all concepts of modality, they immediately become intoxicated. The spirit overflows with zeal and joy and the heart feels excessive excitement.

Sobriety means that the intoxicated ones return to their former, normal state. Like intoxication, sobriety is also an undeniable part of the journeying toward the Almighty. Whenever the Truth invades the very being of the intoxicated lovers of God the Almighty, who spend their lives immersed in spiritual pleasures in the valleys of absence, they feel as if they have immediately fallen into an ocean and have vanished like a drop into the world of feelings, or that they have been burnt away like a dried, flammable object and that their nature has changed. Furthermore, the ways and bridges of sensing are demolished one after another and He alone can be felt everywhere and in everything. There are many who see a relation between such a state and what is meant in the verse (7:143): *As soon as his Lord displayed an exclusive manifestation for the mountain, He made it crumble to dust, and Moses fell down in a swoon (as if struck by lightning).* Just as Mount Sinai, or a part of it, was rendered dust, despite its immensity, and just as Prophet Moses, upon him be peace, fell down in a swoon as if struck by lightning, despite his being one of the five greatest Messengers of God, people of ecstasy feel as if they have changed their nature, they take up different attitudes, act as if intoxicated and utter words that suggest intoxication:

> O cup-bearer, pour wine into the cup, it is time to break the fast;
> Restore this ruin; it is time to display the favor we receive.
>
> (M. Lutfi)
> This day Nasimi displays intoxication with the grace of the cup-bearer;
> I have always seen Mustafa in the wine which intoxicates me.
>
> (Nasimi[78])

There are many other words uttered that concern intoxication, but it is beyond the scope of this book to cite them all. Only consider that the famous Hafiz al-Shirazi begins his *Diwan* with the verse, *Beware, O cup-bearer, bring a cup and pass it around*!

Intoxication is a state in which one is enraptured with pleasures; of sobriety the main characteristics are knowledge and self-possession. A traveler is in waves of unintended, unpremeditated joy and pleasures in the state of intoxication, while in sobriety, he or she is

---

[78] Imadeddin Nasimi (1369-1417), Azerbaijan's outstanding poet of the 15ᵗʰ century, wrote in Azerbaijan along with Arabic and Persian. He was very successful in lyric poems. (Trans.)

conscious, self-possessed, and makes deliberate efforts to feel the All-Holy Truth.

Some consider intoxication to be when a heart boils with extraordinary joy and excitement in the moment when the person feels deeply the All-Beloved One. We may interpret this state as the human self being immersed in joy and pleasures in the face of the gifts coming from the Unseen World or when an initiate loses him or herself, being overpowered by love. If the human self gets intoxicated because of immersion in joy and pleasures, this is regarded as a natural state of intoxication which an initiate gets into. If love drives the person into intoxication, this is the state of intoxication into which God Himself draws him or her. However, whatever the reason for intoxication, the traveler to the Truth lives wonder-struck and acts in tides of zeal and joy. As seekers deepen in intoxication, they begin to wander in the valleys of amazement and astonishment. Sometimes their will-power may even break down, with the result that they begin to feel as if they were a shadow of the Light of His Existence. Those who have reached this point are called the "willed ones." Their finite attributes are replaced by the manifestations of the Attributes of the All-Permanent One, and they become a polished mirror of the fact that *he sees by Me*.[79]

Indicating this highest point, it is said in *Thamarat al-Fuad* ("The Fruits of the Heart"):

> My voice, which sings like a nightingale, has been made to speak by Him;
> My eyes, which see, see by Him, and I have heard speech from Him.
> He has favored me with speech, with which He has brought mysteries to light.
> By the all-brilliant Light of God, my heart has been made extremely bright,
> And by the light of Muhammad, I have become one with a pleasant heart.

Some have disapproved the use of the word intoxication for a spiritual state as it celebrates a concept that is scorned by both reason and the Shari'a. But intoxication, which we can describe as the state of losing oneself due to the depth of love and ecstasy, is a met-

---

[79] See, footnote: 66.

aphor used to express being exposed to or being favored with the rays or gifts of the Almighty which enrapture. Initiates enraptured by these gifts or rays cannot distinguish anything because of the depth of the waves of joy and pleasure in which they are drowning. In a hadith concerning repentance, God's Messenger, who is the most advanced in reasoning and sensibility, tells us that a man of the desert expresses the excessive joy he feels with the words coming from his mouth unintentionally: "My God! You are my servant and I am Your Lord."[80] This may be a good example of what may happen within the ecstasies that one experiences due to being favored by the Almighty's stream of gifts.

There have been numerous people overpowered by this state, who burn with love and yearning. With his words, "O singer, play the instrument, for tonight I am intoxicated!", Muhammed Lutfi Efendi, taking advantage of the permissibility of metaphors, declares nothing more than the joy and zeal of a lover.

As it has been to date, many travelers to the Truth will from now on murmur the same things each in their own style in the face of the Divine lights, colors and forms that they observe everywhere. In fact, when a heart falls in love with the Eternally Beloved One and is invaded by ecstasies, and in its conscience feels His company, only those who have Prophetic insight and resolution can save themselves from confusion. Other faithful lovers, who dive deep into the cataracts of love (or who flow abundantly like a river swelling with rains,) will sometimes overflow their limits; they will let themselves into the huge waves of love due to the rejoicing originating in feeling in His company, and always live in wonder, uttering "He!"

The feeling of absence that a traveler to the Truth has during intoxication is expressed by "He!" Although some suggest confusion, the following verses are beautiful in expressing this:

> The lights of my eyes are He, and the direction for my reason is He;
> My tongue always utters He is He, and I sigh and groan with He.

---

[80] Al-Muslim, "Tawba," 7.

> My heart goes on an excursion in He, the love of my soul is He.
> Those who are lovers and intoxicated are always with He.
> My soul has sacrificed itself in the way of its Beloved,
> Its union is with He, its parting is with He;
> And the cure for its afflictions is He.

Sobriety is the condition when one favored with knowledge of God comes to after having gone into an absence of feelings and consciousness, or, as with the Prophets, when one spends a lifetime in wakefulness and consciousness. It is the opposite of intoxication. The following couplet of Tokadizade Sekip is worth quoting in this respect:

> The people of peace intoxicated with intimacy in Your Presence,
> Do not want to exchange their rapture with sobriety.

Intoxication is a state, while sobriety is a station and is more objective, secure, and straightforward when compared to intoxication. While intoxication comes from a subjective consideration of the Truth, sobriety is based on the consideration of the All-Exalted, Majestic Being known by His Names and outlined by His Attributes and Whose Essence cannot be perceived. From another perspective, an initiate is out of his or her senses when in a state of intoxication, but is sensible in sobriety. Intoxication suggests "self-annihilation in God," but sobriety implies "subsistence with God," which is subsistence by His Subsistence and is defined as "subsistence with God and being in His company."

Some prefer intoxication to sobriety, yet this is the view of the intoxicated when over-powered by the state or induced by traveling through the valleys of coloring. There is absence in intoxication and in sobriety there is peace and rest. Sobriety is a few steps higher than intoxication. Intoxication means being overpowered by state; it is accompanied by coloring, and is the way of some saints, while sobriety depends on consciousness, is accompanied by self-possession, and is the way of the Prophets and the purified scholars. The Qur'an declares (15:99): *Worship your Lord until certainty, which is bound to come, comes*. An approach to this Qur'anic declaration is:

"Continue on the way to God until you are fully awakened by death to the truth of the belief's pillars, for traveling toward the Infinite One is endless."

In addition, sobriety is closely connected with the consideration of life and requires strong will-power. While in intoxication, the considerations of one's feeling annihilated in (God's) Existence and one's feeling annihilated in the Witnessed or in His manifestations, sometimes keep the will-power under pressure, there is in sobriety special assistance and protection that come from the company of God, such as that which is expressed in: *He hears by Me, and sees by Me, and holds by Me, and walks by Me.*

> *Our Lord! Grant us from Your Presence a special mercy and arrange for us in our affairs what is right and for our good!*

> *May Your peace and blessings be upon our master Muhammad and his family for ever.*

FASL AND WASL
(PARTING AND REUNION)

In the language of Sufism, *fasl* (parting) denotes renunciation of the world and the hereafter with respect to their own being in themselves, but not to their aspects that indicate the Creator. It also denotes that in order not to become entangled in self-pride and vanity, one must also renounce thinking that one has renounced the world and the hereafter and indeed renounce the idea of renunciation.

Parting begins with resisting the domination of the carnal self over one's life and letting the faculties of true humanity prevail. Parting continues with the heart severing its relations with all else other than the Truly Desired One by mentioning Him and by being occupied by Him in proportion to the heart's relation with Him. Parting continues by an initiate abandoning all types of love other than love for the Divine Being—loving other things because of Him is another way of loving Him—by being saved from all types of fear and worries by taking refuge in the clime of fear and awe of Him, by turning to Him alone in one's expectations, by seeing, knowing, and mentioning Him alone, and by annihilating oneself in Him.

So, the first step in parting is to turn to God with deliberate intention and be saved from all worries that concern the world and the hereafter. The steps that follow are to completely forget that one has turned to God wholeheartedly; for, if one were to remember, vanity might arise, be it ever so faintly. One must also never be heedless of the reality that there is no power and strength save with God. The final step in parting is to be free from all considerations of duality with respect to the true existence and creativity. One be-

comes annihilated in considerations of Him, and by feeling that
will-power and its results are the reflections of the Attributes of the
All-Glorified One, one lives immersed in the lights of Unity. People of certain temperaments who have attained this rank tend to
confuse what is universal with what is particular, and the original with
the shadow. Although they speak about the Unity of Being, what
they feel and experience can only be the pleasure that comes from
witnessing Him throughout creation.

Wasl (Reunion) has been interpreted as the meeting of an initiate with the Truth through knowledge that comes from witnessing Him in His signs. It never means that a servant is united with
the Creator or that the Creator becomes one with a servant. The
Eternal One cannot be and is not the same as anyone who comes
into existence within time and who perishes within it. Nor can one
contained in time provide any means for the Eternal One. Since
such conceptions as union or reunion can cause some misinterpre-
tations, some exacting scholars emphasize that the True Being does
not admit union and parting and such scholars have interpreted the
Qur'anic expression (57:4), *He is with you wherever you are*, as saying that the Divine Being is present every-where, but without being contained in one place; that is, that He has nothing to do with
matter, place or time. They regard reunion as a feeling that arises in
the conscience of a seeker of the Truth as a result of the dark veils
being removed from the insight, and the eyes of the heart gaining
familiarity with the mysteries and lights of Divine company. Such
company and nearness to God cannot be reconciled with the concepts of combination (*ittisal*) in the sense that a created being is
combined or unified with the Creator to form a single entity, and
separation (*infisal*), in the sense that any part from the Creator separates and forms a new entity. For seekers are in a continuous process of becoming and driven by the Divine Will and Power. For this
reason, they are recipients, acted upon, affected, like a mirror that
reflects, not one that has creativity or is a source. Jalal al-Din al-Rumi says in this respect:

If we come with ignorance, ignorance is a prison for Him;
If we come with knowledge, knowledge is His garden.
If we come in a stupor, we are intoxicated with Him.
If we smile, then we are His lightning.
If we come with rage and struggle, then this is the reflection of His "wrath;"
If we come with peace and excuses, this is the property He grants.
Being doubled in this world, what are we worth
that we can claim existence next to Him?
We are like an alif[81] which has no value worthy of consideration.

Reunion has degrees:

The first degree is reunion accompanied by holding fast (to God), which also has connotations of reliance, asking for help, commitment and seeking refuge. It is connected with ranks of belief and submission and is based on verses, such as: *Whoever holds fast to God, he has certainly been guided to a straight path* (3:101); *Hold fast altogether to God's rope* (3:103); and *Hold fast to God* (22:78).

Reunion that is accompanied by witnessing God in His signs is the second degree. This denotes the attainment of salvation through action and sincerity, and is independent of such reasoning processes as deduction and induction because one has attained certainty, and one has been saved from wavering on the way by setting one's heart on the only, true goal. This is related to the rank of perfect goodness or excellence—worshipping God as if one sees Him.

Reunion in existence, which is the third degree, is when the lights of an indescribable nearness to God embrace the seekers from all sides. Love is transformed into an intense love or passion, and the passion takes on the form of a brightly burning fire, with the result that the breezes that come from God's company pervade the soul, and the inner world overpowers the outer one. Those who cannot attain this degree can neither feel nor comprehend it. When the way comes to this point, the travelers find themselves in poverty of thought, and inability of perception, and lacking in words. They can only utter, "There is no power save with Him;" and cannot help but say,

---

[81] *Alif* is a short vertical stroke, the form of the first letter of the Arabic alphabet, by which Jalal al-Din al-Rumi implies the nothingness of the created. (Trans.)

"One who does not taste does not know." They travel in the world of their feelings resembling the Garden of Eden, and if they can find any power to form speech at all, they speak like Mawlana Jalal al-Din al-Rumi:

> If you would like to see this meaning become wholly manifest,
> Come and strike the sword of No! on the head of all else save Him.
> After negating the created, affirm the Creator;
> If you are able to do that, then you will drown
> in the ocean of the manifestation of the Being of the Truth.
> Then "I" and "we" no longer exist, and one poor in oneself
> becomes rich and like a king by His help.
> When the realm of Unity becomes manifest to you,
> You will believe in all that we say.
> The words of him who has knowledge of God
> are not based on conjuncture and imitation,
> But they are verified and confirmed and are based on certainty.

O God! We ask You for forgiveness, health, and approval; and may Your peace and blessings be upon our master Muhammad, and on his family and all of his Companions.

MA'RIFA (KNOWLEDGE OF GOD)

Ma'rifa is a special knowledge that is acquired through reflection, sincere endeavor, using one's conscience and inquiring into one's inner world. It is different from (scientific) knowledge (*'ilm*). (Scientific) knowledge is acquisition reached through study, investigation, analysis, and synthesis, while *ma'rifa* is the substance of knowledge attained through reflection, intuition, and inner perception. The opposite of (scientific) knowledge is ignorance, while the opposite of *ma'rifa* is denial.

Knowledge means comprehending or encompassing something thoroughly, while *ma'rifa* means familiarity with or recognition of something—that something may be the Divine Being— in some of its aspects. For this reason, the One of Unity is called the All-Knowing (*'Alim*), but He has never been called the One having familiarity with something (*'Arif*). In addition, the exacting scholars of truth view *ma'rifa*, which also means information, talent, and skill, as the culture acquired by conscience or one's conscious nature. It has other meanings such as the ability to feel something with the spiritual faculty that humanity has been endowed with, the image of something known in the mind, and the knowledge kept in the memory which gains strength through repetition. From another perspective, it is consciousness, perception, and sufficient information which helps distinguish one thing from another. *Ma'rifa* can be summed up as having concise knowledge about something or someone through their acts or works and attributes—knowledge which can be developed and detailed.

In order that one can be among those who have knowledge of God and who are regarded by God as being one of such people, one should know God and the ways that lead to Him, recognizing

the obstacles on the way, and knowing how to overcome these obstacles. One should also have enough will-power to apply what one
knows. One who has true knowledge of God is a perfect human being who knows the Unique One, Who is the Eternally-Besought-
of-All, with His Acts, Names and Attributes, and is a person in whose
everyday life this knowledge shows itself. He or she is also one who
always keeps the heart purified and pursues sincerity and purity of
intention, who can remain free of negative moral qualities as far as
possible, overcoming whatever dark emerges from the spirit and
threatens to darken one's horizon, and thereby demonstrating loyalty to the All-Protector. Such a one can bear everything that befalls
on God's way to obtain His approval, and invites others to the way
of the Prophets, which shows itself through God's confirmation in
every step, and whose lights he or she always feels with pleasure.

There is another approach to the meaning of *ma'rifa*, namely
the ability to perceive something as exactly what it is in itself, in its
quiddity, distinct from any and all things not directly connected with
it. According to this approach, knowledge of God is knowing the
Divine Being with His Essential and Positive Attributes beyond all
conceptions of modality. This is different from comprehending, perceiving and establishing other things, and is based on perception
and the feeling of conscience. This feeling and perception should not
be confused with modern intuitionism. The Divine Being is beyond
all concepts and cannot be comprehended, perceived or scientifical-
ly known, although a certain knowledge or familiarity can be acquired
of Him through His acts, Names and Attributes.

The acknowledgment that *The inability to perceive Him is the
true perception*, excellently expresses the inability of anything limited to perceive Him and the imperceptibility of the One Who is Infinite. The same meaning is exquisitely expressed in the saying, *We
are unable to know You, O Known One, as knowing You truly requires*.

It is only God Whose existence is absolute, and the greatest truth
is acknowledging His Existence and Oneness. The first step in acquiring knowledge of Him is the attainment of belief, being a Muslim, and excellence—worshipping Him as if seeing Him. In realiz-

ing such a blessed aim, one should continue one's traveling to the True Source of all gifts and blessings without turning to anything else as a source. One should be able to feel a new joy of reunion in every gift and blessing with which one is favored, and as the final point, gain familiarity with the mysteries of His Names and Attributes, and, if possible, of His Being.

This consideration is expressed as follows in *Lutfiya Wahbi*:

> Try your hardest and be one who has ma'rifa of Him,
> One favored with knowledge of Him!
> For the All-Loving One declared, "so that I may be known;"[82]
> Knowing God is the ultimate cause for the creation of the two worlds;
> And knowing God is the adornment of humanity.
> Those devoid of knowledge of Him are low in rank.
> Knowing Him is a spiritual kingdom,
> And Knowing Him is a Divine gift and blessing.
> ....
> When you, O moving spirit, receive this gift and blessing;
> The two worlds will be yours.

The following words, which are narrated in books concerning Sufism as a *hadith qudsi*—a saying, the meaning of which is from God and the wording of which was inspired in the Messenger—are the gist or kernel of all explanations concerning knowledge of God:

> O humankind! One who knows his self also knows Me; one who knows Me seeks Me, and one who seeks Me certainly finds Me. One who finds Me attains all his aspirations and expectations, and prefers none over Me. O humankind! Be humble that you can have knowledge of Me; accustom yourself to hunger so that you can see Me; be sincere in your devotion to Me so that you can reach Me. O humankind! I am the Lord; one who knows his self also knows Me; one who renounces his self finds Me. In order to know Me, renounce your own self. A heart which has not flourished and been perfected is blind.

---

[82] Here there is a reference to the Qur'anic verse, *I have not created the jinn and humanity but to worship Me* (51:56). *To worship Me* has usually been interpreted as "so that I may be known and worshipped." (Trans.)

Knowledge of God sometimes becomes a source of wonder and astonishment for an initiate, as has been said, "One who knows the Truth becomes dumbfounded and tonguetied." But it sometimes becomes a means of expression for the traveler to the Truth, as has been said, "One who knows the Truth finds his voice." The voice finds its overflowing expression in one's excitement and speech and echoes in one's ears. Although opposites, both the saying of Muhammad Parisa,[83] "There is none who knows the Divine Being other than Himself," and the saying, "I know none else save God," are true.

There is none other than Him who has a true, substantial existence, and there are no true acts other than those performed by Him. Other beings have a relative existence when compared with Him, and other acts are also relative. Whatever takes place in the cycle of causality is of a relative nature. For this reason, knowledge of God is when an initiate melts away in the light of the Truth and gains a second, true existence. This may be viewed as self-annihilation in God and subsistence with Him. I think the author of *al-Minhaj* stresses this fact in these verses:

> If you can see with the lights of certainty,
> Then do not see one who knows and the One Known differently.

Fuduli[84] expresses this depth of knowledge of God as follows:

> One who knows God is not one who knows
> the wisdom of the world with what is in it,
> One who knows God is he who does not know
> what the world is with what is in it.

Sufis have made other descriptions concerning knowledge of God. According to these descriptions, knowledge of God is know-

---

[83] Muhammad Parisa (d., 822/1419) was a great scholar and saint from Bukhara. He passed away in Madina. Among his books *al-Fusul al-Sitta* (Six Chapters) is famous. (Trans.)

[84] Mehmed Fuduli (1490-1556). The greatest poet of the Turkish literature. He lived in Iraq. His *Diwan*, ("Collection of Poems"), *Layla wu Majnun* ("Layla and Majnun"), and *Hadiqat al-Su'ada* ("The Garden of the Holy Ones") are some of his other well-known books. (Trans.)

ing the truth of the Divine Names and Attributes, grasping the phenomenon of the manifestations in existence and the discovery of the existential mystery, deeply perceiving the truth of existence with its originality and shadows, and understanding and representing in life the truth of religion according to the Will of the Desired One, Who is the final goal of those who set out to reach Him. Each of these descriptions requires a voluminous work to explain and is therefore beyond the scope of this study. We will only cite here some verses from *Diyaiya* ("The Book of Light") which point to some dimensions of the subject matter:

> The third chapter is about knowledge of God, O valiant young one;
> To describe it the wheel of speech is unable to work.

....

> There is no scribe nor a pen to write about it;
> One cannot get his tongue around it to express it.

....

> The mirror of reason is veiled from understanding it;
> The ability of perception has nothing to say in it;
> Only the bird of imagination can fly toward it;
> There is no example that we can coin to explain it.

....

> Here the gift comes only from God;
> This is a light-diffusing, sacred rank.

....

> The whole of creation is immersed in this realm,
> Which is more spacious than all the worlds.

....

> There is no true existent save He Who is the One,
> Perceiving this is the real vision;
> Do not interpret this vision in another way, or else,
> It will mean unbelief and heresy, O one with body of light.
> It is not the eyes in the head which have this vision;
> The All-Loving One is all-free from vision by these eyes.
> The innermost faculty—secret—discerns this truth,
> When you find this faculty in you, you can understand it.
> Human scientific knowledge and perception have nothing to say;
> The merit is in wonder and helplessness in this field.

> Perception of one's helplessness is perception of the Truth;
> Listen to what Abu Bakr, the truthful one, says concerning it.[85]

The rank of knowledge of God (*ma'rifa*) is a rank of wonder, utter astonishment, and awe. It is possible to see this in almost all the reflections of the scholars of Sufism on knowledge of God. Some of them see it in direct proportion to the excess of the feeling of awe and have concluded that the deeper one is in knowledge of God, the deeper one's feeling of awe is. Others regard knowledge of God as being the base of serenity and peacefulness and emphasize that inner peace and self-possession increase in proportion to the depth of knowledge of God. Still others consider knowledge of God as the heart's attainment of friendship with God and the initiate's following a way to nearness to God. The approach of Shibli[86] opens new windows on the knowledge of God. According to him, it means that an initiate has an essential relation with none save God, making no complaints when burning with His love, is a sincere, obedient and faithful servant of God who avoids any claims of superiority, and one who worries about his or her end. A person with true knowledge of God and who has a strong connection with the sources of this knowledge, one who has taken refuge in the guidance of the spirit and meaning of the Prophethood, and who has built sound relations with the truths that lie beyond human horizons, cannot feel any essential interest in transitory things nor does lower him or herself to feel attachment to other than the Lord. The Qur'an alludes to this highest point in (35:28), *Only the knowledgeable among His servants have true reverence for God*, reminding the traveler of the relation between knowledge and awe or reverence of God. The greatest of those who have knowledge of God, upon him

---

[85] The writer refers to Abu Bakr's saying: "The inability to perceive Him is the true perception." (Trans.)

[86] Abu Bakr al-Shibli, of Khorasan by origin but born in Baghdad or Samarra, son of a court official and himself promoted in the imperial service, as Governor of Demavend. However, giving up governorship, he joined the circle of Junayd al-Baghdadi, and became one of the leading figures in Islamic Sufism. He died in 846 at the age of 87. (Trans.)

be peace and blessings, said concerning the same point: *I am great-er than you in knowledge of God, and more intense in fearing Him.*[87]

In the books on Sufism, in which the intellect guided by Rev-elation is operative, and which contain numerous gems of wisdom concerning the "garment of piety" of those who have true knowl-edge of God, with Whom their hearts are deeply connected, we can find many gems concerning knowledge of God. The following are only a few of them:

- In the view of one favored with knowledge of God, the world with its material aspect becomes so small that it seems no greater than a cup.

- The souls that have gained profundity in knowledge of God expand to the extent that it is as if they have no limits.

- Those who taste the pleasure of knowledge of God, which is regarded as the sweetest of all honey, pursue no other wealth than nearness to the Truth.

- The richness of the honeycomb of knowledge of God in the heart is one of the most essential sources of love and zeal. An initiate burns with the zeal of reunion in propor-tion to how much this source overflows its banks, which he or she sees as the price of the favors received.

The following points which differentiate those who have a sound knowledge of God from others are important. The former have no selfish expectations from whatever good they do, never think of competition for either material or spiritual ranks nor feel jealous of anybody. They do not see themselves as being greater than anyone else, nor do they moan because of missed opportunities, anymore than they feel arrogant because of their accomplishments. Even if they were granted the kingdom of the Prophet Solomon, they would only seek God's company, regarding it as futile to turn to other things. They feel no relation with beings other than the Al-mighty with respect to their worldly existence and corporeal self,

---

[87] Al-Sahawi, *al-Maqasid al-Hasana*, 21.

and know that one moment of God's friendship is worth the entire world. They consider being with God among people as a victory that has been granted to their will-power, and see the Divine Will reflected in the face of their determination, recognizing the help of the Lord in the result of their endeavor, alongside many other instances of wisdom and God's extraordinary gifts. They observe the manifestations of the Divine Oneness in the multiplicity of the creation, and thereby they grasp how a drop is transformed into an ocean, and a particle into the sun. They witness in their conscience how nothingness or non-existence is a fertile land, to be planted with existence and live drowned in ecstasies and intoxication.

Self-possession, steadfastness, seriousness, profundity, and resolution are the clearest and most important signs of perfect knowledge of God. Those who have this degree of knowledge live under the shower of the manifestations of God's friendship and company. No sign of any flaws can be seen in their inner or outer world, nor is any laxity witnessed in their behaviors. They never show impertinence or conceit, even when favored with the most abundant gifts. On the contrary, they always act in a self-possessed manner, trying to lead a self-disciplined, spiritual life.

Obviously, everyone cannot have the same degree of knowledge of God. Some travel on the horizon of perceiving the Attributes essential to the Divine Being and the favors that accompany His acts. They observe and avail themselves of His proofs that are found within themselves and in the outer world, with the result that their love of truth and their relation with the Greatest of Truths are witnessed in their manners. They travel between the Divine acts, Names and Attributes and are thrilled with the different melodies of belief, knowledge of God, love, attraction and the feeling of being attracted by God to Himself. They feel in their conscience the reflections of the Divine acts or operations in the universe and pursue more and more the pleasure entailed in observing ever new colors and aspects. This is a way bequeathed by the Prophets and it is a way that can be followed by everyone. One who travels along this way of objective truth travels toward the Truth under the arches of His compliments.

On this path there are others who feel all the dimensions in existence ending in one dimension, who feel that everything is annihilated in God. It is as if they have reached a point where the lights and manifestations of the Divine Being and Attributes come together and annihilate their very being in the Divine Being, attaining a new existence with the Self-Subsistence of Him Who is the All-Knowing and the Ever-Existent.

While those belonging to the former group travel in the realm of the Divine Attributes and Qualities, others have already directed themselves to the Source of these Attributes and Qualities. Therefore, their observations and sensations are not aimed at either the Attributes exclusively in such a way as to veil the Being in their minds or spirits, nor at the Being exclusively in such a way as to suggest the denial of the Attributes. For this reason, such an approach has been regarded as the way of the perfected and most advanced, and the main path that is followed by those who travel to the greatest nearness to God.

The Book, the Sunna, reason, and the Divine system in creation and human primordial nature bear witness to the truth of this way along which God's works of art show themselves brightly. Initiates who have firmly established their feet on this path witness at every step that God witnesses His Existence and Oneness, and they cannot help but utter, *God bears witness that surely there is no deity but He* (3:18). They hear in their conscience the confirmations of angels and those possessed of knowledge as a reflection of God's witnessing, and continue to utter: *and the angels and those possessed of knowledge (also bear witness to the same truth)* (3: 18). Then, they see that all means and causes that are not essential to His Being having vanished, and they are able to be at perfect rest and to find perfect peace.

There are others who have such abundant knowledge of God that proofs of God are no longer needed in their world; all the things that witness Him are humbled in the face of their being in the

Presence of the True Witness; all the means tremble with the shame of making distant whatever is near, and all the heralds are silent and busy with correcting the words that they have uttered. At this point, where everything is seen by the conscious nature as witnessing Him beyond all concepts of modality, the eyes are dazzled by the brightest manifestations of the Face, and all other identities save His are lost. Those who have reached this point see that the True Source of existence and knowledge surrounds everything from all sides, tasting the pleasure of perceiving every being's perception of Him according to their level, and feeling that everything is annihilated in Him. They sense the way in which the manifestations of the Divine Names are combined with those of the Being, Attributes and Acts. The conscience is saved from any feeling of dependence on causality and reaches the horizon of *Surely we belong to God (as His creatures and servants), and surely to Him we are bound to return* (2:156). But this never means, as some have assumed, "absolute annihilation" or "union with God."

Our Lord! Grant us from Your Presence a special mercy and arrange for us in our affairs what is right and for our good! And may Your peace and blessings be upon our master Muhammad, by whom the mysteries came to light and the lights shone brightly upon his pure Companions.

FANA FI'LLAH (ANNIHILATION IN GOD)

F*anâ fi'llah* (annihilation in God) has connections with some of the other concepts that we have discussed. For example, sincere repentance requires annihilating one's resistance to acknowledging sin, asceticism requires annihilating carnal pleasures, the highest point of loyalty and love is the annihilation of the expectation for a pleasing life in both this and the other world, and absence (*ghayba*) as a result of intoxication is apparent annihilation. Each of these is an attitude, a feeling and state of pleasure for a traveler on the way to God, while being at the same time, with respect to the Divine Being, Attributes and Names, manifestations of the lights of the Divine Oneness in the sphere of contingent things and beings. Initiates live in tides of existence and non-existence. This life is known as devastation. Their melting away before the Existence of the Truth is known as destruction, and their feeling that their deeds are mere shadows of the acts of the One Who does whatever He wills is known as effacement. Devastation, destruction, and effacement are dimensions of annihilation. They remind one of the fact that everything other than He is a shadow of the True Existence and Knowledge, having no essential value inherent to itself. These states also function as a bridge between the relativity of truth and human perception, feeling and understanding.

The absolute truth never changes; it is always what it essentially is. Neither the assumptions of union or incarnation on the part of the Divine Being nor human absolute annihilation in God bear anything of the truth. Things and events are created by God. Human beings are His created servants, and He possesses absolute Existence and Knowledge. Every existent thing is a ray of the manifestation of His Existence and Knowledge, and humanity feels, witnesses, and interprets these manifestations. But humans can make mistakes, which should be corrected. Humankind are like the conductors of choirs singing the praises of the Creator. They interpret what constantly pours into their horizon or is presented to their view, reviewing it, and adding new melodies taken from the depth of their emotions and sensations. These melodies are sometimes in accord with the truth being played, but sometimes it happens that the state, pleasures, perceptions, and feelings are in discord with existence in their mirrors of perception and consciousness, resulting in a confusion of views of the Divine Oneness and multiplicity in contingent existence. Utterances such as "I am the Truth" (attributed to Hallaj al-Mansur), or "I am a denier if I pray, and an unbeliever if I do not" (attributed to Shibli), and "The Lord is the servant, and the servant is the Lord, so I wish I knew who is responsible for God's commandments" (attributed to Muhy al-Din ibn al-'Arabi), and "Who is the criminal, and what is the chastisement?" (attributed to Yunus Emre[88]), are examples of this confusion.

God knows the true intention and purpose behind such utterances. However, as far as I understand, while preparing for prayer, Shibli was surrounded by multiplicity. When the lights of the Divine Oneness surrounded him during prayer, he, as an obedient one who is seeking God but has been lost in the One, sought and obeyed, he might have voiced his feelings of wonder and astonishment with the phrase mentioned above. The utterance of Ibn al-'Arabi, which is apparently incompatible with Shari'a, must have been an expression of the pleasure of a similar state. Some common people, who are closed to such states of spiritual pleasure and who take such utterances as literal truth, without considering the state in which they are uttered, might suppose that people, after they have reached a certain level of spiritual awareness, are no longer answerable accord-

---

[88] Yunus Emre (1240-1320). One of the most famous Sufi folk poets who have made a great impact on the Muslim-Turkish culture. His philosophy, metaphysics and humanism have been examined in various symposiums and conferences on a regular basis both in Turkey and abroad. (Trans.)

ing to the Divine commandments. This view is nothing but a deviation from the true path. It is also wrong that certain people have accused of heresy and unbelief the great saints who made such utterances, which are the product of being lost in a state of spiritual bliss and which accordingly need to be interpreted.

If such words are the expressions of a mood of self-devastation and destruction that is beyond love and is identified with the pleasures of annihilation in God—and I believe that to be the case—the persons mentioned above who uttered such phrases should not be held to account for such words; these words must be interpreted. Those heroes of intense love should be perceived as representing and practicing the religion. It was reported that Hallaj al-Mansur used to perform a hundred rak'as of prayer every night, and that the others were also deeply devoted to the Almighty. Their words, which are apparently incompatible with the rules of the Shari'a, should be interpreted according to the basic principles of the Qur'an and the Sunna, and if they have uttered anything that cannot be reconciled with those principles, then a Muslim must, obviously, follow the guiding words of the Messenger, upon him be peace and blessings. However, these great persons are excusable because of the states that they were in when uttering such words; others who willfully imitate them, without sharing the same mood and spiritual state, will be held accountable. The author of the *Lujja* says:

> If you are not together with the good ones in all your deeds,
> What use will it be to you that you bear the same name as them.
> One of the two Messiahs restores the eyes of the blind
> While the other is one-eyed.[89]

Doing as the Prophets did in one's manners and acts is the way of saints, while blind imitation and following those who lead the way to the precipice is bound to end in spiritual death.

---

[89] The poet refers to Jesus the Messiah, and the *Dajjal* who, it is reported, will appear before the end of time as a fierce opponent of Islam. The fact that he has one eye is usually interpreted to mean that he is blind to religion and the Hereafter. (Trans.)

Jalal al-Din al-Rumi expresses the same thought in these words:

> Do not compare pure, virtuous characters to yourself;
> Though the words milk and lion are composed of the same letters (shir),
> They are not at all the same.
> If a perfected one holds dust in his hand, it turns to gold;
> While if another, defective one holds gold in his hand, it becomes ashes.

Self-annihilation in God has been dealt with in the following categories by the Sufi scholars:

- Annihilation in God's acts: Travelers to the Truth who have reached this horizon feel in every act that there is no true agent other than God. On the face of all their moments or conditions of poverty, weakness, helplessness, and need, they discern the traces of His Power and Wealth. They hear constantly the voice of the points of reliance and seeking help ingrained in the depth of their consciousness.

- Annihilation in God's Attributes: Initiates who have reached this point feel that all lives, all knowledge and power, all speech, will, hearing and sight are rays of His Attributes of Glory and reflections of His Light. Seeing themselves without any innate power or strength, they are greatly astonished by the lights of the All-Holy One called by the All-Beautiful Names, and experience extreme wonder at feeling the All-Sacred One having All-Sacred Attributes, and always aspire to meet with Him beyond all concepts of modality.

- Annihilation in the Divine Being: A person of truth who has reached the point of attaining a new existence in which all the directions are united into one direction falls into such a state that he or she cannot help but utter, "There is no really existent one save God." Those who have attained this state see all space and time as having existence in His Knowledge and proceeding from His Knowledge and perceive all existing things as manifestations of the lights of His Existence. Enraptured with the spiritual pleasures, they utter with every breath that everything is from Him, and regard annihilation in the light of His Existence as the price of being favored with existence.

Thus, as declared in the verse (37:96), "God has created you and all that you do," travelers to the Truth receive the first signal of annihilation with respect to the realm of acts. Saying, "Everything is from You, and You are the True Agent," they advance toward self-possession. Then, as pronounced in the Divine declaration (8:17), "When you threw, it was not you who threw but God who threw," they perceive their nothingness, melt away in the shadow of His Attributes and become mirrors reflecting the Attributes. Some even rise to the point where people and jinn begin to turn around them. If they are able to go further, they will go on as far as the realms beyond, as stated in, "There was God without there being anything that existed with Him. Now He is as He was before."[90] They feel themselves to be in an indescribable and all but unattainable state of pleasure, wherein their existence is transient and where they have wholly annihilated themselves on the way to permanence. Such a feeling is akin to that where a drop admits what its origin, capacity and end really is with respect to the ocean. It also denotes that everything subsists by His being the Self-Subsistent and the All-Maintaining and that nothing can come into existence or maintain its existence without being dependent on Him. So, transience and decay are essential to human nature; this is a fact of which everybody should be aware. Permanence is necessary to the Self-Subsisting One. When the journey comes to the end where the servants perceive this essential part of their nature and existence, the All-Holy Sovereign and Owner rewards them with permanence. In the language of Sufism, this favor is called annihilation in God and subsistence by God's Self-Subsistence.

The heroes that follow the way of the people of the Sunna wa'l-Jama'a and who are able to base all their views, words and manners

---

[90] See, footnote: 64.

on God's absolute Oneness, have always viewed annihilation in the endless ocean of Divine Knowledge and Existence according to the above considerations. They have meticulously observed the rules that issue from the Sphere of Divine Lordship, and the manners required by self-possession and wakefulness, even in states of intoxication and absence. Any extreme words or manners contrary to self-possession are not seen in their words and acts, even if the influence of the state and the signs of joy are witnessed. One of them says:

> The moving tunes that come from the wooden instrument and
> Which the singer plays come in fact from Him.

This means that such heroes of both annihilation and self-possession see that all things other than He are but drops from the endless ocean of the Divine Existence and, despite their self-possession, they cannot distinguish a drop from the ocean nor a particle from the sun nor the mirror from what is reflected therein because they are deeply immersed in God's Existence. As was once said,

> O beloved, you have become a river ending in this ocean;
> How difficult it is to distinguish between the ocean and the river!

They become lost in the ocean or in the heaven of the Divine Oneness or Unity into which they have abandoned themselves. Overpowered by the irresistible waves of the ocean and the depths of the heaven, they can neither see the shore nor find in themselves the power nor consciousness to come ashore.

Another one among those intoxicated ones, those who reached the horizon of annihilation in God and was favored with the gift of a new existence by the Lord, saw all existence like a mirror in which he was looking upon himself and in which he was intoxicated, said:

> Sometimes He has condescended to appear arrayed like Layla,
> And sometimes He has honored us in the form of Majnun.
> When the Beloved One has stepped out of the privacy of the meeting room,
> The decoration and ornament of the interior has become most apparent.

The heroes of immersion who have reached this highest point express their sensation of Divine Oneness, joy and pleasure, they express the favor of God's company, and the excitement of feeling Him by sometimes crying or screaming, sometimes by losing themselves and fainting, and sometimes by going into ecstasies and dancing. All of these happen during the spiritual journey on the hills of the heart. One of those who dove deeply into this ocean expressed himself in the flood of the ecstasies of his heart as follows:

> I am such a falcon of love that
> I have no place in either world.
> I am such a phoenix of secrets that
> I no longer display any trace of my essence.
> I hunted the two worlds in a pleasant way
> With my eyebrows.
> Look and know that
> I have neither an arrow nor a bow.
> I have become a voice to speak
> And an ear to listen.
> But how strange it is,
> For I have no ears nor a tongue.

The leading Sufi scholars have also dealt with annihilation in the following four categories:

- Annihilation in renunciation of people: an initiate is saved from fear of people and from having expectations of them.
- Annihilation with respect to the desires: this is the renunciation of selfishness and all worldly desires, aspirations, and bodily appetites.
- Annihilation of will-power: total submission to God's Will.
- Annihilation of reason: this is reason's submission to God in the face of the manifestations of the Attributes. This annihilation comes along with the astonishment and amazement which initiates feel even though they are unable to observe the criteria of thinking, judging, and acting that are valid in the sphere of causality. They usually cannot help

but voice this astonishment and amazement. For example, Junayd al-Baghdadi says: "For a certain time, the inhabitants of the earth and heaven wept for my amazement, and sometimes it occurred that I wept for their amazement. Now I am in such a state that I am aware of neither myself nor of them."

> The amazement of Gedai is also worth noting:
> I did not know myself as I see me now,
> I wonder whether He is me or I am Him?
> This is the point where lovers lose themselves;
> I have burnt away, so give me water!

The words of the author of *al-Minhaj* demonstrate a deeper aura of love and amazement:

> I do not know whether I am myself or Him.
> I am in bewilderment, but I am sure I am not myself.
> I am a lover or the one loved or love itself.
> I am intoxicated from the cup of Oneness, and I am not myself.
> What am I? Am I a phoenix with no fame or mark?
> I am away from my home, and I am not myself.
> I am transient in soul but permanent by the Beloved.
> I am flying high, and I am not myself.

If we consider what annihilation is, these words are natural for a hero of annihilation. Annihilation means that they see, according to their level, none save God and set their hearts on Him alone. When they advance to the point where their inner and outer worlds, perception, and consciousness are illuminated with the knowledge of truth, then they begin to see clearly Who holds the reins of everything, and they always turn to Him in Whose Hand lie their existence and subsistence. Then, while they become more deeply immersed in truth by concentrating all of their thoughts on Him and endeavoring to reach Him, then they perceive that all existence is a manifestation of the light of His Existence. They reach the horizon of viewing all things and events differently with the consideration of Divine Oneness, and they are favored with being able to feel and interpret everything with the essential characteristics that the veil of corporeality hides. This can be regarded as the first step on the way of annihilation to the Truth.

Travelers on the way to the Truth take a further step and are able to perceive with the certainty of conviction that all the events in the universe, including human acts and endeavors, depend absolutely on God's Names and Attributes, and that everything has come into existence and has blossomed in the heart of these Sources. They also perceive that whatever happens happens by His Power and Strength and see more clearly the limits of their will-power in all of their deeds. Abandoning all shadowy existence, they take shelter in the protection and ownership of the True Existent One, and gain a new existence by Him.

If the traveler can take a further step, then he or she can feel with some certainty, a certainty that comes from experience, that all things and/or beings with their being, attributes and characteristics are transferred from their existence in God's Knowledge and clothed in external existence by His Power as a manifestation of His Existence. Becoming more profound in their feelings, the travelers are immersed in the vision of the truth that everything exists and subsists by Him. They perceive in their consciousness that the truth of (55:26), "All that (exists) is transient by nature (except He)," undulates throughout the universe like a flag, and everything created is bound to decay, and is maintained by the manifestation of God's being the Self-Subsistent and All-Subsisting One. They also feel in their consciousness that if a being suffers a moment's interruption of this manifestation, it will perish, and they reach a further horizon of perception of the Divine Oneness.

The first step belongs to the verifying scholars, the second to those traveling on the way to the Truth who have strong, inflexible will-power, and the third to those who have true knowledge of God and vision.

Those who are at the first step are annihilated to the extent of the depth of their consciousness of God and enter the way to "a revival after death." Those who have left this step behind experience absence and immersion with respect to their inner world by means of a spiritual vision and discovery; they find seclusion in crowds and silence in noise and uproar. Others, who have reached the third step, renounce all human desires and aspirations, and wherever they look are immersed in the manifestations of the Divine Knowledge and Existence; they feel fully surrounded by His signs, as stated in (2:115), *To whatever direction you turn, there is the "Face" of God*. Whatever they see, they feel awe when enveloped by His rays, and whatever they observe they feel astonished at the burning manifestations of His Face and they mention Him with many allegories.

When travelers to the Truth have gone beyond all these steps and have become heroes of annihilation in God, the colors of subsistence with God begin to appear to them from all horizons. They also go beyond one dimension of "there is no deity." This new dimension confronts them every moment during their journey and they reach a new dimension of "but God." Due to their taking larger steps and due to the uninterrupted shower of Divine favors, the universal Lordship and complete Subsistence begin to manifest themselves on their horizon. A time comes and they feel that His Throne has embraced the whole universe, and rising by the stairs of repentance, penitence and contrition, which comprise the way of turning to Him completely, they are immersed in the lights of His Divinity. They drown in the extraordinary pleasures of feeling awe and fear of Him in their acts of worship. They take a great pleasure in listening to the Divine Speech—the Qur'an. Finding themselves sometimes in the clime of self-possession that is embedded in fear, and sometimes on the hills of alertness that are embedded in awe, and sometimes in the oceans of mercy, they experience fear and expectation, sadness and rejoicing, all together at the same time, and try not to fall away from His door. Unburdening themselves to Him in every thought, concept, utterance and breath, they become heroes of following the Divine commandment (15:99), *Worship your Lord until certainty comes to you (by death)*, and without being content with their worshipping, they advance further and further. They know that when they stop, both the way and the journey will come to an end, and they can no longer have the ambition of reaching their destination. For the journey is toward the Infinite One. Unending endeavor in this world is reflected as endless favors from the realms beyond.

> *Guide us to the Straight Path, the path of those whom You have favored, not of those who have incurred (Your) punishment and condemnation, nor of those who have gone astray. And let God's blessings be upon our master Muhammad, his family and all of his Companions.*

BAQA BI'LLAH
(SUBSISTENCE WITH GOD)

Subsistence with God denotes that the servant of God regards all existence, including him or herself, as being non-existent in and of itself, and discovers in his or her consciousness that every being, living and non-living, is a manifestation or shadow of the light of the Divine Knowledge and Existence. Initiates who experience destruction and effacement with respect to their corporeal self and gain a new existence by God's permanence or subsistence exist by His Existence, subsist by His Subsistence, live by His Life, know by His Knowledge, will by His Will, and hear and see by His Hearing and Seeing. They see and hear what other (normal) people cannot see or hear, and receive favors that come as a result of such hearing and seeing. Initiates who have reached this rank, which marks the near completion of the journey, and where they feel themselves to be in the most pleasurable state of being freed of their name and existence, are in relative terms qualified with any of God's Attributes in heaven and earth. Those who have contact with the spiritual realms can feel in their consciousness a reflection of this favor. This state is also regarded as persons of heart being called according to their own perception of themselves. Only those with purified souls who see and think of nothing but the True Beloved One, and whose hearts always beat by His Existence and Subsistence, and whose spirits are continuously reanimated with a new flash of His manifestation, can experience this state. So long as they can keep their relation with the Truth at the level which has carried them to this summit, and only if the Truth continues to treat them in this way, do they perceive even the slightest falling under the influence of others in knowledge, perception, feelings, and consciousness as a spiritual eclipse, which may end in their spiritual spark being extinguished. If they feel they have suffered such a terrible falling-off, they will, in order to save themselves from it, be on the lookout for the All-Beloved One's opening a window in their spirits.

From another perspective, subsistence is, after the total disappearance of things that are transient and visible in the sight of an initiate, either a temporary permanence dependent on its own conditions, or an uninterrupted continuity due to the extraordinary confirmation of Divine grace. That is, while a traveler continues his or her journey with the guidance of the signposts and the enlightenment of teachers, after a certain point, which is determined by the impressions and discernment of the traveler, the signposts will no longer be needed and are no longer visible. This stage, where the One Who is indicated by the signs and proofs shows Himself with the lights of His Existence, making signs and proofs no longer visible, and where His witnesses are the only instruments for His praise and exaltation, is a different point of breathing and turning to a different direction. If the initiate has the ability and resolution to continue journeying toward further goals, the breezes of annihilation will begin to blow in both the person's inner and outer world. When the journey is almost exceeding time and space, the initiate feels in the consciousness complete annihilation ready to turn into subsistence. One cannot say anything, nor think of anything, nor attempt to perceive anything. Despite the brilliance of the witnesses that point to Him throughout the universe, they disappear when faced by the lights of His Existence, like stars sinking when the sun rises. As stated in (55:27), *There subsists the Face of your Lord with Majesty and Munificence*, only the Divine Being continues to exist beyond the scope of human perception, understanding and feeling.

Initiates can view His subsistence or permanence in three stages: the first is based on knowledge, the second on vision, and the third on the pleasure of experiencing His Existence. While traveling through these stages, any information that has been acquired by the known means of acquiring knowledge loses its significance and utterly disappears into what is known. All instances of seeing and feeling vanish while the meaning and content based on or reached through seeing, feeling and knowing remain intact. While all relative truths no longer exist, the absolute truth prevails and the natures of existents, each different from the other, are surrounded by the lights that emanate from their annihilation in the True Existence. In all of these stages, annihilation provides a way to subsistence and wherever an initiate attains subsistence, it can address itself to different levels of feeling and perception, producing relative effects of its own on things. For this reason, this rank has usually been called "subsistence by God together with God," and not only "subsistence by God."

We can view this stage from two angles:

- Travelers find and feel things and events annihilated with respect to their own selves and existence. No thing exists any longer with respect to its own being. When the travelers are surrounded by the atmosphere produced by this, they no longer feel the existence of anything except Him and find everything annihilated in Him.
- A wakeful initiate can always distinguish between the essential, absolutely true Self-Existence and relative instances of existence. So, all things have relative existence dependent on the unique Self-Existence in the initiate's sight. Concerning these two kinds of feeling, perception, and experience, the leading Sufi scholars comment that for a traveler who feels all things annihilated in Him everything ceases to exist, while for one who has the ability to distinguish between the Absolute Existence and the relative existence all things continue to exist.

If we deal with the matter from the approach of the Companions, nothing exists by itself nor does it have any essential existence. Everything has relative, insubstantial and accidental existence as a manifestation of the Existence of the Eternal Truth, according to its receptivity. Things, as dependent on the Absolute Truth, have a constant, relative truth. In the beginning, this consideration is doctrinal belief (or dogma) based on acceptance, and in the end it is based on the certainty that comes from knowledge and vision.

In the spiritual journey, the whole of existence no longer has any value or significance in the heart of an initiate and vanishes in the infinite light of the True Existence in the same way that the light of a firefly fades when the sun rises. The initiate gives no place to anything else but God in his or her heart, and leaves him or herself in the cataracts of his or her spiritual pleasures immersed in the ownership and guidance of His Will and the lights of His Existence. The utterance always on the initiate's lips is "He."

Travelers who feel themselves in a state of pleasure when they find themselves annihilated in their own acts, advance toward the attainment of a new existence and permanence in the acts of the Truth. By feeling transience in their own attributes, they taste the pleasure of permanence in the Attributes of God. By forgetting their own selves—though forgetting has been interpreted in different ways—they attain a new existence by the lights of the Truth's Existence. While they sometimes refer to the relative, existential truth of things and emphasize its difference from the absolute, True Existence, they sometimes can find everything annihilated in the absolute, True Existence. There is left only one rank to be reached by the travelers who have arrived at this point, namely God's company. Every initiate who has attained subsistence with God can attain this rank according to the individual's capacity. Attainment of this rank sometimes brings with it a feeling of wonder and sometimes an intoxication and sometimes astonishment. Mawlana Jami' expresses this feeling of wonder beautifully as follows:

> Love is not without the flute-player, and we are not without Him.
> He cannot be without us, as we cannot be without Him.
> The flute always beautifies its tunes, but in fact
> The beauty of the tune comes from the breathing of the flute-player.

The following verses, belonging to another hero of subsistence by and with God, are concerned with a feeling of wonder and astonishment:

The light of my eyes is He, and the direction for my reason is He;
The recitation of my voice is He, and I sigh and groan with He.
My heart goes on an excursion in He, and the love of my soul is He.
My greatest secret is He, and my brightest sun is He.
Those who are lovers and intoxicated are always with He.
Their fasting is He, their festive day is He, and their rituals are He.
My soul has sacrificed itself in the way of its Beloved,
Its union is with He, its parting is with He, and its cure for afflictions is He.

Those who have attained subsistence with God always feel and think of Him alone, they are always with Him alone, and they begin with Him alone. Attracted by Him, they leave themselves in the overflowing pleasures that come from experiencing His Oneness throughout the universe, and always act according to His good pleasure and approval. In the face of the rays of His Knowledge and Existence, which totally eliminate all others save Him and His friends from their hearts and sight, they cannot help but utter "O All-Living One!" and feel as if they are talking about themselves. They utter "O True One!" and melt away in the light of His Existence.

> *O God, O All-Living and Self-Subsisting One! O One with Majesty and Munificence! Pour unto us knowledge of You and give us from the drink of Paradise, and enable us to be steadfast on the Prophet's way and true guidance. And let God's blessings be upon our master Muhammad, Who teaches the true way, and on his Companions, the noble, godly ones.*

TAHQIQ (VERIFICATION)

In the language of Sufism, *tahqiq* (verification) means that not only does an initiate who has almost come to the final step of the journey know the Unique Being that is Eternally-Besought-of-All with His Existence and Perfect Attributes in accordance with the Qur'anic presentation of Him, but also that the truth of Divinity is felt beyond all concepts of modality and His special manifestations in the individual's consciousness and other spiritual faculties. Those who have found the truth and reached this level continue their journey in the horizon of journeying to God or journeying from God, according to their capacity, without suffering doubts or hesitations any more. They are no longer exposed to any feelings of being eclipsed by God's permission, for they see by God's Seeing, hear by His Hearing, and feel everything in the light of His Attributes. In other words, such heroes of verification are always on the way to God and live for His sake and feel His constant company. This is a rank which is regarded as the rank of being loved by God and implies a special favor of the All-Beloved One. One who has attained this rank is loved by the Almighty and, as a reflection of this love, by the inhabitants of heaven and by people with sincere hearts on the earth. The visible sign of this invisible Divine love is attachment to the performance of supererogatory acts of worship in addition to faultless performance of the obligatory acts.

Lovers of truth who perform the obligatory acts of worship perfectly and punctually, later making up those which they were not able to perform at the correct time with a serious, sincere feeling of remorse, and who feel great, heartfelt concern for the supererogatory acts, always feel the Truth, always "see" Him, walk toward Him, and uphold truth in life. It is inconceivable that anything else save

Him can find a way into such persons' hearts and anything or any-one that is lovable from the heart can catch their eye. Even if some-times a mist may appear on their horizon, it comes and goes like the mists of spring, indicating new expansions of spirit. Such peo-ple always advance, whether they are in distress or whether they are rejoicing.

Ismail Haqqi Bursawi depicts such heroes of verification as fol-lows:

> The people of truth have clearly found in their souls,
> That the Light of Truth is extremely near to the creation.
> The Truth declared: He hears by Me and sees by Me,
> For one that was created from water and dust has found His Light.
> If that one of water and dust had not found that Pure Light,
> The meaning would not have been manifested so clearly.
> Those people of the heart who have found the Light
> Belonging to neither east nor west have become the lamp of this Light.
> The people of truth have found Unity in multiplicity,
> They are safe and secure, and in prosperity.
> O Haqqi, submit to the Truth and commit your affairs to Him,
> Then you can find the One Who does whatever He wills,
> How excellent a Helper He is.

From another perspective, verification denotes that initiates deepen their belief with the knowledge of God and their knowl-edge of God with the love of Him, and pursues only God's approv-al and good pleasure in all the stations that they call at. This exalt-ed truth is felt differently at each step of the spiritual journey. For the belief, knowledge, love and yearning of each traveler to the Truth is in direct proportion with the individual's certainty and grada-tions in belief, knowledge and love of God, and the spiritual pleas-ures are the results of gradations in verification. Belief based on the-oretical knowledge, no matter how strong, cannot be, as stated in the saying, *Hearing something is not like seeing it*, like certainty based on vision and spiritual discovery, even though the object of belief and certainty belongs to the unseen world. Such certainty cannot, likewise, be the same as a perfect conviction that has been deeply ingrained in the heart and become a part of human nature. Theoretical knowledge can only be "a capital of scant worth" (12:88) for the Divine grace expected to come on the way to verification. It is possible to bring certainty based on vision and spiritual discovery to fruition with the munificence of the All-Munificent One, despite such certainty being relative. As for perfect conviction, it is the pure fruit, even the juice, that the rays of His Existence have first annihilated and then given a new existence to with different characteristics. There is reference to the beginning of verification in the Prophet Abraham's appeal, "My Lord, show me how You will restore life to the dead," and in its summation of why he made such an appeal, "So that my heart may be at rest" (2:260). We should point out here that it is not possible for us to understand either the certainty of this noble, great Messenger that came from his knowledge, or his certainty that came from his observations and seeing, or his certainty that came from experience. We can only cite him as an example in order to offer a point of comparison and a perspective that will enable us to explain the subject matter. Our Prophet, peace and blessings be upon him, stresses this fact by declaring, *We are more liable to such a doubt than Abraham;*[91] lest doubts appear in people's hearts concerning the certainty of Abraham in particular, and the certainty of all the Prophets in general. Everyone has a relative horizon and final point of certainty particular to their individual capacity, and everyone needs rest and contentment according to their individual horizon. The smallest degree of certainty of a Prophet is much greater and stronger than the greatest degree of the most spiritually advanced of all other people.

The heroes of verification turn to and concentrate on the Divine Being alone with their belief, love, yearning, zeal, and spiritual pleasure. Accepting His approval and good pleasure as their sole aim, they never consider the blows of Majesty as a cause of suffering nor the breezes of Grace as a means of joy. In their view, whatever comes from Him, be it reprimand or favor, is the same. They consider all

---

[91] Al-Bukhari, "Tafsir Sura al-Baqara," 2; Al-Muslim, "Iman," 238.

His treatment of them as a necessity of being on the way to Him and, without becoming entangled therein, regard everything apart from the true goal to which they have been dedicated, as a transient shadow, and are resolved to reach Him.

Heroes of verification bear all suffering, resist all carnal impulses and meticulously observe the religious orders and prohibitions. They rise without stopping toward heaven with "He" as their sole goal. They feel that they are welcomed with a new trial at every turn and with a different manifestation of Divine approval at every station. They feel the following melodies echoing in their outer and inner senses:

> A call has come to me from the Truth:
> "Come, O lover, you have intimacy with Us!
> This is the place of intimacy;
> I have seen you as a faithful one!"
>
> (Nasimi)

This is truly such a rank that one who has reached it feels that his or her belief comes from Him, just as his or her knowledge, love and zeal also come from Him. What confirms these feelings is the impressive acknowledgment (2:32), *Glory be to You, we have no knowledge except what You have taught us,* and the sole truth felt in consciousness is, *He is the All-Permanent, the Eternal, the Perpetual.* Many diverse things catch the eyes and ears until they reach this rank. However, when the steps end here and the state is transformed into a station, human nature melts away voicing (40:16), *All the commandment belongs to Him Who is the One, the All-Overwhelming,* and the truth (55:27), *There subsists the Face of your Lord with Majesty and Munificence,* echoes from all sides. The human logic which has divided time into the past, the present and the future, becomes lost in the truth, *You are the First with none preceding You, and the Last with none to succeed You.*[92] It even occurs that the consciousness makes the initiates' relative existence sink into oblivion and allows them

---

[92] Al-Muslim, "Dhikr," 61; Abu Dawud, "Adab," 98.

to feel deeply the meaning of *There was God without anything that existed with Him.*[93] They whisper, "Neither union nor incarnation is true; the true existence belongs to You only, and all else is a shadow of Your Light," and feel honored by being attributed to Him. Despite their modesty, humility and feeling of nothingness, they taste in their spirit the virtues of being favored with being the best pattern of creation.

> *O God! We ask You for forgiveness, health, approval, favor, and the breezes of Your friendship, and Your love and company! And let God's peace and blessings be upon our master Muhammad, Your servant and Messenger, and on his Companions who loved You and made him near to You.*

---

[93] Al-Bukhari, "Tawhid," 1; Ibn Hanbal, *Musnad*, 4:431.

TALBIS (SELF-CONCEALMENT)

albis (self-concealment) means that the perfected servants of God who attribute to God whatever good or virtues that they may have, try to be known as ordinary people by constantly keeping secret the special blessings and extraordinary attainments with which the Eternally Generous One favors them, and the blessed times when they come. But such an attitude is by no means false pretense or deception. It is usually felt during the tides between seeing everything annihilated in God and distinguishing the Existence of the Truly Existent One and the relative existence of others. Those who are seeking self-concealment are in constant pursuit of sincerity and frequently question themselves to ensure that they are really preserving their devotion and loyalty to God. They do their best to keep God's special favors to them that come in different forms as sacred secrets between themselves and their Bestower, out of respect for Him, and they consider whatever comes from Him as a secret gift. Whatever good or blessing has been attributed to them, they always draw attention back to the Almighty and, if there is not anything to make them absolutely obliged to display their blessings, then they will always try to find ways to conceal such, as in the allusions of the Prophet Abraham, who said, *I am sick* (37:89) when he was invited to the religious festival of his people, implying that he was sick of idol-worship, and, *Rather, he did it; that is their chief* (21:63), when he was asked whether he had smashed the idols. They shy away from becoming a person who is sought after in the same way as others shy away from snakes and other vermin.

Perfected persons of self-concealment are extremely careful not to display any inward riches and spiritual profundity. Even if they should sometimes feel they are really profound in spirituality, they try to persuade themselves of their essential insignificance. However, in trying to impress on others that they do not have any extraordinary virtues, they avoid causing Islam to be criticized for being a religion that brings dishonor and ignominy to its followers. Without saying or doing anything to suggest that they have been specially favored by God, they are always deeply devoted and loyal to Him. They regard attributing to themselves whatever good or spiritual attainment that others may discern in them as usurpation. Even if at times they are in the center of the Divine favors, they always act with good manners and modesty, saying to themselves: "You are neither the source nor the owner of these favors. These gifts which sometimes appear to you and then disappear can in no wise belong to you. As you can clearly see that it is not you who has brought them about, nor is it you who takes them away, you must see that you cannot own them. Your position with respect to them is that you are essentially a dark mirror; therefore you must attribute these gifts to the Eternally Generous One and draw attention to Him." When they have been deprived of such favors and blessings that were abundant, they think: "You must conceal the Divine secrets and His treatment of you. You must be able to do so in order that His transactions with you may continue, and so that these gifts, which are beyond your capacity, may not lead you to gradually perish because you think that you own them." Such people appear quite ordinary among people; they are extremely careful to keep their inner world pure and they are very sincere in their exclusive devotion to God, ensuring that they do this so as not to attract anyone's attention.

Heroes of self-concealment follow a secure way to verification and always pursue God's approval and good pleasure. They never think of others' approval or appreciation and they expect nothing from others. They try to make their feelings and devotion deeper and to rise higher and higher without stopping; they are in a state of continuous self-supervision. They always control themselves so that they can be with God even while mixing with other people. They try to direct others to the way of the light, which is the way of knowledge and love of God and a source of spiritual pleasures, although those pleasures should not be sought. They show the way to Paradise to those who linger at the crossroads between Paradise and Hell, and they try to inculcate lofty ideals in the hearts of those who are living aimlessly. They can establish good relations with all, be they from any segment of society, without any difficulty or ceremony.

Heroes of self-concealment are always in self-negation and self-denial and try to attract the attention to the Almighty in everything they do. But some scholars, like Harawi[94] and Ibn Qayyim,[95] went to extremes in evaluating this virtue; the former asserted that it is the Almighty, not the servant, Who conceals His servant from others, while the latter denied this state altogether. For this reason, I would like to remind the reader once more that self-concealment denotes that travelers to the Truth, who have attained spiritual purity by carefully performing their obligatory religious duties, have become deeper in their attachment to supererogatory acts of worship in order to be favored with God's company and have become polished mirrors reflecting His manifestations of Majesty and Grace. The All-Generous One becomes the eyes and ears of His servants who have reached this point; they see and hear with Him, and He never leaves them to suffer loneliness and helplessness without anyone to claim them. By means of the criteria which He inspires in them so that they view life, things and events appropriately, He causes them to reach the best results in both this world and the hereafter. He causes them to see things that others cannot see and to hear things that others cannot hear, and he employs them to carry out His will in the human realm and to convey to people the things which He is

---

[94] Abu Ismail 'Abdullah ibn Muhammad al-Harawi (1005-1089) was born in Herat in Afghanistan. He was a Hanbali devoted to the Qur'an and Sunna. He was also well-versed in Sufism. *Kitab al-Manazil al-Sairin* is his most well-known work on Sufism. (Trans.)

[95] Ibn Qayyim al-Jawziya Shams al-Din 'Abdullah Muhammad ibn Abi Bakir (1292-1350) is the most famous pupil of Ibn Taymiya (1292-1350), one of Islam's strictest religious thinkers He lived in Damascus. He followed the Hanbali School in Islam. *Kitab al-Fawaid al-Musawwiqa ila 'Ulum al-Qur'an wa 'Ilm al-Bayan* is among his well-known books. (Trans.)

pleased with and the things He wills others to do. The Qur'anic statements, *When you threw, it was not you who threw, but God who threw* (8:17), and *Those who swear allegiance to you (O Muhammad), swear allegiance only to God. God's Hand (of aid) is over their hands* (48:10), refer to this point, in that those who have reached this rank are absolutely convinced of Divine Unity, but sometimes they see everything annihilated in God and sometimes they are able to distinguish the absolute (Divine) Existence and the relative existence (of other beings) from each other. Although the rank indicated by the verses belongs primarily to the Prophets, who are the purest of all and incomparably superior in self-concealment, as in all other virtues, other heroes of self-concealment have a share in it. However, the self-concealment experienced by travelers on the way to God is concerned with and should be attributed to the Divine Attributes, not the Divine Being, and the unchangeable rules of Shari'a determine its limits and nature. The throwing and hitting, seeing and speaking, and exalting by participating in allegiance, which are mentioned in the verses just cited, signify that the Truth manifests His Attributes of Majesty and Perfection, not His Divine Being, on the chosen, matchless being, upon him be peace and blessings.

This consideration is expressed in the following words of Jalal al-Din al-Rumi, although they also suggest to some extent annihilation in God and subsistence with Him:

> Noah said: O people leading rebellion to God, I am not myself;
> I am dead with respect to my soul, but alive to the Beloved One.
> I died and was annihilated with respect to some senses of Adam,
> the father of humanity,
> And the Truth has become (a means of) hearing,
> seeing and perceiving for me.

From the very beginning, the people of truth have stressed that existence arises from self-annihilation and that the assertion of self-existence ends in annihilation. The best and most appropriate approach in this respect is that travelers to the Truth annihilate them-

selves with respect to their carnal selves and ego and that they find
a new life in spirit and heart.

> *Our Lord, do not let our hearts swerve after You have guided us, and
> bestow upon us mercy from Your Presence. Surely You, only You, are
> the (Munificent) Bestower. Let God's blessings be upon our master
> Muhammad and upon his family and Companions to the fullness of
> the earth and heavens.*

WUJUD (FINDING AND EXISTENCE)

*W*ujud (finding and existence) is not what is meant in Qur'anic statements like the following: *They assuredly find that God is One Who truly returns the repentance of His servants with acceptance and extra reward, and All-Compassionate (especially toward His believing servants)* (4:64); *He will find God All-Forgiving, All Compassionate (especially towards His servants who seek forgiveness for their evils and sins)* (4:110); and *In the end he will find God and meet with Him, and He will pay him his account in full* (24:39). These are, respectively, more concerned with how those who have sinned or lapsed somewhat into deviations on the way, beg God for forgiveness, and how the unbelievers will find God or how God will treat them. Rather, finding and existence denote the finding of Him with His truth beyond all concepts of modality, as referred to in, *O son of Adam, seek Me that you may find Me,*[96] and some allegorical sayings of the Prophet, upon him be peace and blessings. When travelers to the Truth attain this rank of finding, they feel and achieve a state of melting away in the presence of the manifestations of His "Face," with nothing being left behind except that state and the pleasure it gives. One who starts with this belief and advances toward knowledge and love of God is called "an initiate." Such initiates continue their journey by understanding the language of His signs in the outer and in their inner world and by feeling that their witnessing of Him is that of "a seeking one." Finally, when they have reached the ultimate point where they have found the truth in their consciousness according to the capacity of that consciousness, beyond all concepts of time, space and matter, each becomes the

---

[96] Ibn Kathir, *Tafsir al-Qur'an*, 2:302.

"one who has found." The beginning of this journey demands belief and perfect resolution, and its continuance requires being driven and led, and reaching the end according to the capacity of each, melting away and total annihilation in the face of the rays of the Realm of the Holy Presence. This final point in no way denotes incarnation or union (with God) or God's taking on a corporeal body or His being transformed into another being. It only denotes the state and pleasure of feeling as a drop in relation to the ocean and as a particle in relation to the sun. Abu'l Hasan al-Nuri[97] expresses the state of those who have reached this point vividly: "I have been going to and fro between finding and losing for twenty years. When I enjoy meeting with my Lord Whose Essence is unknown, I lose my heart; and when I feel my existence in heart, I then suffer a loss of Him."

Certainly, it is not possible for those who are still at the beginning of the way to feel the state described by al-Nuri. For this state, which is frequently felt and frequently disappears, resembles the state of a diver who feels the water when diving into it, and lets the water pull him or her deeper, and who feels only the water when he or she becomes "lost" in the depths. If such a feeling that appears on the way to reaching the truth of something is based on the knowing of the heart or consciousness, it is the culture of consciousness or cognizance in consciousness. If it is of the kind obtained with vision or insight, then it is sight. If travelers are in constant pursuit of increasing research, analysis, and synthesis, then the result is spiritual discovery and vision. Finally if they see everything annihilated in God, then their state is annihilation in God and subsistence with God, and they feel no need whatsoever for anybody else save Him.

At the beginning or in the first stage of the journey, travelers are saved from all doubts and hesitations and attain in their consciousness such a degree of knowledge of God that they no longer need deductive or inductive reasoning in the name of "finding," even

---

[97] Abu'l-Hasan al-Nuri (d. 1499) is one of the famous Sufi ascetics. He was mostly concerned with the matter of *wujud*. (Trans.)

though they sometimes refer to things and events when expressing the truth. Based on a knowledge that comes directly from the Divine Presence to aid finding, they rise to the horizon of knowledge of God they inwardly experience, and this knowing is above the kind of knowledge acquired by rational arguments and the observation of His "material" witnesses in the universe.

In the second stage, travelers reach the point where they feel and have the vision of the Eternally Existent One, which is in effect knowing Him with a knowledge based on spiritual observation of Him, without restricting Him with such considerations as body, substance, matter, time and space.

In the third stage, which marks almost the end point of the journey, travelers are in a state of experiencing the Truly Existent One without seeing any other existents save Him, and they attain annihilation in Him in their world of feelings.

This systematization of the journey is based on the assertion that spiritual knowledge of God is higher in value than the knowledge acquired through scientific or rational arguments, and that the spiritual vision of God is above the spiritual knowledge of Him, and that finding Him in self-annihilation in Him is more valuable than the spiritual vision of Him. However, this needs to be revised according to those who see the vision beyond finding.

There is another consideration based on the concentration of the Divine Existence only. This consideration, which has been called the Unity of Being, is sometimes reduced to a mere philosophical view, although it arises from a spiritually experienced state. It will be useful to give some information about it here.

* * *

In fact, all of existence is nothing more than a shadow or a manifestation of the Names and Attributes of the Unique One, the Eternally-Besought-of-All. Travelers favored with the knowledge of the truth behind things and events sometimes go into a state where they experience only His absolute Existence to such a degree that they become completely lost in It and all other existent beings disappear from their sight. Although this is a state experienced spiritually, it is sometimes reduced to a mere philosophical view or to a matter of speculation, in imitation of others who have experienced this state spiritually, and it can be confused with several other approaches, such as the Unity of the Witnessed, Monism, and Pantheism. Although a discussion of these approaches and their substantial difference from the Unity of Being is not among the topics which will be discussed in *The Emerald Hills of the Heart*, it would be useful to note some of the important points, as this is a matter open to misunderstanding and misrepresentation.

Existence is related to being and/or identity, nature and the existent beings themselves, and is unquestionably manifest. This is a view shared by numerous Muslim thinkers, as well as by many modern philosophers. However, existence is different from the existent beings, identity, and nature. Identity and nature must be conceived of before existence. For example, we can conceive of an amount of water with its identity and nature, even if it does not exist here. Its existence is additional and accidental to its being or identity. Something cannot exist without its essential qualities being combined with certain accidental elements. As regards our example, different states and qualities of water are additional to its essential being or identity. Although the essential identity always remains as it was, without any changes, accidental and additional qualities can be replaced with similar others. Water, while remaining as water in essence, can change into ice or vapor.

Just as a physical substance like water has an essential identity and nature, metaphysical beings have also an essential identity and nature. However, in saying this, we should not confuse the Being Whose Existence is Essential and Absolutely Necessary with contingent beings. Muslim thinkers have accepted the Absolutely Necessary Existence as the Being Who is Absolutely and Uniquely Self-Existent, and have also agreed that His Being is absolutely free from requiring a nature or a form or a composition; need is essential to all other beings whose existence is contingent and created. The Self-Existent One is free from such accidental qualities. It is not permissible to associate the Necessarily Existent One with a different, additional nature or existence. We cannot even conceive of nor mention such a possibility with regard to Him; it would be supposing the inconceivable to be conceivable to explain the question.

It is He Who is discerned in the universe. All things, each individually and all as a whole, are signs of His Existence. Things and events run in a gurgling flow and clearly point to Him at every juncture of their being. In one respect, the universe and humanity are the title of the continuity of this flow, and human consciousness is that which hears, views, and reviews it.

From this perspective, all existence (creation) comes from Him and continuously flows like a river with uninterrupted manifestations. Because of the order, coherence, and speed of this flow, we cannot discern the interruptions in our nature or in the lives of things. Since the "film" of things and events is projected extremely swiftly and the very thin lines between the frames on the film strip cannot be discerned, we cannot feel the alternation of coming into existence and disappearing. Like separate pictures on a film being projected on a screen, things and events are projected on the screen of existence, one after the other, but we cannot discern the lines separating the frames.

> They come and go, one after the other, with the only Unique One remaining;
> That which comes, goes, and that which goes does not come back again:
> this is a mystery.

Those who cannot penetrate this mystery spend their lives like an insensate person, who cannot see, hear, or feel anything. While others who have familiarity with this mystery sometimes refer to vision or to witnessing when observing the creation, they sometimes mention only the absolute Existence in interpreting their observation, or they sometimes utter some words that are apparently incompatible with the rules of the Shari'a that suggest union and incarnation. They do this because of their inability to find words that express their vision and discovery. It will even sometimes happen that there appears a person who is stuck in monism and who commits great sins by seeing the absolute Existence as if it were a permeating spirit that manifested itself as the creation. It is possible that the universe may be viewed as an image or a shadow, as it is a reflection of the Light of the absolute Existence, and that things and events, including humanity, can be seen as being unstable, transitory images. However, this does not by any means imply that the universe is He. The truth is that it is He Who eternally exists without anything else eternally existing with Him. He willed the objects or identities in His eternal Knowledge to be clothed in an external, sensible existence in accordance with the measures He determined for them. This happened along with or within time and space; in other words, time and space began or appeared together with His bringing forth the objects or identities existing in His Knowledge into external existence. He observes the manifestations of His Existence that are indescribable and beyond-all-concept with the eyes of others—the creatures He has created. He favors everything with the rank of being a polished mirror to Him.

He has done all this with the single command "Be!" and with this command He has clothed the archetypes in external existence and displayed them in different forms. As He has done all this with a single command, He can destroy everything in a moment with another single command.

> He said "Be!" once and the whole universe was;
> If He says, "Do not exist any longer!"
> everything will immediately be destroyed.

Since the universe did not exist eternally along with Him and since it was brought into existence by His peerless, inimitable creation, and since it continues to exist by His Sustaining, then its existence is relative and dependent and can be viewed as being essentially non-existent. Everything owes its existence and subsistence to Him absolutely. The Eternally Existent One willed that His perfections be observed in innumerable mirrors and so created existence as a shadow of the shadow of His Knowledge and Existence; this has included us as a part of creation. Our identities as "I," "you", and "he" or "she" had not been thoroughly distinguished with respect to our existence in His Knowledge. Destiny or His "Pre-Determination" identified us as individuals, and His Power clothed us in our "ego," thus distinguishing and bringing us into external, sensible existence as complete individuals with different natures particular to each one of us. As He has manifested on us all His Attributes, He has entrusted us with a restricted will-power. He has also endowed us with different potentials which we can develop or realize as abilities. He has determined goals for us according to our abilities and endowed us with inclinations to realize those goals and has given us the ability to make use of or direct these inclinations. Thus, in addition to His Attributes of Knowledge and Existence, which He has manifested on us, He has also honored us with the manifestations of His other Attributes. So what behoves us is to willingly resign ourselves to this great, Divinely-willed honor and act accordingly.

Those who attain the horizon of viewing existence in a certain spiritual state regard their existence as essentially non-existent in the face of the essential, absolute, eternal, and everlasting Knowledge and Self-Existence of God. This means the non-acceptance of a transient shadow in the face of an Eternally Self-Existent One. Feeling that the whole of existence is as a single unit is different from that the whole of sensed existence is essentially identical with the absolute Existence. Divine truths are never the same as relative truths. Although the Divine Names and Attributes, such as God (*Allah*), the All-Merciful (*al-Rahman*), and the All-Providing (*al-Razzaq*) seem to point to a single truth concerning the Being called by or described by these, they are different both from the perspective of the concept to which each points and the impression that each causes to rise in minds. For this reason, one who has true, substantial knowledge of God considers the relation between the Truly Existent One and other beings whose existence is relative and dependent in proper terms, and observes the true criteria in thinking, while those who are in a certain state of experience and spritiual pleasure may lapse into confusion.

In the realm of the relative truths—the facts related to creation— there are manifestations with different names or titles, such as living and non-living, and in the living realm, there are the animals, humankind, angels, and jinn and Satan. All the existing beings that are called by such collective names can be traced back to a unity that arises from a stage or rank in the process of creation, which we call "the first determination" or "the Pure Realm of Divine Dominion" or the "Truth belonging to Ahmad" (the name of the Prophet before his coming to the world). The overall Divine manifestation in this stage is viewed as His overall manifestation over the whole of creation with all His Names (*Tajalli Wahidiya*), though some prefer to call it *Tajalli Ahadiya*. This manifestation caused the archetypes in God's Knowledge to develop and, with the concentration of the manifestations of certain Divine Names while others remained subordinate—the manifestation which we usually call *Tajalli Ahadiya*—the archetypes were individualized.

One with a true knowledge of God and a true vision of the truth behind the appearances can discern the relative truth and its relation with the Divine truth and God's absolute Oneness and His overall manifestation over the whole of creation with all His Names at the same instant. They do not lapse into confusion. Even though they feel that everything goes back and ends in an essential unity, they can see each individual being in its particular nature and therefore can distinguish between the absolute, necessary and essential Existence and the relative one. This does not cause them either to ignore the gifts coming from spiritual vision and discoveries or to remain indifferent to the acquisitions of feelings and sound reasoning. Those who have set up their royal tents on this horizon express their perceptions in their true nature and with a true distinction between those things that are absolute, essential and original and those that are relative and dependent. They conclude that although there is an absolute, essential truth, its manifestations as sensible existence are numerous. They never lose their bearings or true direction and therefore do not fall into deviancy.

In addition, the Existence of the Truth has usually been viewed from two perspectives. Looking from one perspective, the Attributes are ignored and therefore the differences among them or their manifestations are not considered. Those who view the Existence of the Truth from this perspective are people of state and vision, who concentrate only on the Divine Being Himself. Some view this perspective as that of the Pure Being, but leading scholars of Sufism give to it such designations as Uniqueness, the Pure Divine Realm, the Realm with No Determination, and the Unknown Identity. Those who have acquired this perspective, which is also a rank from where the Divine Being can be viewed, experience this state each according to his or her capacity. Looking from the other perspective, the Divine Being is considered with all His Attributes in the differences of their particular characteristics and manifestations. This perspective, which is also a rank, is designated as the Oneness, the Pure Realm of Divine Dominion, the First Determination, or the Truth of Muhammad.

God's being the One or Oneness, which denotes, in connection with His relation to the creation, His overall manifestation of all His Names throughout the universe, has an inward and outer aspect. We can call the former His being the Deity or Divinity and the latter His being the Lord or Lordship. Although these two aspects are two faces or aspects of a single truth, there is a slight difference between them which initiates can discern, according to their personal experiences during the journey. For this reason, initiates of varying states, perceptions, and pleasures can interpret the states differently. For example, some initiates tend to do away with their carnal selves and egotism, freeing themselves from the considerations of their relative, self-existence, which they regard as an obstacle to feeling the All-Holy Existence with all their hearts. They are rooted in annihilation in God and absorbed in subsistence with God, sipping peace and contentment from the pure water of His company. Others have melted away in the face of the rays that come from the All-Holy Existence to the extent that they are unaware of their own relative existence and their surroundings. More than this, they regard the ability to discern the relative existence of others than the Absolute One as a dream and the attribution of existence to others than Him as covert polytheism.

It is natural that those who have different perceptions and feelings should voice these and interpret the issue of existence differently. Some may suggest pantheism in their styles, some monism, some may assert the Unity of Being, while still some others clearly adopt the Unity of the Witnessed.

Now let us see how the theologians and the scholars of Sufism themselves view the matter:

Sa'd al-Din al-Taftazani[98] deals with the Sufis in two categories from the viewpoint of their perceptions of existence. According to him, some Sufis are quite sensible in their view of the Unity of Being. Although they accept the multiplicity of other things in existence other than the absolutely Existent One, when they reach the final point in their journey and see themselves totally immersed in the infinite ocean of Divine Oneness with their being absorbed in the Divine Being and their attributes in the Divine Ones, all else save Him disappears from their sight; the result of this is that they can only see the All-Holy Existence. This state is regarded as and called the annihilation in Divine Oneness, which the one who is the most advanced in belief in Divine Oneness, upon him be peace and blessings, indicated in his report from God, Who said: "My servant gets nearer and nearer to Me until I love him by fulfilling the supererogatory acts of worship. When I love him, I become his ears with which he hears, his eyes with which he sees, his hands with which he grasps, and his feet on which he walks. (His hearing, seeing, grasping, and walking take place in accordance with My will and commandments.)" Those who have almost completed their journey in this rank cannot find words to express the scenes they witness nor the feelings that arise in their consciousness, and therefore they may utter words whose meanings are beyond their purpose and which sometimes suggest union and incarnation.

According to Taftazani, there is another group of Sufis. They claim the Unity of Being and project it as a philosophy or theory. They

---

[98] Sa'd al-Din al-Taftazani (d. 1390) was a famous scholar of logic, rhetoric, grammar, theology and jurisprudence of Samarqand during the rule of Timur. His *Sharh al-'Aqaid al-Nasafiyya* is among the basic works of the Muslim theology. (Trans.)

regard whatever there is in the name of existence as comprising the Divine Being only. According to them, there is no other kind of existence save the Existence of the All-Originating One in the universe. All other things or beings that seem to exist are no more than a mirage or an illusion.

As Mustafa Sabri Effendi[99] also pointed out, the first group are called Sufis, while the second group are known as pretenders of Sufism. The expressions of the first group that suggest Unity of Being arise from a spiritual, ecstatic state and an inability to find the words to express it. The consideration of the others is a distinct philosophy or theory.

Jalal al-Din al-Dawwani[100] tries to base the considerations of the Unity of Being on a theoretical foundation. He explains: Since it is inconceivable that all other beings save Him can come into existence by themselves, every contingent being (i.e. whose existence is not necessary or absolute) must depend on an absolute, necessary existence. In addition, as any contingent, created being cannot have come into existence or subsist by itself, it cannot oppose the point on which it is dependent in coming into existence and subsistence. So, all things and/or beings and causes or means of their coming into existence can continue to exist by the point (the First Cause or Creator of Causes) on which they are dependent. This leads to the conclusion that the existence of every other being save Him is relative, even nominal. Although such beings have relative existence that is dependent on the absolute Existence, we cannot regard them as having an independent self-existence.

According to this approach, although there are numerous, relatively existent beings in the universe, there is only One with a true,

---

[99] Mustafa Sabri Effendi (1869-1954) was a Turkish scholar and shaykh al-Islam. He lived in Turkey and Egypt. *Mawqif al-ʿAql waʾl-ʿIlm* is among his most well-known works. (Trans.)

[100] Jalal al-Din Muhammad ibn Asʿad al-Dawwani (1426-1502) was a prominent philosopher and theologian from Shiraz. He combined elements of illuminationist and Peripatetic philosophy and possibly also interests in Ibn al-ʿArabi. His *Lawamiʿ al-Ishraq fi Makarim al-Akhlaq* ("Lustres of Illumination on the Noble Virtues") is famous. (Trans.)

independent, self-existence. All the things we observe are the manifestations of that All-Originating One's acts.

Muhy al-Din ibn al-'Arabi goes a step further and observes:
Nothing has anything worth mentioning in terms of existence other than that it is something originated, or manifested, or reflected.
These manifestations or reflections occur (like the frames on a film)
so quickly, and follow one another so fast, that we wrongly perceive
this occurrence as being uninterrupted. After all, all that (other than
the Absolutely Existent One) we regard as existence consists of this
seemingly-uninterrupted manifestation. Jami' shares this consideration, saying: "Whatever there is in the universe is either an illusion
or imagination or shadow-like reflections in mirrors." Badr al-Din
al-Simawi[101] refers or reduces everything to matter and cannot be
considered to be among even those who have a theoretical view of
the Unity of Being worth studying.

The considerations of some concerning the doctrine of Unity
of Being are based on a state of pleasure, while some fix their eyes on
the True Being exclusively, and others have only a theoretical or philosophical approach to the matter, having provoked different thoughts,
comments, and expressions. Despite all of these, those who share
this view at all times and places are agreed that there is no existent
being that exists and subsists by itself save God. For this reason, attributing existence to others than God is done because their existence or subsistence depends upon God, not because they exist or
subsist by themselves. There is a single true existence, with all things
and events being manifestations of it. From another perspective, if
existence is an ocean, objects and events are the waves. However, each
wave has a unique characteristic, distinguishing it from the others,
while it is seen to be lost in the ocean by those who are immersed
in a state of spiritual pleasure.

---

[101] Badr al-Din al-Simawi was born in Simavna town in today's Greece. He is generally known for his materialistic views of existence. He was sentenced to death because
of his participation in revolts in the political scene in the Period of Interregnum
(1402-1413). His *Waridat* is famous. (Trans.)

If the Unity of Being is approached from a merely philosophical perspective without considering that it is a view based on a state of spiritual experience and which sees the creation as a mere shadow of the True Existence, it will inevitably be reduced to the denial of the Divine Attributes and Names and cause many negative ideas to arise concerning religion, morality, knowledge, and wisdom. It can even cause one to fall into a hidden association of partners with God in the name of Divine Unity.

With its essential principles, such as *Say, "There is no deity save God," and attain salvation*, and *Say, He is God, the One and Unique* (112:1), and *Your deity is the Deity Who is only One* (2:113), the religion of Islam has continuously insisted on the absolute Oneness of God, never mentioning ideas or concepts such as the Unity of Being or the Unity of the Witnessed, as doctrines it has sanctioned. For this reason, such concepts have been regarded as arising from spiritual states and experiences and have not been considered as objective or binding teachings.

Actually, the concepts of the Unity of Being and the Unity of the Witnessed arise from certain feelings and perceptions that people who are of a particular temperament and way of journeying, and who have reached a particular rank of knowledge of God, develop in the state in which they have been favored during their spiritual journey. When they get out of, or are awakened from, that state of pleasure or intoxication, which has caused them to voice these concepts, review their feelings and perceptions in the light of the essential doctrines which the Messenger brought and preached. Nevertheless, it is also a fact that some sayings uttered by those favored with true knowledge of God in moments of intoxication and immersion, and some others which, even though they have been uttered in wakefulness, have caused confusion due to the choice of words, have led those with ill opinions of these people to make philosophical speculations about the Absolute Self-Existence and the existence of contingent beings. A mind devoted and obedient to the Shari'a understands from the dictum *There is no existent being save Him* that there is no true self-existent and self-subsistent being except Him, while those who deal with the matter purely from a philosophically speculative approach understand that whatever exists is God. According to the former group, only God has a substantial existence, with every other being than Him having only a relative existence or as a shadow. As for the others, all existence, visible or invisible is He. It is clear that such a view or consideration entails polytheism and has nothing to do with the doctrine of the Unity of Being, which the Muslim Sufis perceive and express in a spiritual state of spiritual pleasure. It has almost the same meaning as pantheism and/or monism, which is related to union and incarnation. Such deviancy has been continually responsible for the most abominable forms of the association of partners with God, such as Ezra is God, the Messiah is God, 'Ali is God, Baha'ullah is God, the Pharaoh is God, and Nimrod is God.

* * *

The issues concerning God, the universe and humankind are obvious when looked at from a viewpoint of Qur'anic disciplines. However, a number of ignorant persons and a number of ones who are ill-intended have adopted deviant approaches, have tried to prove existence and to substitute the world for God. They have distorted the truth of Divinity or denied Him any attributes or regarded Him as a spirit that pervades existence. They have also offered views that God takes on bodily forms (incarnation) or that there is a created being that is united with God and becomes God (union). They have distorted the Divine truth in the ugliest way possible by claiming that the statement that "There is no deity but God" is the same as "There is no existent being save Him," meaning that God is identical with the visible universe.

In my view, in this respect we should adopt an approach such that we regard the concept of the Unity of Being, which negates the existence of beings other than God, as being based on a state of spiritual pleasure and as arising from being over-powered by absorption and being lost in God's Existence along with an inability to find the words to express this state. We cannot accept the philosophically speculative theory that existence comprises God and that His Existence consists of the existence of all beings. We must protect Muslim minds from such theories. We should also bear in mind that if the doctrine of the Unity of Being is not outlined by and kept within the essential principles of Islamic belief, it may lead to an incorrect conception of God, His Existence and His relation with the created. It is a only with a correct conception of Divine Unity that people can be favored with a special knowledge that stems from Him and in which they perceive the true character or reality of things and events. Then they turn away from these events to the Eternal Witness, and in indifference to His signs and the signposts that show the way to Him, become immersed in the lights of His absolute Existence and melt away with respect to their carnal self and ego. But to adopt speculative theories or views that ascribe divinity to things and events means the association of partners with God and this implies going beyond one's limits of perception and knowledge. Such views or theories can even amount to the denial of God, the Truth, He Who is known by His Names and qualified with His eternal Attributes, and Who infinitely surrounds all things with His majestic Attributes such as Knowledge, Power and Will.

The two views or approaches mentioned here are worlds apart from each other. One is based on seeing everything, not excluding the human ego itself, as being, with respect to its existence and subsistence, absolutely dependent on the Divine Existence and Self-Subsistence. Those who adopt such an approach are annihilated in the Almighty and subsist by Him, believing that everything comes from Him. The other is the view of the self-conceited ones who are unaware of what a spiritual state is or what spiritual pleasures are. They speculate that all things, including themselves, are united with Divinity or with a part of it. While the former regard themselves in the face of the Divine Existence as a drop in the ocean or a particle in the sun, the latter consider that the ocean is the drop itself or the sun is the particle itself. They maintain that the universe is an appearance of Him. The former are self-possessed, always feeling in awe of Him and pursuing Him as the final goal. The latter are, on the other hand, loose, inattentive and lack any goal. The author of *Mizan al-'Irfan* describes the former as follows:

> Those who have reached the final point in their journey,
> Are all self-possessed and people of perfection.
> Their state is described as "finding,"
> And they have no interest in whether they exist or not.
> The voice cannot express their state,
> Only those who share their state can understand them.
> For they have reached annihilation in the Divine Being,
> Having been freed from their corporeal existence,
> Since they have been annihilated in the Existence of the Truth,
> Absorbed in states of exhilaration and ecstasy.
> They cannot see another existence save that of the Truth,
> His love invades through their hearts,
> Yet they are aware that still they are His servants.
> The states of others do not resemble theirs.
> These are the ones, O brother, who maintain
> Their relation with God as His servants;
> The one who writes about them no longer has any say.

According to these people, all things exist because the Necessarily Existent One exists. The relation of the Divine Being with things and events is that He brings them into existence and maintains and cares for them. But it is not possible for us to know the character of this relation, or how this relation takes place and is maintained. What we know is that it is He Who originates all things and maintains them. Nothing can "be" without Him; nothing can come into existence or maintain its existence without Him. For this reason, everything is from Him and it is He with all His Attributes of Perfection and Grace Who is the Originator of all things. In this approach, there is no room left for the duality of cause and source.

The prince of lovers (Jalal al-Din al-Rumi) says:

> Certainly, there is no duality concerning the Almighty,
> I, We, You have nothing to do with that Holy Being.
> Incarnation and Union are inconceivable for Him.
> Thinking of duality for the Unique One is obviously an error.

There is a point to be mentioned here. The doctrine of the Unity of Being maintained by some Muslim Sufis as being based on a spiritual state of pleasures and absorption is not contrary to the Islamic belief of Divine Unity. However, we should admit that there are many utterances which have been made due to intoxication and immersion which are apparently incompatible with the principles of belief. What follows is one such utterance by an intoxicated one that suggests monism:

The Almighty has declared: "I am nearer to you than your jugular vein."
That is, the ocean and a drop it contains are the same.
O human being, you have fallen away from your own self.
If you but know, all are the same—
the one who witnesses and the one witnessed,
And the place where witnessing takes place; and also the same are
The owner and protector and the one owned and protected.
Though the universe is the result of the manifestation of
God's All-Beautiful Names,
There is only one Greatest Name among those Names.
O Lord! You are the One Who absolutely exists; as for other existing beings,
They are no more than images or illusions.
For this reason, whatever You create is one and the same.
Though the beauty of all beautiful things is
because of Your all-enchanting Beauty,
Still there is only one uniquely Beautiful Being.
Every sedition and seduction in the world is because of His love.
It should be known that
the chief cause of this sedition anddissension is the one and the same.

It is true that the style of these words is also seditious and seductive. Some have tried to comment on such words so as to make them compatible with the spirit of religion, while others have wandered in the pits of monism when interpreting them.

Like natural sciences, such as mathematics, physics, chemistry, and medicine, and the religious sciences, such as jurisprudence, Qur'anic interpretation, and Hadith, Islamic Sufism has some concepts peculiar to itself. Those who do not know the true meaning and contents of these concepts will never be saved from errors. It is not possible to know and understand Islamic Sufism correctly without knowing these concepts.

To sum up: the concept of the Unity of Being comes from a spiritual state marked by personal spiritual experiences and the pleasures and ecstasy that arise from an initiate's knowledge of God and His Oneness. An initiate who has this degree of attainment feels inwardly that the truly existent one is the only True One, and regards all other beings as a shadow or as having an imaginary existence. The Muslim Sufis who possess this concept have experienced such a degree of knowledge of God in their hearts and have made it a dimension of their conscious nature, trying to express it in proportion to their power of expression. Their expressions concerning unity in multiplicity and multiplicity with respect to unity are the utterances of these inward feelings and experiences, based on the consideration that unity is the foundation and source of everything, while multiplicity is illusory. In fact, it is not possible for a hero of state and pleasure who witnesses the manifestations of His Names and Attributes in every thing and event to think or act otherwise. They feel the omnipresence of that All-Exalted Being far beyond the horizons that are within the reach of human reason and imagination. They feel that they are always in His company and they turn to that Being Who eternally exists and who cannot be known with respect to His Divine Essence. What follows is an excerpt from how they put their experiences into words:

> The All-Beautiful One Who wills to see
> His Beauty through innumerable faces,
> Should be in innumerable parts, like mirrors broken.

As for another view of the Divine Being in His relation to the universe, which is known as the Unity of the Witnessed and which has become a separate school led by Imam Rabbani Ahmad Faruq al-Sarhandi,[102] although it is nearer to the thought of the Prophet's

---

[102] Imam Rabbani, Ahmad Faruq al-Sarhandi (d. 1624): Accepted by many as "reviver of the second millennium." Born in Sarhand (India) and well-versed in Islamic sciences, he removed many corrupt elements from Sufism. He taught Shah Alamgir or Awrangzeb (d. 1707), who had a committee of scholars prepare the most comprehensive compendium of the Hanafi Law. (Trans.)

Companions than the Unity of Being, it cannot be considered as being fully compatible with the consideration that is a way of perfect self-possession and complete wakefulness, because it also originates in a state of intoxication and absence and is combined with ecstasy and absorption. By contrast, those following the way of the Companions present to their audience their experiences, which even when experienced in a state of intoxication and absorption, with extraordinary self-possession, never falling into confusion.

The Unity of Being, which is known in the West as pantheism and, with its variations, monism, is a philosophical school. This approach, based on seeing the universe as God Himself or His appearance, cannot be reconciled with Islamic Sufism. Furthermore, it is impossible to reconcile it with any Islamic philosophical movement. As mentioned before, while those who share this approach have strayed from the right path by admitting a pervading divinity and sharing it among all things, the Muslim Sufis following the Prophetic way have always believed that everything is from Him, not that everything is He.

> *O God! Show us the truth as the truth and enable us with the observance of it, and show us the falsehood as falsehood and enable us with the avoidance of it.*

> *And let God's blessings be on our master Muhammad, who is the guide to the truth, and on his family and Companions, the noble, godly ones.*

TAJRID (ISOLATION)

Literally meaning to separate, abstract, peel away, or to isolate oneself from every occupation and engagement, *tajrid* (isolation) denotes the state where one isolates oneself from worldly things and abandons all carnal or bodily desires. It also denotes turning away from all else save God and being freed from any attachment to wealth, status or position or any worldly expectations, and setting one's heart totally on Him without expecting anything in return.

The scholars relate isolation to the Qur'anic statement, *Take off your shoes* (20:12), and interpret this as the purifying of the heart, which they call the home of God, of all worldly and otherworldly considerations, and preparing it for the visit of the Holy Sovereign. Some go a step further and regard this as turning to the Light of Lights with all one's heart and setting one's heart totally on Him without leaving any room for anything else in one's feelings, according to one's capacity. From another perspective, isolation has been approached as resistance against all carnal or bodily appetites and impulses and against the attractions of the world with whatever is in it. Initiates who have not been able to isolate themselves from carnal appetites, the attractions of the world, the attachment of the heart to anything else save Him, or from any worldly or otherworldly consideration, cannot attain His private company and the spiritual pleasure inherent in this.

Concerning this significant point, the author of *al-Minhaj* says:

So long as you do not isolate yourself
from considerations about everything save Him,
You will not be able to reach privacy with the Beloved in His private room.

Ibrahim Haqqi expresses the same point, as follows:

The heart is the home of God; purify it from whatever is there other than Him,
So that the All-Merciful may descend into His palace at night.

Isolation, which, in the words of Sayyid Sharif,[103] is cleaning the heart and other innermost faculties from the dirt and dust of attachment to anything save Him, requires that the people favored with a vision of Him should isolate themselves from what-ever they see or hear, and that they live immersed or absorbed in the lights of the Existence of the Eternal Witness. Every initiate feels this and is favored with its gifts according to the individual's capacity.

When those who are in the initial stages of the spiritual journey find themselves growing in the knowledge of God that is developing in the heart, acquired information concerning Him gradually fades, and they begin to receive glimpses from things beyond. Then all of their material or bodily necessities, and even the entire world with whatever is in it, gradually lose their importance and value for them and they become polished mirrors to the truth, or function as some misty medium to reflect Him. One who feels this favor sometimes says, like Fuduli,

> The way of isolation is a home
> requiring full renunciation and sacrifice to settle in,
> So abandon whatever worldly things you have, and do not have a house.

or sometimes cries, like Yunus Emre:

> I have found the unique, matchless honey;
> Let everybody come and plunder my existence.

One who has reached the final point of the spiritual journey is freed from all considerations concerning other existent beings save God, and is left with no trace that belongs to anything else except Him. If those favored with this degree of isolation do not follow the principles of the Prophetic way or the rules of Shari‘a in their considerations, they may lapse into negating the "reality of things"—the (relative) existence of other things than God the realities of which originate in God's Names; this is a rank where many initiates live in a

---

[103] Sayyid Sharif al-Jurjani (1339-1413), was one of the leading theologians of 15th century. He lived in Iran and taught in Shiraz. He visited Istanbul in 1374. *Sharh al-Mawaqif* is his most famous work. (Trans.)

daze. Whereas, those who strictly follow the signposts and lights of the Prophetic way during their entire journey, though admitting the reality of things, see in everything only He Who is the One, only know the One, only mention the One, only call the One, and only turn to the One in thousands of signs of "dawn", turning their eyes from all others.

Ahmadi[104] describes this rank according to his feeling as follows:

> I have submitted all my being to that Friend, having no home any longer;
>> And purified my hands of any worldly things I had,
>>> being left without both of the two worlds.
>> For God's love has come and drawn me to itself:
> Opening the eyes of my heart, awakening me from an intoxicated sleep.
>>> His Unity has become manifest to me,
>>> so that I have seen Him with all certainty.
> I have driven away polytheism, having no doubt any longer.

As for the state of those who have completed their journey toward God, it is such a deep, indescribable state of pleasure, where efforts toward isolation have ended in perfect isolation and they have all but lost their own being, that those who do not experience it cannot know or describe it. Anybody who attempts to describe it cannot be saved from confusion. Such a relation between the Almighty Truth and an initiate whom He has favored with such a degree of spiritual attainment must be a mysterious gift of secrecy of His to His distinguished servants. What we should do is to feel respect for this gift of secrecy.

> *O God! Show us the truth as the truth and enable us with the observance of it, and show us the falsehood as falsehood and enable us with the avoidance of it. And let God's blessings be on our master Muhammad, who is the guide to the truth, and on his family and Companions, the noble, godly ones.*

---

[104] Emir Muhammed ibn Emir Ahmadi lived in the same age as Jalal al-Din al-Rumi. He lived in Bayburt, in the Eastern Turkey. He was also the leader of the Ahis (The Brotherhood of Craftsmen and Tradesmen) in the region. (Trans.)

TAFRID (INDIVIDUALITY)

T*afrid* (individuality) means seclusion from society or going into retreat to devote all one's time to worshipping God. More particularly, it denotes that even when initiates have attained states or stations that others cannot, they never see themselves as such, because of their conviction that whatever attainment they have is, in fact, a gift from the Truth, submitting themselves wholly to Him, and always being in His company. The verse (24:25), *Surely God is He Who is the manifest Truth*, contains an implicit indication of this rank.

Although resembling each other in coloring, individuality and isolation express different ranks and states of pleasure. Isolation is the state of cutting off relations with everything else save the Beloved and of always being with Him, while individuality is being favored with total self-negation. Because those who have attained it never think of the spiritual states they have reached, their consciousness and nature always indicate the Truth. Isolation is marked by the zeal and pleasure of devoted servanthood to God, while individuality is the consciousness of being a servant bound to worship Him. The depth of this consciousness is in proportion to one's capacity and varies in degrees with respect to the things people feel during their spiritual journey.

Those in the initial stages of the way to individuality— which is called *individuality on the way to God*—are constantly in quest of Him, trying to feel Him and making strenuous efforts to find and see Him. While doing this, they never consider what being in constant quest of Him denotes nor what kinds of things are used as means to reach this goal. Even if they make use of these means in a natural way, they are concentrated on the goal with the whole of mind and heart, and are always thinking of it. They use all their abilities of thinking and contemplation on the way to making contact with Him, and endeavor to reach Him, thus spending their whole life in the climate of this sweet dream.

Travelers dedicated to reaching the goal to such degree always feel the gifts or radiations of individuality coming from their turning to God, from their love of Him, and from their visions during the journey. They also feel the pleasure of seeking only He Who is the One and concentrating all their love on Him alone. Being freed from wasting their faculties of loving, feeling, and seeking, they sip the sweet water of unity in multiplicity. They find themselves turning to Him with a great zeal and thirst, and in waves of annihilation of their love, and in privacy with Him that is freed from all others than Him when they reach the peak of the vision of Him.

When halfway on the road to individuality—summarized as *individuality in the company of God*—they feel that they are being favored with abundant gifts from the All-Holy One. However, they should not feel vain on account of these gifts; rather, they should be ever conscious that it is not themselves who are the origin of such gifts, but they have come purely from the All-Holy One. With this consciousness, they remain full of thanks and praises for Him. Those reaching this rank of being perfected or of becoming universal human beings and the most polished mirrors to the Almighty Truth, cannot help but express that this is purely His favor. The following couplet of Hassan ibn Thabit, a famous poet during the Prophet's time, is an excellent example of this:

> I have not praised Muhammad with my words;
> Rather, I have praised my words with Muhammad.

He means that his words are praiseworthy because they are about Prophet Muhammad, upon him be peace and blessings. Such a favor should be proclaimed in attribution to God as declared in the verse (93:11), *As for the grace of your Lord, proclaim it*. Some sayings of the Prophet, such as, "I am the lord of the children of Adam, and the first to be resurrected on the Judgment Day, and I am the one who will first intercede (with God on behalf of human beings) and whose intercession will be accepted; but there is no pride,"[105] and comparable utterances of some of His Companions about themselves belong to this category. They do not express self-pride, but rather proclaim God's favors and are overflowing with the feelings of thanking and praising Him. Such a favor can be regarded as a threshold to the perfect knowledge of God that is for the heroes of knowledge, love of God, and spiritual pleasures. The rank of individuality beyond this threshold marks a different depth of their knowledge of God and suggests an unimaginable attainment.

This rank, which is called *individuality on the way from God*, and which is supported by God's unique and most comprehensive appreciations of those who have attained it, is the rank where initiates are favored with the constant company of God due to their perfect expansion, knowledge of God, and feeling of awe and reverence beyond all measure. The heroes of this rank feel in their inner worlds that the whole universe has been annihilated in God, they feel His constant company even when among people, and convey to the creation what they have received from the Creator, opening the door for people in order that they may be enabled to meet with the Truth. The main characteristics of such people are that, because of their modesty, they are like other human beings in appearance, they always pursue God's good pleasure and approval in all their acts and dealings, they live in this world by concentrating on the next one, they always feel the exhilarating company of God, they convey to others what they hear, see and feel, they take an interest in every thing other than Him only because of Him, and they see every other thing as a shadow of the light of His Existence.

Those who are in the first rank of individuality are dedicated to reaching the goal of their journey. Those who have attained the second rank voice, as a proclamation of the Divine favor, the fact that they have been favored with the rays of His "Face" and the lights of His Existence that they feel in the hills of their hearts. They are

[105] Al-Muslim, "Fada'il," 3; Abu Dawud, "Sunna," 13.

constantly thanking and praising God. As for others who have attained the peak of this journey, which is in fact beyond all ranks, and who share the indescribable depth of those of the second rank, we can approach them only with respect to their missions and their consciousness of these missions. They receive messages from the Truth or the True One and convey these to the people, calling people to meet with God, trying to remove the obstacles between the people and God. They put up with living only for the life of others, and if they cannot do anything for the life of others, they experience life as an unbearable suffering. These are perfect guides and conveyors of the Divine messages. Their first rank is composed of the Messengers and the Prophets, and their true successors constitute the second rank.

The initial-rank travelers to individuality are the heroes of belief and knowledge of God who are in constant pursuit and who hasten to sincerity and purity of intention. Those of the second rank are the loyal ones filled with a knowledge and love of God, who have fully displayed their faithfulness and sincerity. As for the others, whom we try to know by their tasks and missions, they are the guides and conveyors of God's messages, those who try to make the Truth known to people and to rouse the spirits to meet with God. Since the heroes of this final rank also have the attributes that are shared by those of the first two ranks, they can also be called the leaders of the heroes of knowledge of God. As for the first and foremost among them, he is our master Muhammad u Ahmad u Mahmud u Mustafa, who is the master of creation and the unique one of all time and space, upon him be the best and most perfect of blessings and peace. There are many other great persons near to his sacred sphere, especially including the other great Messengers, upon them be peace. Each of them has been honored with special favors according to his rank. However, it is the Prophet Muhammad, the leader of the holiest of humankind, who was constantly being honored with such favors. Others have been ready to sacrifice their lives for the sake of one moment of his relation or togetherness with the Light of All Lights. All the beauties and lights with which the others have been honored are mere reflections of the Divine manifestations that he received.

In his famous *Qasida al-Bur'a* or *al-Burda* (Eulogy of al-Bur'a),[106] Busiri expresses this highest grace as follows:

All the miracles that the other great Messenger worked by God's leave,
Were caused by the light that reached them from the light of Muhammad.
What we all know concerning him is that he is mortal human being;
But he is the best and greatest of all that God has created.
If the miracles he worked had been in proportion to his greatness,
The rotted bones would be revived when one prays, mentioning his holy name.

O God, bestow Your blessings and peace upon him whom You sent as a mercy for all creation, and on his brothers among the Prophets and Messengers, and on the angels You have made near to you, and on Your righteous servants among the inhabitants of the heavens and earth. May God be pleased with all of them.

---

[106] The *Bur'a* by Al-Busiri is arguably the greatest classical poem in the Arabic language in praise of the character and exalted rank of Prophet Muhammad. Composed by Imam Al-Busiri in the 13th century in Mamluke Egypt, it has been recited ever since throughout the Muslim lands. (Trans.)

JAM' (ABSORPTION)

J *am'* (absorption) literally means coming and bringing together. In the language of Sufism, it means fixing all one's feeling,
sight and consciousness on the Truth, to the extent that one
is absorbed in Him and does not feel the existence of the world with
all that is in it. To the degree of one's knowledge of God, one only
knows Him, feels Him, sees Him and is saved from preoccupation
with anything else. If this meaning is approached from the concept
of unity, it is the opposite of multiplicity; but if it is conceived of
as one's heart cutting off relations with all else save God, then its opposite is distinguishing (*farq*), which we, God willing, will deal with
as a separate subject.

Absorption is a state or station belonging to those who have
reached the final state of the spiritual journey. Travelers to the Truth
who are honored with the gift of absorption always feel Him, know
Him, and according to the level of the horizon and spiritual pleasures of each, can be aware or not aware of the people around them.
But they always feel and are always conscious of the Truth and live
as if charmed by observation of the meanings that belong to the Truth
and that are reflected in everything. They always see the manifestations of His Names and Attributes in all things and events which
they encounter. Thirsty for the Divine Being Himself, they fly around
the manifestations of His "Face" like moths flying around a light.
In tides of wonder and admiration, they cannot help but utter: *Glory be to You, how exalted You are (as the Divine Being)*!

Two stages further from this state of pleasure is absorption within absorption, which means a total absence for the travelers to the
Truth. Travelers who find themselves in such a whirlpool of feeling
are no longer aware of their own selves nor that of others. Totally

detached from distinguishing, they are completely forgetful of all else save the Truth—as anybody except He is a shadow of the shadow of the light of His Existence—and turn to Him with all their being.

For initiates who base themselves on God's absolute Oneness in all their views and considerations, everything is a shadow of the light of the Existence of the Truth. For one who is in the state of absorption, it is a shadow of the shadow of His Existence's light, while one who is in the absorption within absorption only sees the rays of the manifestations of His "Face" in the name of the creation. Some scholars mention a further degree of absorption, which they call holy absorption. This is the rank which the verifying scholars of Sufism regard as the title of nearness to God, Who is nearer to us than ourselves, by means of supererogatory prayers. The travelers who have attained this level are conscious that it is God Who maintains them, and begin to observe everything more deeply and clearly with their innermost senses, which have become sharper than their external senses. They hear with their spirit, see with their power of insight, review and examine with their conscience, and have the opportunity to see the true faces of theoretical knowledge through the door half-opened by their inner vision and experience. This is the rank where travelers are favored with the full manifestation of the truth contained in *He is the First, and the Last, and the Outward, and the Inward* (57:3), and where they become polished mirrors that reflect it. The servants of God who have reached this farthest point either "travel in God" and rotate around themselves like the North Star, or are turning around their axis in their hearts while being in their bodies among people.

If they have attained the rank of absorption, it means that they have also been favored with "subsistence with God." Those who hold this rank in the final stage of the journey, and who are abstracted from their own attributes in their absorption in God's Attributes and from their own being in absorption in God's Being, gain a new existence through subsistence with God. They begin to feel the bliss of eternality and breathe "absorption" in the delight of being aware that their acts have become lost in God's acts. A stage further, when they observe that their attributes have been annihilated in the all-comprehensive Attributes of God, they become lost in the delight of experiencing absorption within absorption. Finally, as a result of their own being being obliterated in the face of God's Knowledge and Existence, they leave themselves to the consideration of the holy absorption with inner vision and spiritual pleasures, and are immersed in the feelings of wonder upon wonder.

From another point of view, the act of observing the requirements or responsibilities of servanthood to God with the utmost care, devotion, and consciousness is called "distinguishing," while being favored with a shower of Divine gifts that come unexpectedly as a reward for this "small capital"—small because the greatest capital is one's being favored by God—is absorption. In view of this approach, those who have attained a higher spiritual state have observed that one who does not perceive "distinguishing" is ignorant of servanthood, while one who does not feel absorption is unaware of knowing God.

The Qur'anic statement (1:5), *You alone do we worship*, which expresses the individual consciousness developing into and translating the public consciousness, is a voice of distinguishing and servanthood, while *You alone do we ask for help* (1:5) is an expression of absorption and a declaration of human poverty and helplessness before God. Every initiate hears the voice of distinguishing at the beginning of the spiritual journey, and feels the pleasure of absorption at the end of it. The ultimate point, which only those endowed with a particular capacity can reach, is "absorption within absorption" and the "holy absorption." While the former signifies God's concentration of the manifestations of His Names on a certain object, the latter is a sign of the manifestation of His Names throughout the universe.

According to Kashani,[107] distinguishing is the knowledge of God the Almighty and spiritual pleasures of those who have not yet been able to develop their theoretical considerations about God (I personally find this view unacceptable), while absorption is immersion

---

[107] 'Abd al-Razzaq al-Kashani (d. 1335) is one of the interpereters of Ibn al-'Arabi. His *Ta'wilat al-Qur'an* is especially famous and important. (Trans.)

caused by a concentration on the Creator without ever thinking of the creation, and absorption within absorption is the peak of seeing the creation as subsisting by the Creator. This final rank is also the rank of distinguishing above absorption. Since in this rank only God's acts, Attributes and Essential Qualities are observed, the Absolutely True One, for those who have attained this rank, becomes the eyes with which they see, the ears with which they hear, and the hands with which they hold. For this reason, He attributes to Himself what they do by His will and leave and ignore the apparent causes. The Sufi scholars are of the opinion that the verse, (8:17), *You did not kill them but God killed them, and when you threw, it was not you who threw, but God who threw*, besides clearly mentioning a miracle of God's Messenger, upon him be peace and blessings, alludes to this rank.

Absorption can never mean the unity of being—the unity (union) of God and the universe or God's being identical with the universe—as pantheists claim, nor is distinguishing totally the opposite. The One Who is the Eternal is eternal, and the beings who are contained in time and come into existence within time are mortal and different from the Eternal One. The Creator cannot be and is not the same as the created. The relation between them is not that which comes from appearance; that is, the universe is not an apparent form of God. Rather, this relation is that between the Creator and the created. We can also see the creation as the totality of the manifestations of God's Names. These manifestations are completely pure and transparent, while that which issues from the created is usually tangible. Human beings have both a pure, transparent aspect or dimension, and a dense/tangible one. This is why, as declared in the verse (17:84), *Each being acts according to his own standard of measure*, they can display behavior either according to their bodily dimension or according to their spirit. As they are composed of a body, a carnal self, and a spirit, they fix their eyes on nature and corporeality, while they carry inclinations toward spiritual, exalted worlds as well. By means of the ways of rising which the Shari'a has appointed and guaranteed, travelers on the way to God cut their relations with fleeting and decaying things and turn to eternity. *Whosever's breast God expands and opens to Islam follows a light from his Lord* (39:22). So, when travelers to God turn to Him in submission, they travel in the exhilarating horizons with utmost self-possession and awareness under the guidance of the light of their Lord. Even though they may sometimes encounter confusion or bewilderment, they easily overcome these with the assistance of the never-deceiving leadership of the master of creation, upon him be peace and blessings. They always head for the sources of knowledge that God has determined and secured through Prophethood, and never fall into the errors committed by pantheists.

From another perspective, absorption has been dealt with under the rubrics of "absorption with respect to knowledge", "absorption with respect to existence", and "absorption with respect to the (Divine) Being Himself."

Absorption in knowledge means that at the beginning of their journey, travelers to God base themselves on the knowledge that comes from, or that is obtained through, the proofs and indications of God. Then this knowledge develops from the certainty based on knowing into a certainty based on observation and finally into a certainty based on experience. However, only a shadowy degree of certainty based on experience can be reached in the world. Ultimately, this knowledge becomes pure knowledge from His Presence. Although it is the result of following the way of inference, it is not the same as the knowledge acquired through a proof originated in the outer world or in the human inner world. Not is it totally different either. It is a special gift of the Almighty to the free will with which God has endowed human beings, and which is in fact a simple means given to them for the execution of the Divine commandments. However, like all other Divine gifts, this gift is never proportionate to our free will. Like it, all other gifts of God Almighty are many times greater than what we actually deserve.

Absorption with respect to existence is when the travelers to God are perfectly aware in their consciousness of how things and events occur and how they are maintained. All of existence disappears from their vision to the extent that they are no longer aware of which direction is right and which is left. The conquerors of the heart, who walk in this station, feel only the rays of the Eternal Holy Existence and Knowledge and see all else as the motions of these rays. Provided manifestation is not confused with appearance, and shadow with the original, those who have attained this horizon feel or hear innumerable things and/or beings in every part of the universe invoking His Name, saying, *He is the All-Living, the Self-Subsisting (by Whom all subsist)* (2:255).

Absorption with respect to the (Divine) Being Himself means that all the indications and proofs of God that originate in the outer and inner human world are no longer visible in the face of the light of knowledge of God and the spiritual pleasure that the Almighty lets flow into the hearts of travelers to Him. Some have regarded this rank as the final station of the spiritual journey. If they base this consideration on their constant turning to God during traveling from wakefulness to self-possession and thence to repentance, penitence and contrition one after the other, and on the relation between God and humankind as being the relation between the Creator and the created, and the Sole Object of Worship and the worshipper, and the Lord and the servant, there can be no objection. But, if they imply by absorption that things have no reality at all, and it is of no use or significance to use one's mental faculties to infer from things and events the existence of God and therefore to acquire certain knowledge about Him, and that people are no longer responsible for the fulfillment of religious obligations after reaching some point in the spiritual journey, and that there is essentially no difference between I and you and He, then this is most definitely a total deviation in conception and creed. This can be either a fantasy of those who are pursuing "originality" for the sake of fame or a view held by some self-conceited pantheists and monists.

As for the Prophets and the pure, saintly scholars, they have regarded the way leading to the Infinite One as endless, and have experienced the final station one can reach in the journey along this way according to their capacity with the same solemnity, wakefulness, and consciousness as they experienced the beginning. They have always accepted that serving the Truth with the utmost humility is the goal of their lives. The Almighty ordered the master of creation, the most perfect in servanthood to Him, *Worship your Lord until what is certain (to come, i.e. death) comes to you* (15:99). By this, He both emphasizes that death marks the end of this responsibility and consoles the Messenger for the afflictions and tortures he was subjected to by reminding him of his meeting with God. Because meeting with God meant for him reaching certainty based on experience in his own, unique level.

> *O God! Make us among those of Your servants who pursue sincerity, whom You have favored with sincerity and purity of intention, who have achieved piety and abstinence from all forbidden things big or small, and whom You have made near to You, and who are pleased with You and whom you are pleased with. And let God's blessings and peace be on our master Muhammad, the head of those whom You have favored with sincerity and purity of intention, and on his family and Companions, who were austere, near to God, and were pleased with Him and whom God was pleased with. Amen!*

FARQ (DISTINGUISHING)

In the language of Sufism, *farq* (distinguishing) has been interpreted as making a clear distinction between unity and multiplicity. To give a longer and more explicit definition, distinguishing means the discernment of the created, despite having perfect knowledge of the Creator, and despite being among people at the same time as being in God's company. Absorption is marked with knowledge and love of God the Almighty and spiritual pleasures, while it is a distinctive sign of distinguishing that an initiate who has it tries to lead others to the same horizon of knowledge and love of God and spiritual pleasures. For this reason, it has been said that one who does not have distinguishing is imperfect in servanthood to God, and one who does not feel absorption lacks in perfect knowledge of God. This is why one should have both distinguishing and absorption, each of which has a significance of its own. As mentioned before, in the account of absorption, *You alone do we worship* (1:5) is said to indicate distinguishing, and *You alone do we ask for help* (1:5) absorption.

Absorption is a subjective state of pleasure, while distinguishing is objective, in that it depends on the Shari'a. In absorption, one is under a greater influence from one's spiritual state and inner depth than from one's reason and logic, but in distinguishing, reasoning according to the Shari'a is essential. One can pass into the state of absorption from the state of distinguishing. However, to turn back to the latter from the former means becoming distinguished. Those who remain in absorption are immersed in spiritual pleasures according to the capacity of their spirits and know nothing else. Isa Mahwi expresses this as follows:

> One who exists in his non-existence
> does not know non-existence while he exists;

Strangers to this state are unaware of the pleasure
in communion with the Beloved.

If one remains in the rank of absorption and is unable to turn
back to distinguishing then this means that one has not been able
to perceive well what Prophethood is. Ascending is progress, but
descending among people after having completed ascension is perfection. An initiate has individual pleasure in absorption and can be
an individual mirror to the Divine truths, but distinguishing after
absorption denotes a determined attitude, pleasure shared with others and it denotes serving as a comprehensive mirror. Those who
have attained such a station are with God and with people; and they
discern Him in His manifestations in everything, feel unity in multiplicity, and look at multiplicity from and through unity.

Concerning the relation between distinguishing and absorption,
we should also point out the differentiation in absorption. This means
that He Who is the One Who manifests Himself differently in different "mirrors," or rather, those who are usually in a state of pleasure observe Him differently in different mirrors. As for the differences among the mirrors—things and beings that receive and reflect God's manifestations—these are caused by the varying abilities
of people to receive the manifestations.

Distinguishing after absorption is a more sound and perfect state
than the former one—distinguishing before absorption or distinguishing without absorption. It is the state in which travelers to God
cut their heart-felt relations with all else save the Single, Unique
One and completely turn to Him to be annihilated in Him. Like
annihilation in God and subsistence with God, those who have attained this rank do not discern the world and the things in it, although these exist before their eyes. They live in immersion, with
observations made with their insight into the Divine Attributes and
acts in all things and events, and are lost in the manifestations of unity in the mirrors of multiplicity. Like the stars, which, although they
are always there, become invisible when the sun rises—we should
set forth for God the most sublime of examples—the heroes of this
rank cannot see anything else than Him from their observatory in

the atmosphere of the manifestations of the acts and Attributes of the Holy Existence Who is manifest enough to be recognized before all else.

From another perspective, an initiate in absorption is freed from corporeality and the animal dimension of his or her being, while in distinguishing he or she rises to the level of life that is lived at the level of spirit and heart and discovers that his or her ego is made up of elements from the All-Merciful, thus gaining a new existence. In this rank, he/she confesses, "I have lost my carnal ego and attained a new ego from the All-Merciful," and always expresses the idea, "There is no agent save God." Naturally, this is done without excluding the free will of human beings. Being aware of the realities of the Existence and Knowledge of the Self-Existent, All-Knowing One that are contained in the degree of certainty based on experience, he or she is enraptured with the observation of the dominion of the All-Living, Self-Subsisting One over everything.

We should, however, point out that, despite all considerations of annihilation and ecstasy, distinction is essential to distinguishing. Heroes of distinguishing are alert at every step of their journey to the fact that, though it is the Creator of causes alone Who creates both humanity and their deeds, they have free will, even though it consists of a relative inclination. They remain mindful that they have been given free will so that they are responsible and accountable for their sins and errors.

With respect to distinguishing, some people have gone to extremes and become mired in deviations. According to these people— may God protect us from believing in such a thing— every person is the creator of his or her own deeds, and human free will has an absolute effect on human actions. Others hold exactly the opposite view and assert that human free will can play no part in human actions at all in the face of the absolute Divine Will. They have supposed that human beings are like so many leaves blown around by winds by the overwhelming, all-compelling will. Those who have adopted the Straight Way, and who have been favored with true perception of the mystery of the Divine Will in Its relation with human free will, have admitted that everything occurs by God's Will and Power without human free will being excluded. God takes human inclinations and free choice into consideration when determining and creating the actions of humans. Such a belief supports with prayers their inclinations to do good, while also helping them to struggle against their inclinations to do evil by asking God for forgiveness.

Many among the first of the three groups mentioned are naturalists, who attribute every thing and every event to "natural" causes. They do not admit that anything else exists except what they can see with their eyes and hear with their ears.

Overpowered by the spiritual state in which they find themselves and the pleasures they feel, the second group negate free will and display fatalism, making out that people are as senseless objects.

As for the third group, in addition to seeing God's Wisdom and authority, creativity and disposal in everything, in their consciousness that stems from their belief, and with their conscious perception, they admit that they have been endowed with a free will, which in reality consists in an inclination. So, without ever confusing the parts of the Divine Will and their own choices with each other in their acts, they are aware of what is meant when they say "I have done it." In whatever kind or degree of pleasure and immersion they find themselves, they never lose their conviction of this fact.

> *Our Lord, do not let our hearts swerve after You have guided us, and bestow upon us mercy from Your Presence. Surely You, only You, are the (Munificent) Bestower. And bestow peace and blessings upon our master Muhammad, the master of those who ever turn to God in contrition, and on his family and Companions, the noble, godly ones.*

TAWHID (UNITY)

Tawhid, derived from *wahda* (oneness), means unifying, regarding as one, believing in God's Oneness or Unity, and sincerely accepting the reality that there is no deity but God. The Sufis add to these meanings the ideas of seeing only He Who is the One, and knowing, mentioning, desiring, and calling Him alone, and conducting relations with others than Him only because of Him.

The beginning of unity is admitting that the Divine Being is beyond and above all concepts that occur to the mind concerning Him, the result of this being that there is no room for anything else save Him in one's heart, according to the depth of the spiritual state and pleasures, and fixing one's eyes on Him alone. In this meaning, unity is both the foundation of Islam and its fruit. Sufism has considered unity with respect to both its beginning and end. Those who are not included in the fold of Sufism have regarded it slightly differently.

According to such people, unity means recognizing the Almighty as the Lord of all creation, and responding to His Divinity with servanthood or worshipping, and acting with a feeling of responsibility. In other words, unity is something that we must admit to with both our words and our actions, and our attitude should be that God has absolute authority over the whole of creation and disposes as He wills, and He is absolutely above having a like, a rival or an equal. In addition, since He is the One Who absolutely deserves to be worshipped and to be desired, we must serve Him perfectly in a way that contains the meanings of glorifying, exalting and praising Him, and by declaring that He is the All-Holy. To sum up these definitions, we can say that unity has three types or degrees: unity based on knowledge and belief, unity based on spiritual discovery and pleasures, and unity based on the Divine Being's bearing witness to Himself. Being aware of the last one is a special gift granted by the Almighty to His chosen servants.

- Unity based on belief and knowledge is the kind or degree of unity which is acquired through observation, inference or reasoning. Those who have acquired this degree of unity are free from associating any kind of partners to God and spend their lives thinking about God's Oneness, mentioning Him and feeling Him in the depths of their hearts.
- Unity based on spiritual discovery and pleasures means feeling the knowledge of God which has been acquired through observation and reasoning in one's conscious nature, sipping the pleasures originating in this knowledge, and experiencing it in the heart and daily life.
- Unity based on the Divine Being's bearing witness to Himself is so profound that only those whom God has favored with it can feel it, and those who can feel it either become dumbfounded or can express it to those around them only to the extent to which He allows them. In the sight of the initiates who can feel such a degree of unity, all proofs and indications of the Almighty fade away, things turn into a mirage, all existence is reduced to relativity, and the attitude of modesty which initiates must adopt before God tells them to keep silent. For this station is that where an initiate must keep silent and this degree or kind of unity is the unity that brings about silence.

Mawlana Jalal al-Din al-Rumi says concerning the unity of this degree:

> O brother, keep aloof from those
> who are busy with discussion among the scholars,
> So that the Almighty may cause knowledge
> from His presence to rise in your heart.
> When speech comes to this point,
> lips are no longer able to move or close;

And the pen breaks when it reaches the same point.
This is not the station where eloquent words will be uttered;
So, come and give up talking about things; God knows best the truth.

This station, where knowledge from God's Presence has turned into knowledge of God from His Presence, where the consciousness has been awarded special favors, and where travelers to God feel that they are being attracted toward Him by Himself, is the station of being a mirror to God where a drop has become like an ocean, an atom like the whole universe, and things that do not exist are honored with existence. In his introduction to *Harabat*, Ziya Pasha,[108] in his deep appreciation of poetry, describes the state of an initiate in this station as follows:

O You Who exist, and Who have brought existence into existence,
There is nothing which does not exist;
how can it be possible to claim Your non-existence!

Those who are the foremost in this degree of unity, which has allowed an atom to become an ocean, which has caused that which does not exist to gain existence, which has encompassed both the beginning and the end of the journey, and which is a degree that is possible for everybody to attain, are the Prophets. They begin their speeches with unity, and stop where they must stop because unity requires them to do so. The first platform for the travelers to God on their way to God is also this objective consideration of unity, where the beginning and end of the journey are united. All the Messengers and Prophets of God, from the first to the last, who carried out their responsibilities on the way of wakefulness, preached this greatest pillar of belief first, declaring: *Worship God alone: you have no deity other than Him* (7:59, 65, 73, 85 ...). Then they went on to communicate other principles and commandments to explain its meaning and content and to establish these in this world.

---

[108] Ziya Pasha (1825-1880) was one of the influential political and literary figures of the 19th-century Ottoman Turkey. He published *Hurriya* (Freedom) newspaper (Trans.)

This consideration of unity is the first door to entering Islam and is the means to feeling and experiencing Islam with a certainty based on knowledge, and a certainty based on observation, and a certainty based on experience. This is also the first call of God to know Him—according to the individual's capacity—as He makes Himself known. One enters the fold of Islam with such a concept of unity, and those who have the potential to advance, advance by means of it. Studies and mental endeavors gain profundity through this concept, and it is again through it that what lies beyond the relative truths appears. The difference between eternity and what is eternal and what is contained in time can be discerned within this concept. One perceives through this concept the nature of the relation between God as the Creator and the Sole Object of Worship with other beings as the created and those responsible for worshipping and servanthood. Again, it is through this concept that one understands that the Creator is not of the same kind as the created, and that His Attributes are perfect, universal and essential to Him, while the attributes of the created are imperfect, particular, relative and borrowed. This concept of unity causes one to base all one's views on the principles taught by the Prophets. Starting from these principles, one is saved from falling into errors such as, while arguing (in the name of unity) that He is absolutely free of any imperfections that belong to the created, going to the extreme of denying God any Attributes; or (another extreme) assuming that God takes on bodily form (incarnation) or that a created being can be united with God and become God (union). One is also saved, while observing His manifestations, from likening God in any respect to the creation, or, while interpreting His Attributes, likening Him to the created or attributing to Him a body and being that are contained in time and space. Thus one displays the worthiness (and need) to be counted among the people of the Straight Way, when one prays at least forty times a day (in the daily prayers) to God to guide one on this Way.

That conception of unity also serves to guide travelers to God so that they can perceive the sole source and nature of the Divine Destiny and Decree. Turning to Him, they do not waste their lives in the philosophical deviations of the Mu'tazila (the Muslim theologians who maintain that human beings will and create their actions) and the Jabriya (who deny human free will). They serve God sincerely, and feel a deep respect for Him because of His every commandment. Without denying that they have been endowed with free will, they believe that God is the Creator and the eternal origin or cause of everything, and expect from Him the attainment of all their purposes. They always rely on Him, and implore Him for happiness in both this world and the next.

* * *

Philosophers such as Aristotle,[109] Abu 'Ali ibn Sina (Avicenna)[110] and Nasir al-Din al-Tusi,[111] who considered unity as the Existence alone with no identity or Attributes, opened the door to the deviation of monism, which would later evolve as a philosophical system, in turn giving rise to many other falsehoods. Those who have strayed into incarnation and union—which can be said to have been smeared onto the belief-system of Islam by Neo-platonism—have fallen into associating partners with God by seeing existence as the constant appearance or externalization of the Necessarily Existent One, and therefore as being (in some measure) identifiable with Him. Among

---

[109] Aristotle, Greek philosopher, (384-322 BC) was not primarily a mathematician but made important contributions to some other sciences. He systematized deductive logic. He also wrote on physical subjects: some parts of his *Analytica posteriora* show an unusual grasp of the mathematical method. Primarily, however, he is important in the development of all knowledge. (Trans.)

[110] Abu 'Ali ibn Sina (Avicenna) (980-1037) was one of the foremost philosophers, mathematicians, and physicians of the golden age of Islamic tradition. In the west he is also known as the "Prince of Physicians" for his famous medical text *al-Qanun* "Canon." In Latin translations, his works influenced many Christian philosophers, most notably Thomas Aquinas. (Trans.)

[111] Nasir al-Din al-Tusi (1201-1280) was one of the greatest scientists, philosophers, mathematicians, astronomers, theologians and physicians of the time and was a prolific writer. He also wrote poetry in Persian. He was born in Tus near the present Mashhad. The observatory at Maragheh which he built became operational in 1262. His influence on sciences was immense. He wrote one or several treatises on different sciences and subjects including those on geometry, algebra, arithmetic, trigonometry, medicine, metaphysics, logic, ethics and theology. (Trans.)

other groups or movements, the Qadariya and Jahmiya, which deny God any Attributes, have attributed to God impotence and to human will absolute power. On the other hand, the attitude of the Jabriya, who deny human free will and regard humans as if they were dried leaves blown about by winds, is totally contrary to the most rational realities and is a great slander against God. What is true for all such movements, even if there were a grain of truth in them, is that their early followers were not able to save themselves from going to extremes and they prepared many points from which those who followed them and the ideas they promoted might stray.

As for the overwhelming majority of Muslims, who have accepted the truth of the Messenger and his Companions, they have learned unity (as well as other aspects of Islam), from, once more, the expressions, attitudes, visions, and spiritual discoveries of the true successors of the Messenger and the Companions, experiencing it in their inner and outer worlds. According to them, unity is the bedrock of Islam, a fact which the Qur'an and the Sunna give the greatest importance to with respect to the Creator's Lordship and recognition of our being His servants who must recognize and worship Him. The Qur'an and God's Messenger frequently refer to the Divine Being and His Attributes, Names, and acts, including the establishment of Himself on the Throne—the nature of which is unknown to us— His speaking to the Messengers and Prophets, and honoring whomever He wills with speaking to Himself, and reminding us of His absolute, unconditioned Life, Knowledge, Hearing, Seeing, Power, Will, and Speech. They also teach us that God is the Creator and the One Who takes life and revives after death, and that He is the All-Providing. All these Attributes and acts of God have a close connection with God's being One and Unique.

God's Lordship and the lights of His Existence and Lordship which shine on things and events are stressed in many verses of the Qur'an such as: *God, there is no deity but He; the All-Living, the Self-Subsisting (by Whom all subsist.), Slumber seizes Him not, nor sleep.* (2:255); *Alif-Lam-Mim. God, there is no deity but He; the All-Living, the Self-Subsisting (by Whom all subsist.)* (3:1-2); *Say (O Messenger):*

"O God, Master of all dominion! You give dominion to whom You will, and take away dominion from whom You will…" (3:26); *(He) the All-Merciful, established Himself on the Throne* (20:5); *And say: "All praise be to God Who has neither taken to Him a son, nor has He any partner in His dominion (of the whole creation); nor does He need, out of weakness, anyone to own and protect Him; and exalt Him with all His limitless greatness."* (17:111), and *Say: "He is God, the One; God is the Eternally-Besought-of-All. He has not begotten, nor been begotten. There is nothing equal to Him."* (112:1-5). A consciousness that discerns this majesty of the Divine Lordship, feels deeply and eagerly the necessity to worship Him in the face of this all-encompassing scene or in these concentric scenes of Lordship, and responds with: *All praise and gratitude is for God, the Lord of the Worlds. The All-Merciful, the All-Compassionate. The Master of the Day of Judgment. You alone do We worship and from You alone do we seek help.* (1:1-4) It demonstrate its readiness to serve Him in response to the Divine proclamation, *O humankind, worship your Lord* (2:21); receives from the warning, *Worship your Lord until certainty (death) comes to you* (15:99), the message that His eternal Lordship requires perpetual servanthood; and understands from the declaration, *Worship God, devoted to Him alone in all your religious practices* (39:2), that we must fix our eyes on Him exclusively.

The banner of the declaration, "O unbelievers! I do not worship what you worship" (109:1-2) undulates over our head, and determines the nature of our position with all else save Him. We demonstrate the purpose for our creation by proclaiming, *You alone do we worship* (1:5), and we acknowledge with utter modesty and a feeling of insignificance that We rely on Him alone in order to realize this purpose, declaring, *And You alone do we ask for help* (1:5). In order to fulfill the task that is required by nearness to Him and to reach the rank of speaking to Him directly, we reinforce our acknowledgment of His being the sole Deity in the two above declarations, with the prayer: *Guide us to the Straight Way, the way of those whom You have favored!* (1:6-7). Following this, we exhibit our care and sincerity in this petition, continuing: *Not (the way) of those who*

have incurred (Your) wrath (severe punishment and condemnation), nor
of those who are astray (1:7). Thus, traveling at least forty times a day
from our acknowledgment of God's Unity in Lordship to His Unity in Divinity, and thence to His Unity in being the Sole Object of
Worship, we try to fulfill what is required by our having been created as the best pattern of creation.

In short, the Qur'an is extremely clear and precise concerning the
matter of unity. It orders that we should admit that God is both the
sole Lord of creation—the One Who creates, maintains, protects and
provides—and the sole Deity. In all its chapters, from the longest (*Surat al-Baqara*, 2) to the shortest (*Surat al-Ikhlas*, 112), the Qur'an
declares, teaches and reiterates unity explicitly or implicitly. In *Surat
al-Ikhlas*, in addition to emphatically teaching that God is the sole
Lord of creation, it is also emphasized that He has Attributes of
Perfection and is above having any imperfections. *Surat al-Kafirun*
(109) warns us that only God is to be worshipped, and calls on us
to turn only to Him in our beliefs, lives, and expectations. A careful
study of the Qur'an will show that it turns on the axis of unity. All
the verses mentioning God and His Names, Attributes and acts are
proclamations of His being the sole Deity, while the declarations referring to worshipping the Absolute Object of Worship, Who has no
equals, opposites or rivals, and which forbid the worship of any thing
or being other than Him, are indications of His being the One and
Only Lord.

From another perspective, believing in God's being the sole
Lord of creation, which is also called "unity in knowledge" with respect to our position with unity, means confirming all the truths pronounced by the master of creation, upon him be peace and blessings.
As for believing in God's being the one and only Deity, which is also known as "unity in practice," this denotes doing the religious
commandments as they should be done, avoiding those things that
have been prohibited. Unity in knowledge is perfected by knowing
the All-Holy One as One Who has Attributes of Perfection and in
believing that He is above all imperfections. Unity in practice can be
realized by worshipping and loving the All-Majestic, All-Exalted One,

by being sincere toward Him, and by preserving the balance between fear of and expectations from Him.

Travelers to God who are at the beginning of the journey, a journey of which they are expected to reach the end, advance in the company of proofs, indications, and observations of their inner world and the world around them. These are the strongest groundings of unity. At every stage of their journey, travelers feel and sense the signs that come to them according to the rank and capacity of each, and review them. To the extent that they reach deeper perceptions and experiences, they can feel or see in the proofs and indications the One indicated by them. They reach through witnesses to the One Witnessed. Then, in the broad atmosphere of spiritual discoveries, pleasures and feelings, they begin to feel, see and hear the messages brought by the Prophets beyond the normal scope of the senses and feelings. They experience delight in observing the truths that are demonstrated by proofs and indications, but without needing them any longer, for they have passed beyond all concepts of quality and recognition through examples, and beyond the normal scope of perception.

So, this concept of unity—unity which becomes visible as God's special stamp on things and events by means of the proofs and indications that are observed and experienced in the inner world of people and in the outer world—is an objective concept, and an observatory from which everyone can attain certain knowledge of God. One who admits of it can, if possessed of the necessary capacity, advance as far as being able to perceive the true nature of apparent causes (in nature) and the means of knowing the Almighty. One sees that all those causes and means are lost before their Creator, Who is the real agent beyond them, and one witnesses that all proofs and indications end in an inner perception beyond the scope of the senses. The deeper the state one gets into and the greater the pleasure one feels, the more profound and vivid the degree of the concept of unity one can reach. Travelers to God who have reached this point live immersed in the special favors that come as a reward for their inner perception and the insight they have attained by starting from the proofs and indications. Because of the light which the Eternal Witness has placed in them, all their thoughts, speeches and acts become "light." They walk intoxicated by the manifestations of the "Face" of Him Who has created the light. When proofs and indications have developed into the voice of their state, they no longer need them, nor do they seek an apparent cause to rely on the Creator of all causes, nor run after other means. Rather, they begin to see, know, and love by Him, and to transform whatever they see and hear into knowledge and love of God, and into attraction and the feeling of being attracted by Him. They spend their life in the tides of absorption and distinguishing.

At this point, where the initiates feel as if they are seeing the Necessarily Existent Being in everything with their eyes, apparent, external causes fade away and lose the ability to be a means for happiness or salvation, although they continue to exist as mere causes. Whereas the internal causes of belief, confirmation, and the knowledge and love of God are felt more deeply. It is for this reason that, so long as the travelers to the Truth advance on the spiritual journey, they feel an increasing passion for worship and other acts of obedience to God. As they grow in the knowledge and love of God, they feel that they are overflowing with prayers and invocations and they become like a nightingale singing ceaselessly in the court of God. They always mention Him with the voice of their heart. In addition, neither their being able to observe from here the worlds beyond, nor crossing distances by flying through the heavens, can harm the self-possession that they maintain in their humble servanthood to God.

As for the unity the Necessarily Existent Being has assigned to Himself—a unity based on His bearing witness to Himself—it is an attainment belonging, first, to the Prophets, and then to their true successors. It is not possible for us to perfectly perceive such a horizon of knowing and feeling God. It is an extremely great favor from Him by which He endows the perfectly pure hearts with the necessary capacity to feel that perfect conception of unity, which He expresses in verses such as:

God, there is no deity but He, the All-Living, the Self-Subsisting (by Whom all subsist) (2:255).

God bears witness that surely there is no deity but He (3:18).

Surely, I am God, there is no deity but I, so worship Me (20:14).

He is God: there is no deity but He (59:22).

It is a great favor that He grants, enabling those so favored to voice this perfect conception of unity with their hearts, and causing them to understand and express their poverty and helplessness before Him and the fact that whatever they have is from Him, with confessions such as follows:

We have not been able to know You as knowing You requires, O Known One.

We have not been able to worship You as worshipping You requires, O Worshipped One.

We have not been able to mention You as mentioning You requires, O Mentioned One.

We have not been able to thank You, as thanking You requires, O Thanked One.

He makes them express this favor in consideration of the requirement to know Him as He must be known, and with a consciousness of servanthood, and an attitude of helplessness and poverty, and with a yearning for thankfulness and praise. It is not possible for others to perceive this. How can it be possible, seeing that this is a special gift from the Giver of Gifts, no matter how it was prompted or if prompted at all? Only those who can bear the weight of His gifts are loaded with them.

Only the Prophets and their true, pure successors can feel this degree of unity in the perfect form, and they can reveal to others only the part of it that they are allowed to reveal. The pure, perfected scholars, who are the true successors of the Prophets, run in the spacious field of this unity and try to breathe it out with certain ambiguous symbols according to their capacity. Saints who follow them whisper it to themselves when they deem it necessary, but none of them reveal the state they are in nor the pleasures they feel. They consider its revelation to be a grave error committed against the honor of Divinity, and tremble with fear at giving away the secrets with which they have been entrusted.

What should be done here, in this respect, is to regard the messages of the Prophets as sufficient, and by admitting that acknowledging the inability to perceive is perception itself, attribute to God the knowledge of truth and the concept of unity that belong to the most distinguished among the elect.

It is essential that while thinking of unity as viewed by the elect, either with respect to creed or as an expression of the spiritual state and pleasures, one should strictly follow the guidance of the master of creation, upon him be peace and blessings. For it is always probable that even the lights brightest in appearance, and the deepest pleasures and any knowledge of God not found within the Prophet's guidance are no more than carnal pleasures and ostentation.

It would be appropriate to end our article on unity with a verse from Calabizade Abdulaziz Efendi[112] found in *Gulshan-i Niyaz*, which resembles the poem of Ibrahim Haqqi of Erzurum concerning the Islamic creed, which begins "My Deity, my Lord; my Prophet is God's Messenger:"

> I have a conviction that the Divine Being is one,
> And I confirm that He has Attributes.
> Knowledge, Power, Life, Hearing, and Seeing,
> Are concealed in His All-Holy Being.
> Though the Attributes eternally exist in the Being,
> They are neither the Being Himself nor separate from Him.
> Those who attempt to qualify You are unable to understand Your Attributes.
> We have not been able to know You as knowing You requires.

---

[112] Karacalabizade Abdulaziz Effendi (1591-1658) was one of the Shaykh al-Islams (the highest religious authority) in the Ottoman State. His *Gulshan-i Niyaz* ("Rose-Garden of Invocations") and *Rawdatu'l-Abrar* ("The Garden of the Godly") are famous. (Trans.)

He has no equals nor likes in His Oneness,
And He needs no assistants in His sovereignty.
You are not a substance or a body;
Nor are You composed nor shaped.
You are the All-Holy Being from nowhere.
Your Attributes are not of the kind of those of the created;
You have no eyes, nor ears, nor any other organs;
You are One without number; and You have no limits;
You are not composed, or separable or dissolvable.
Neither time nor space, O Exalted One,
Has any meaning in relation to You.
It is also inconceivable that You have any relation with
Eating, drinking, getting dressed, or sleeping.
He is All-Majestic and absolutely pure in His Majesty;
He is absolutely above all desires and lusts.
The verses, "He has not begotten nor been begotten,"
Have put an insurmountable barrier before His having parents and children.
You have undoubtedly no beginning or end.
He is the First without a beginning,
And the Last without an end.
He is the Eternal Being Who brought the universe into existence,
And each of His creatures is a ray from His all-comprehensive Grace.
His work is the universe and Adam—humankind;
Existence and non-existence are according to His command.
All creation, including the heavens with all the celestial bodies, and the earth
Have come into existence by His command, "Be!"
If He had not given existence to the universe,
We could not have known Him or known how to bear witness to Him.
He it is Who creates both good and evil;
He it is Who is the origin of all deeds.
He has established what is right and what is wrong.
And it is He Who will reward or punish.

O God! Show us the truth as the truth and enable us with the observance of it, and show us the falsehood as falsehood and enable us with the avoidance of it. And let God's blessings be upon our master Muhammad, who is the means for attaining unity, and on his brothers among the Prophets and Messengers, who had strong self-possession.

YAQADA (WAKEFULNESS)

In the language of Sufism, *yaqada* (wakefulness) means that an initiate must be aware, careful and sensitive with respect to God's commandments at the beginning of the journey, and, without falling into any confusion, must be straightforward in thought, preserve spiritual balance, and act with insight in the face of the gifts that come as a result of advancing to the final point.

There have been somewhat different approaches to wakefulness. Some scholars have interpreted wakefulness as being where initiates perceive the Divine purpose in His prohibitions, especially at the beginning of the journey. When they have reached the final point where they are on the journey "toward God and with God and in God," which denotes "subsistence" or "maintenance with God," they should act with self-possession as if seeing God and as if being in His company. In the consciousness and knowledge of God that is required by the rank where they are, and thinking of themselves as humble servants of God Whom they need at every breath and of Whom they should not be heedless even for a moment, they should always fix their eyes in humility and awareness on the door of God in expectation of His favors and in fear of any reproach from Him. They should be in constant wakefulness, thinking as Ibrahim Haqqi of Erzurum did:

> Does sleeping in heedlessness behove a humble servant,
> While the All-Merciful calls (His servants) with affection at nights!

Wakeful travelers to God act with insight at every step of the spiritual journey and represent the truth expressed in *Say (O Messenger!): "This is my way: I call to God based on conscious insight and sure knowledge—I and they who follow me"* (12:108). They receive beneficial advice from whatever they hear, and see every thing and event as being a different tablet of instruction, and continuously travel on the horizon of thinking, reflecting, and pondering. There is wisdom in their speeches, and a lesson in their silence, and their manners inspire awe. They remember God in the face of what they encounter, and their own faces reveal Him.

Such a degree of wakefulness can be also viewed as the deepening of insight and the revival, with respect to the reason, of an initiate who is occupied with and skilled in the matters of the hereafter. Some have considered it as an aspect or dimension of the heart. One of the important means of reaching this point is frequently reciting *O All-Living, O Self-Subsisting One, there is no deity but You*. Frequent repetition of *There is no deity but You, I appeal to Your help for the sake of Your Mercy*, is another means. In attainment of this rank, it is also important to have adequate knowledge of the "days of God." That is, we should never forget why and how God favored His obedient servants in the past and how He punished the rebellious.

Having a sound and sincere intention and viewpoint and being free from prejudices are among the important conditions needed to preserve wakefulness. Those whose minds are under the influence of their carnal impulses, whose eyes are closed to the lesson given by the "days of God," and whose viewpoint is wrong, can have no insight, nor can they be wakeful. If wake-fulness is seeing deeply and becoming acutely aware of being observed, then this can only be possible by having deep insight, by observing God's rights, and by acting in awareness of always being seen by God. Those who cannot keep their eyes away from the "pictures" of others and their hearts from memories shared with others cannot be wakeful ones, nor can they be safe from falling, no matter what rank they have achieved. Safety is a special gift of God given to those who have spent their lives in quest of it. This is why those who regard themselves as safe are by no means safe.

Having a wakeful heart and eyes is dependent on the awareness of the fact that the Truth always sees and knows us in the state in which we are and always knows with what we are occupied, and on turning to Him with all our being, and spending our lives in consciousness that we are always in His Presence. The author of *Nazm al-Maqamat*, observes:

> Always turn to that Most Exalted Being in humility,
> And with utmost poverty and helplessness;
> To the extent that even if yourself were to give it up,
> Your heart should never falter and should remain fast in its place.
> This is what people of truth call "presence,"
> And this is the reason why we always mention Him.

Wakeful travelers are deeply conscious that the Truth always sees them, and think that, since He always sees them, they must therefore remain alert and self-possessed—that is, wakefulness has a connection with "perfect goodness" (depending on the awareness of always being seen by God and acting as if seeing Him). Like hunters who keep a close, even secret watch on their prey, the travelers journeying to God are in constant expectation of the gifts that come from Him, all but never blinking. In perfect reliance on the truth that *there is no power or strength save that which is with God*, they never appeal to anyone other than Him in order to meet their needs, and always petition Him and find ways that lead to Him. God never leaves them by themselves, helpless.

The greatest hero of wakefulness, upon him be peace and blessings, says, "My eyes sleep but my heart does not," indicating constant wakefulness. To warn those who live unaware of this truth, 'Ali, the Fourth Caliph, who was one of the most distinguished students of his school of light, declares: "People are asleep; they wake up when they die."

> O God, we ask You for forgiveness, health, and Your approval, favors, friendship, and nearness to You.

> And let God's blessings be on our master Muhammad, the master of those made near to You, and Your Messenger, and on his family and Companions, who had great yearning to meet with You.

MUJAHADA (STRIVING)

A ccording to people of the heart, *mujahada* (striving) means doing what is required by having been endowed with will-power. It includes struggling against the carnal self and seeking ways to defeat it, always preferring to fulfill the religious obligations without neglecting even the secondary ones, when they clash with carnal appetites; never being satisfied with one's worshipping, acts of obedience to God and doing good, yet being content with what is absolutely required for worship and obedience by way of disciplining one's eating, drinking, sleeping and speaking.

Those having a certain degree of knowledge of God have always dealt with striving in two categories: one, the major or greater striving (*jihad*) and the other, the minor or lesser one. The former means struggling against the carnal self and Satan and striving to have a sound belief and to be endowed with virtues or good morals, being able to worship God well, and struggling against evil morals, bad habits and tempers, while the latter denotes being alert against and, when necessary, fighting the enemy. People who serve people with knowledge and thoughts, by imbibing and internalizing belief, the truths of Islam and the morality of Muhammad, upon him be peace and blessings, and by representing them in their daily lives and conveying to others, encompass both kinds of striving, and therefore need to have the "endowment" necessary to fulfill both.

In every work or article written on austerity, communication of the Divine messages, and physical or minor striving (*jihad*), the subject is discussed in the light of relevant verses such as *Strive in God's way in the way that striving for His sake requires* (22:78). Here we are interested in major striving.

Major *jihad*, or striving, in the language of Sufism, denotes that in the face of the mean impulses of the carnal self, the whisperings of Satan, and the excessive desires and pressures of the body or corporeality, we should demonstrate that we are beings endowed with will-power. We should also try to show due respect for the heavenly faculty that we have as human beings, which is a composition of our inner senses, our consciousness, perception, and heart. *Jihad* in this meaning is the greatest of all strivings, and one who performs it is great and esteemed in God's sight; such a person is favored with His company. It can be said that it is more difficult to rebel against the impulses and desires of the carnal self and to lead a life in worshipping and performing other acts of obedience to God in piety, sincerity and abstinence in order to obtain God's approval and good pleasure, than to fight against the enemy under a shower of bombs and shells at the front. It is because of such difficulties that God's Messenger told the soldiers returning from fighting, *Now you have turned from the minor jihad to the major one.*[113] It was in this way that he instructed his Companions in such a vital matter. On another occasion, saying, *A true fighter is one who fights against his carnal self for God's sake,*[114] he taught that the major or greater *jihad* consists in the struggles against Satan and the impulses of the carnal self.

While the minor striving can occasionally be necessary or compulsory, a believer must continuously fulfill the major one. In addition, success in the minor striving depends on success in the major one. For this reason, everyone must purify their inner world, so that they may acquire harmony and accord in all their acts—sitting, rising, thinking, speaking, working, etc.—doing these for the sake of God. It is only by success in this striving that one can be supported by God's Will, which is the real factor in making human endeavors on God's way beneficial and fruitful.

For those whom belief has not guided to an appointed goal, who have not disciplined themselves with Islamic principles of spir-

---

[113] Hatib al-Baghdadi, *Tarikh al-Baghdad*, 13:523.
[114] Al-Tirmidhi, "Fada'il al-Jihad," 2.

itual training, who have not deepened in doing good consciously so that God sees them, who cannot lead a life of unwavering sincerity nor live in the consciousness of God's constant supervision, it is not possible to be people of the truth; they cannot restore rights nor display coherent attitudes in social relations. Those imprisoned in the cycle of eating, drinking, and sleeping can neither keep their corporeality under control nor direct their spirits to lofty ideals for spiritual victories nor keep the doors of their consciousness open to God to be rewarded with His company. What is most impossible for them is to free themselves from hatred, rancor, and other malicious feelings in order to embrace all existence only because of God.

A perfect society can only be made up of perfect individuals, and an individual cannot be perfected without spiritual training. It is therefore useless to try to build a sound community with individuals who suffer from mental and spiritual shortcomings. The perfect individuals needed to compose a perfect community are shaped in the crucible of striving.

Such a striving is based on controlling carnal desires and impulses and on having an operative mechanism of conscience. A spiritual journey is the safest way of striving. Concerning what a mortal enemy the carnal self is, Hakim al-Busiri[115] says:

> How many lethal delights there are that
> the carnal self presents to humankind as pleasant;
> Almost no one has ever been able to perceive that
> it presents poison within the butter.

It would be appropriate to end this section with a poem by Hüda'i,[116] which is regarded as a bridge to the spiritual journey:

> O carnal self! Give up your many mistakes and errors,
> Relent and be just and fair from now on!

---

[115] Muhammad ibn Sa'id al-Busiri (1211-1295) was an Egyptian saintly scholar, calligrapher and poet. He has poems in which he expressed his deep love for the Messenger and his Companions.

[116] Hüda'i was the father of Shahidi Ibrahim Dede (see, footnote: 121). He was from Mughla in the western Turkey and lived in the 15th century. He belonged to the Mawlawi Order. (Trans.)

Abandon cherishing these long-term ambitions,
Relent and be just and fair from now on!

Why do you have these habits and innovations?
Why such fondness for fame and adornment?
Why expend so much effort that way?
Relent and be just and fair from now on!

One day the wind of death will blow,
To ruin the garden of the body;
So fulfill your obligations in sincerity;
Relent and be just and fair from now on!

Do not be obstinate, O Huda'i!
Submit yourself to Divine orders.
Come and mention the Master,
Relent and be just and fair from now on!

O God, we ask You for forgiveness, health, and Your approval, favors, friendship, and nearness to You.

And let God's blessings be on our master Muhammad, the master of those made near to You, and Your beloved one and Messenger, and on his family and Companions, who had great yearning to meet with You.

CHILA (SUFFERING)

D enoting abandonment of all (worldly) pleasures and delights, and the affliction and hardship one bears when overcoming corporeality, *chila* (suffering) is used to express an initiate's spending at least forty days in strict austerity and self-discipline in the name of spiritual training. During this period, initiates keep to the absolute bare minimum in meeting such bodily needs as eating, drinking, sleeping and speaking, and spend most of their time in worshipping, mentioning God, thinking and self-supervision. As if they had died before dying, they concentrate on death and are annihilated with respect to their carnal self and prepares for a new, spiritual life with the necessary endowment to be persons devoted to God.

Dervishes spend the period of suffering either in a silent corner of a dervish lodge or in a quiet room in their homes. Associated with austerity and even serving to fulfill some of its functions, suffering is an attempt to gain nearness to God or an active expectation of meeting with Him in the spirit. The original word used, *chila* in Persian and *arba'in* in Arabic, means forty, because such a period lasts at least forty days, although it may last less or more than forty days. It may even occur that the dervish feels obliged to suffer the whole life long in order to surmount the animal aspect of his or her nature. Regarding all hardships that dervishes suffer in God's way as His precious gifts, they like life more as its griefs and hardships increase, and they welcome afflictions in the delight of living a conscious, deeply felt life. Some people of the heart consider misfortunes as Divine favors presented in that form, and desire more. Fuduli expresses his thoughts in this respect in the voice of Majnun as follows:

> Never reduce Your grace on people of affliction;
> That is, make me addicted to more and more misfortunes.

Jalal al-Din al-Rumi likens suffering and afflictions to a guest knocking on our door every morning and stresses that the dear guest should be welcomed and entertained:

> Every moment a grief comes upon your heart like a dear guest.
> When that emissary of grief visits you, welcome it as a friend;
> In fact, it is not a stranger to you, for
> You and it are acquainted.

Ibrahim Haqqi voices the same thoughts, dressing them in the style of his age:

> If grief and melancholy come upon your heart,
> Suffer it and know that it is acquainted with you.
> If anything occurs to you from the Truth,
> Accept it with warm welcome.
> Sorrow is a guest, entertain it, so that
> God may find you welcoming every misfortune.
> ....
> Hold not back from affliction so as not to become unmanly;
> Many people relying on God are happy with affliction.

Ashrafoghlu Rumi[117] advises that poison should be accepted as if it were honey or sugar:

> Ashrafoghlu Rumi, this is what behoves those who love the Beloved,
> They should swallow poison as if it were sugar for the sake of the Friend.

In this way, it is essential to be very welcoming toward misfortunes, and to welcome with the same contentment whatever comes from God—good or bad, happiness or suffering. Moreover, there are

---

[117] Ashrafoghlu 'Abdullah Rumi (d., 1484) was a Sufi scholar and poet who lived in Iznik in the North-Western Turkey. He was taught by Haji Bayram Wali in Ankara and Husayn Hamawi in Hama, Syria. He wrote several books, the most well-known of which is *Muzakki'n-Nufus* ("The Book Which Purifies Souls"). (Trans.)

some other principles which dervishes should observe during certain periods of suffering that they spend in retreat.

Suffering, which usually lasts for forty days, is the most direct way for travelers to God who are in pursuit of lofty ideals to purify their minds and hearts and to deepen in thought and feelings in consideration of the world beyond, and to rise to the level of life in the horizon of the heart and spirit where they will share the same aura with spiritual beings. Suffering exists in all the heavenly or unheavenly religions and religion-like spiritual systems; it is necessary in order to discover the innate power of the spirit. But here we will not discuss that aspect of it, which rather concerns mystical movements and parapsychology.

Muslim Sufis base their consideration of suffering on the forty days which the Prophet Moses spent on Mount Sinai before being addressed by God (see, the Qur'an 2:51; 7:142). They also refer to the forty years the Children of Israel had to spend in the desert of Sinai as a punishment for their refraining from fighting and as a preparation for their future life. In Christianity, there is the time of Lent (a period of forty days before Easter), which shows that suffering is common to almost all religions and religion-like systems. Furthermore, even if it only lasts ten days, retreat into a mosque without going out during the last ten days of Ramadan for the purpose of more devotion can also be considered as having some relation with suffering.

In the Muslim, Christian and Jewish worlds, and in different schools of thought in Islam, there have always been retreat and seclusion for the purpose of spiritual refinement and training. While such refinement and training have been performed in special rooms of retreat and seclusion, called houses of suffering, followers of others religions have performed the same in the seclusion of their places of worship.

Dervishes are taken into a retreat or a house of suffering by their spiritual guide. There they live alone, eating, sleeping, and speaking little, and spending most of their time in worship. They hold themselves under strict control and self-supervision, continuously breathing life into the heart, and traveling in the mind between their inner world and the outer world. Wholly dedicated to attaining a purely spiritual life, they try to feel the Lord with all their being and to see beyond the door half-opened on the heart. Endeavoring to discern and attain unity, they fear missing any signs of the Divine manifestations that may dawn on the hills of the heart. They express the limits of their capacity and the insufficiency of their will-power with sighs of poverty and helplessness, and become more hopeful with their reliance on the limitless Power of the Truth. When left with no means at all, they expect to be surprised by the opening of a door, and unburdens themselves to their Lord, Who sees everything, in the manner of a poor beggar, saying:

Be kind to me, O my Sovereign,
do not abandon favoring the needy and destitute!
Does it befit the All-Kind and Munificent to stop favoring His slaves?

As long as they grow in knowledge and love of God, they deepen in relationship with the Lord, and devote themselves wholly to feeling and thinking of Him. Keeping the satisfaction of their essential needs to the barest minimum, and overcoming their corporeality, they become confidants of heavenly beings in their states, attributes and being, and begin to breathe the breezes of friendship with the Sovereign.

Although suffering always takes on the same form, dervishes experience it differently according to their capacities and their powers of resistance. Some are almost completely freed from corporeality and worldliness, and are content with extremely little to meet the essentials of life, spending all their time in worship, thinking and mentioning God. Some others try to live consciously every hour, minute and second, letting no part of life pass without an effort to attain His nearness. Hours pass, weeks follow one upon another, and hunger, thirst and other hardships continue, without any sign of ending, but a dervish who has been accustomed to suffering as a way of life never desires the periods of suffering to come to an end. However, when the first period of forty days ends, the guide investigates to see at what stage the dervish is. The guide looks into the heart of the individual or reflects upon any dreams or visions reported. If the dervish has reached the point of being able to lead a life at the level of the heart and spirit, the guide will then put an end to the period of suffering with certain ceremonies. But it is always possible that new periods will be assigned if the guide considers that the dervish still needs more suffering in order to complete the spiritual purification.

In addition to the Mawlawis—followers of the Sufi order attributed to Mawlana Jalal al-Din al-Rumi—Persians, Azerbeijanis and even some Baktashis—followers of a Turkish mystical order—have ceremonies of their own for suffering. To whatever spiritual order or way a dervish belongs, the purpose of suffering is that travelers to God should purify themselves, discover their inner world and advance toward new horizons through the steps that are to be taken during the spiritual journey, leading a life at the level of the heart and then deepening through their other innermost faculties, such as "the secret" and "the private," and "the more private," observing their relations with and duties to the guide, perceiving the significance of obedience to orders, and endowing their spirit with humility and a feeling of nothingness, sincerely adopting the principle of being a simple human being among the people. This is what the guides, who teach dervishes suffering, and the dervishes who suffer, are seeking and what they expect from suffering. The final goal is to become true, perfect human beings.

However, it is not inevitable that one must suffer a certain period in order to attain what is expected from suffering. It is possible to obtain the expected result by abstention from doubtful things, being content with the pleasures inherent in the lawful sphere under the supervision of a guide who has truly succeeded God's Messenger, upon him be pace and blesssings, and who has achieved the degree of great sainthood, by the acknowledgment of one's innate poverty and helplessness before God, by thankfulness to Him, by zeal in serving His cause, and by exceptional piety, abstinence, and sincerity. What is absolutely essential in this way is that we should not approach the forbidden things, we should be careful about doubtful things, and we should benefit from the lawful only to the extent of what is necessary.

For those who succeed the Prophets, suffering is, rather than preoccupation with worship and the recitation of God's Names in seclusion, and the abandonment of an easy life for the sake of torment, the pursuit only of God's good pleasure and approval, always being aware of God's company even while among people, arousing in hearts zeal for worshipping God with sincere Islamic thoughts, feelings and attitudes, representing Islam in daily life in the best way possible, stirring up Islamic feelings in others, and by developing in others the desire to believe. This is the way of the Companions.

Suffering in this sense becomes, beyond our own spiritual progress, the dedication of our lives to the happiness of others in both worlds and living for others. In other words, we should seek our spiritual progress in the happiness of others. This is the most advisable and the best approved kind of suffering: that is, we die and are revived a few times a day for the guidance and happiness of others, we feel any fire raging in another heart also in our own heart, and we feel the suffering of all people in our spirits. Rather than only being aware of selfish considerations, such as "One who has not suffered does not mean what suffering is," we groan with the afflictions and pains which others in our immediate and distant surroundings endure.

Actively expecting (exerting the necessary efforts for) the subsidence of the storms of denial and heresy is a great suffering, while enduring with humility and grace life among rude and ignorant people in order to enlighten them both mentally and spiritually is double suffering. The struggle with the cruel people who take belief in and submission to God as a sport and who reject Islamic values is suffering upon suffering. Finally, in an atmosphere where all the causes of suffering already mentioned exist, and where friends are unfaithful, where time and conditions are pitiless, where troubles are numerous, where cures are extremely scant, where enemies are powerful, and where the wheel of events turn in the opposite direction, to always breathe in the atmosphere of the Truth while having to live every moment of life as if sipping poison is the greatest of sufferings. All of this will help travelers to God to reach the final point in a very short time.

Those who suffered the most in this sense are the Prophets, and on their right and left are the pure, verifying scholars who succeed them and the saints. The hadith, *Those who are subjected to the greatest afflictions and suffering are the Prophets, and then come others (according to the depth of their belief)*[118] indicates this fact and reminds us that the intensity of suffering is directly proportional to the resistance of the sufferer.

There are few who really suffer in the sense that has been discussed here. It is not genuine suffering that people are subjected to in daily life. Those who really suffer feel suffering and bear it in their private worlds. It cannot be shared by others. The Prophet Joseph, upon him be peace, whose suffering began when he was cast into a well, experienced suffering doubly in a foreign county when he was sold as a slave and thrown into jail, and left among a people who had a different culture and language, and who did not sympathize with him. The suffering he experienced purified and perfected him in the name of his mission as a Messenger; and God made him nearer to Him. The Prophet Adam bore his suffering with tears, and Noah had to breast terrible disasters and destruction, while Abraham, whom God took to Himself as an intimate friend, always had to travel in rings of fire. The Prophet Moses, whom God addressed directly, struggled fiercely against the rebellion of brute force. Jesus, a pure spirit from God, called people to God under the fatal shadows of the gallows. And finally, the master of creation, upon him be peace and blessings, suffered all that the other Prophets and Messengers suffered. He wept tears, groaned and burnt inwardly for the salvation and happiness of others, but without displaying any sign of suffering.

Hundreds of sufferers from the first day of human history have tasted the pleasure of suffering for the salvation and happiness of others in both worlds in utmost submission to God and have been

---

[118] Al-Tirmidhi, "Zuhd," 57; Ibn Maja, "Fitan," 23.

wholly dedicated to the life of others, without ever considering that they have been made to experience the greatest of sufferings. More than this, they have welcomed such suffering and have been intoxicated with the pleasure thus received.

Suffering of thought is also another great suffering. Thinking, leading others to think, setting themselves to solve the severest problems and world-heavy enigmas, including that of existence, is a form of suffering. Thought does not yield, but rather builds bridges between and composes the Divine Revelation and human thought, presenting to "hungry" and "thirsty" hearts and minds the pure extract produced from this composition. This is the suffering in which the heroes of suffering, who are as sincere as angels and who have followed the Messengers, have found an antidote for poison in the poison itself, peace and coolness in the fire, having experienced such with the greatest pleasure. Such people are fortunate that there is no end to their periods of suffering; they cannot be pleased with the idea that such suffering is bound to come to an end. If you attempt to take them out of gardens of suffering, you will not be able to do so; if you were able to do so, you would extinguish their fire and leave them to die.

It is this suffering which is the purest source that feeds the spirit of a true dervish, and which is the most powerful means for travelers to the Truth to reach eternality.

> *Our Lord! In You we trust, and to You we turn in contrition, and to You is our homecoming. Our Lord! Pour out upon us patience, and set our feet firm, and help us to victory over the unbelievers. And let God's blessings be upon our master Muhammad, our leader, and on his family and Companions, who were the patient and faithful.*

SOHBA AND MUSAHABA
(CONVERSATION AND COMMUNION)

Sohba (Conversation) means making effective speeches to direct people to the Almighty, enlightening others with words and thoughts, using other's good opinions of oneself to guide hearts to eternity, and always wishing well for others. The famous Turkish Sufi poet who lived in the 13th century, Yunus Emre, stresses the vitality of conversation and communion (*musahaba*) in this sense, saying: "What sets the soul right is the conversation of saints."

With respect to the relationship between a guide and the initiates on the Sufi way, there are two things which lead initiates to the truth: a guide's conversation and communion with his disciples and their serving in the lodge where the guide teaches. Serving is a means of being favored with the guide's special attention, and conversation or communion, which has been considered as an important means employed by the guide that is greatly beneficial, is a way to feeling and experiencing truth with all one's inner and outer senses. Nevertheless, benefiting from the guide so that one is "colored" by him depends on the rank of the guide. Every guide has an influence upon his disciples in proportion to the degree of his rank. The most perfect and greatest guide is the Almighty Himself. That is why the master of creation, upon him be peace and blessings, took on the universal, brightest color due to his being addressed by Him in the Revelation. The verse (2:138), *Take on God's color perfectly; whoever can be more beautiful in color than God?*, indicates this fact. After him come all the other Prophets and pure, verifying scholars and saints, who vary in the colors they have taken on, according to the rank of guides and the capacity of each to take on the color. All the scholars and saints who have and will come after God's Messenger have been and will be dependent on him and his guidance, both in taking on color and coloring their disciples. However, as mentioned before, both the coloring of others and taking on color varies according to one's capacities:

> Everyone benefits from God's enlightening gifts according to his capacity;
> A snake receives poison from April rain, and an oyster a pearl.

Service denotes seeking God's good pleasure and approval with sincerity and purity of intention, and putting oneself in the hands of one with whom God is pleased for teaching and guidance. As for communion, this means attending the courses of a friend of God with a heart whose doors are opened to Divine favors and blessings, and sharing his aura of holiness within which the Divine manifestations of grace pour forth. The Companions of God's Messenger were the most advanced of all in serving, and were accordingly favored with the most enlightened communion. This was due to the fact that the one who taught and held communion with them was the greatest of creation, whose single look was enough to cause the souls endowed with the necessary capacity to rise to the high horizons of perfection. We should also point out that his disciples, those heroes of steadfastness, who put their hearts, senses, consciousness, and will power into orbit round that sun, had the necessary capacity and performance.

Every friend of God is favored with coloring those around him or her to a certain extent. The range of this favor is very broad, from a friend of God whose light may be likened to a candle in darkness, to those whose light may be likened to radiant stars that light up whole galaxies. In addition, as pointed out before, as with every guide or friend of God, those who benefit or receive light from them vary in their capacity. This means that the extent or degree of coloring on the part of guides varies to the number of the capacities. So there are as many ranks or degrees of coloring and being colored as there are Prophets, spiritual guides and initiates who benefit from them, from the greatest of creation, who is the most polished mirror of the Light of Lights, to the one who has just taken his or her first step on the spiritual journey. The communion or conversation of the one who was universally favored with coloring others was so influential and so great a blessing for him that no one has ever been, nor will ever be, able to attain it. Consider the fact that those who were honored with the conversation and companionship of him, who said, "The first thing which God created is my light,"[119] were and have been called with the title of *Ashab* (meaning the friends with whom he communes), not with another title even though they were the fortunate ones who traveled to God most eagerly and sought His good pleasure and approval most of all.

Everyone listening to or sharing the atmosphere of a guide, observes in his every manner his belief in the Single, Besought-of-All, his knowledge and love of Him, and the degree of his relationship with Him. Influenced by all these blessings that the initiates observe in the guide, they find themselves in an indescribable mysterious spiritual atmosphere. Those flying toward the "Sun of Suns," attracted by the centripetal force of a guide, both benefit from his knowledge of God and follow in his footsteps to reach every point that he has already passed.

I think this is also the reason why people gather around spiritual guides who are sources of radiance, and develop as particular spiritual institutions or schools. It is because of this that in the early periods of Islam, the Muslim Sufis who sought to strengthen or consolidate their individual relationships with the All-Radiating One, came together in dervish lodges or similar institutions of enlightenment where the Truth could be "observed" beyond all concepts modality. In those buildings of light, which they saw as being similar to the hall adjacent to the Prophet's Mosque in Madina, where those of the Companions stayed who had dedicated themselves, during his lifetime, to studying the Qur'an and the Sunna. They sought the way to develop an atom into a sun, a drop into an ocean, and to change the darkness of corporeality into light. As this was the main reason for the appearance of dervish lodges and distinct spiritual orders in

---

[119] Al-Ajluni, *Kashf al-Khafa'*, 1:265.

later centuries, it is not possible to claim that they are incompatible with the spirit of Islam. Moreover, since everyone has weaknesses or shortcomings of character that they cannot overcome alone, being in the company of others seeking the same goal attracts God's special help and protection. A member of a community or group thinks with many heads, turns to God with a collective heart, strengthens the entreaties of one voice with the entreaties of many, and turns his or her individual notes into the melody of a chorus. In the words of Bediuzzaman, by participating in the other-worldly deeds of a community, the individual can transcend the normal level of attainment in acts of obedience to God.

Those who have come together around the same feeling, thought and goal have such a depth in their turning to God in unison, such a richness in their consciousness and feelings, and such a profundity in their thoughts and concepts, that individuals of even the greatest capacity and perfection cannot attain the least of the blessings that come their way in their community. In the illuminating atmosphere of communion, benefiting and causing to benefit, enlightening and being enlightened, feeling and causing to feel occur differently and in an abundance peculiar to that atmosphere.

In fact, the most important purpose of communion is that belief should be supported with a knowledge of God, a knowledge of God that is based on any of the degrees of certainty, by making journeys at the levels of life of the heart and spirit under the guidance of the Truth of the Prophet's being Ahmad, and these journeys are accompanied by a conscious observation. The most important capital and endowment of the initiates during such journeys and observations is that the inner faculties are aroused with the actions of the heart and voice, for example, the recitation of God's Names and reflection, and the demonstration of their deserving Divine gifts. Since deserving such gifts can only be acquired by following the Message of the master of creation and therefore bears witness to the truth of this Message and the Messengership of him who brought and preached it, this decisively proves that he was absolutely truthful in all his speeches and actions.

Benefiting from the communion or conversation of spiritual guides depends, in one respect, on the initiates' humility and feelings of nothingness, and of their being freed from the influence of their carnal selves. If travelers to the Truth have not been able to completely free themselves from the influence of their carnal selves and to rise to the point of always preferring God's commandments and obtaining His good pleasure and approval over their own views and desires, they may commit the error of attributing to themselves being favored with some gifts or the development of some of their faculties. Instead of always being thankful to God, they may become conceited. Furthermore, if they are sometimes and temporarily favored with the feeling of attraction and being attracted (toward God by Himself), they may roll into the valleys of uttering words of pride that are incompatible with the rules of Shari'a, and therefore suffer loss upon loss, although a spiritual journey should be a means of gain after gain.

In fact, those who do not converse or commune with their disciples in accordance with the rules of the way of God's Messenger, upon him be peace and blessings, cannot always maintain the balance in the spirit of Islam and may display relaxed attitudes or make utterances that cannot be reconciled with their rank or position. They may even go so far as to prefer sainthood to Prophethood and, favoring the principles and manners established by the founder of their orders over those of the Prophetic way, commit such great errors that it as if one chose to be illuminated by a candle instead of by the sun. Besides, those unfortunate ones who prefer sainthood to Prophethood will naturally see their guides or masters as being greater than the Companions, who were the foremost and most distinguished students of Messengership. This will denote that communion has changed places with gossip, that spirituality has become darkened in its own home, that the essentials originating in the Divine sources have been replaced by those of personal choices and desires, and that there no longer remains the sacred power of attraction which the spiritual guides and their aura must have. As Muhammed Lutfi laments:

Those who were valiant have melted away like butter;
Lovable personages have all been reduced to dust.
Thorns have grown in the place of flowers;
Honeycombs have shrunk and been emptied of their honey.

The communions and conversations which resemble idle talk in cafes bring nothing in the name of Divine gifts and never assist the disciples to attain the truth. Rather, Satan intervenes in their frequency and sends out sparks. So, every action that is in the guise of a spiritual interaction in these places, which appear to be homes of spirituality, but have long since expelled sincerity and the feeling of being seen by God, is only a deception or even perdition, and expecting God's special favors is nothing more than mere illusion. Those who attend such places as if they were attending a united congregation are only joining in a spiritless ritual. In addition, if they regard criticizing and quarrelling with others, rumor-mongering and slander, and cherishing ill-opinions about others as religious services, then they are gravely mistaken; the places they attend are only places of hypocrisy and their guides are not Sufis, but rather bigoted highwaymen. Who knows that such attitudes did not cause Destiny to allow the banning of such and the closing of the ways that led to their collapse?

Autumn winds have blown and the vineyards have withered away;
And there no longer exist the gorgeous roses in the gardens.

O God! Favor us with a happy end to our affairs, and protect us from loss and humiliation in the world and punishment in the hereafter. And bestow Your blessings and peace on the master of creation, Muhammad, and on his family and Companions, the noble, godly ones.

SAYR U *SULUK*
(JOURNEYING AND INITIATION)

In the language of Sufism, when used together, *sayr u suluk* (journeying and initiation) denotes becoming free of bodily and animal appetites to a certain extent within the framework of certain principles, searching for ways to reach God and traveling toward Him by the heart in order to lead a life at the level of the spirit and heart. It also signifies becoming refined from evil nature and morals and adopting Qur'anic morals in order to be able to travel toward and meet with God.

Journeying and initiation have connotations with regard to the Divine manifestations that come during the journey. From the viewpoint of these manifestations and an initiate's being favored with them, journeying has been dealt with in two categories:

Journeying downward: in order for a restricted, conditioned, and transient existence to emerge, the Absolute, Necessary Existence manifests Itself with mercy and blessings. In other words, the Almighty, True One graciously condescends beyond all concepts of modality to manifest Himself. He does so universally, with all His Names, and gives existence to, and maintains, beings and things, and He does so particularly, with some of His Names, and bestows its particular shape, character, quality and capacity on, and maintains, each being and thing. This can also be regarded as the expanding manifestation of the Necessary in the spheres of the contingent, and the Absolute in the spheres of the conditioned. This journey extends from the earliest determination of beings and things in the Divine Knowledge to the step expressed in the Prophetic saying, "The first thing which God created is my light," and from here to all degrees of existence in the whole of the universe, and finally to the realm of humankind.

Journeying upward: Human beings, the most comprehensive fruit of the tree of creation, set out for a spiritual journey with their will-power, senses, consciousness, and heavenly faculty (the core of the heart) to return to their original home or source. They find that the original home toward which the journeying is, is in one respect the spirit in its primordial purity. When the spirit finds its original home, it is annihilated in respect of its bodily associations or appetites in the Light of the Existence of the Absolutely Necessary Being. It is this journey that we deal with here in four steps or stages:

The first stage is journeying toward God, which is also called the first journey as it is the beginning of traveling toward God. It begins in the realm of the manifestation of the Divine acts and continues through the realm of the manifestation of the Divine Names and ends in reaching the Name which determines a traveler's existence with all its peculiarities. There are many who set out for this journey, but few who can continue it. Whether this journey is made in the outer world—through reflection on God's works in the universe—and called journeying in the outer world, or it is made in the inner word of travelers—through self-purification—and is called journeying in the inner world, when it ends the travelers no longer feel interested in anything save God and find themselves in tides of annihilation in God. This favor has been described as minor or lesser sainthood.

The second stage is journeying in God. Since it requires another determined attempt and beginning, it is regarded as the second journey and is sometimes called the absorption. Travelers at this stage are freed from evil morals and mortal attributes and acquire praiseworthy or Qur'anic qualities, and represent the Divine Names according to their individual capacity. They reach a higher horizon where they begin to discern what lies beyond material existence and feel that a knowledge from the Divine Presence flows into their heart. They gradually melt away in the face of the rays of knowledge that concern the realms of the Divine Names, Attributes and Qualities that are essential and indispensable to the Divine Being, and that are favored with a full perception of what belonging to God means. This favor has been called subsistence with or by God.

The third stage is mentioned with different names, such as journeying with or in the company of God, the third journey, and distinguishing together with absorption. One who has reached this final point only sees Him beyond all concepts of modality, knows Him, and feels Him, and is surrounded by the lights of knowledge of Him. The manifestations of His "Face" destroy everything and everywhere it is echoed: "All that is on it (the earth) is perishable, and the very Being of your Lord possessed of Majesty and Munificence remains permanent" (55:26-27). All other existent beings, and kinds of knowing, seeing, and feeling begin to be reduced so that they are of only a nominal nature in the initiates' deep knowledge of God and their overflowing spiritual pleasures. Feeling the existence of all others, even if only temporarily, is distressful to the heart. Travelers who are not among the successors of the Prophet in his mission of representing, conveying and practicing the Divine Message in its universality, are lost in the depth of their spiritual pleasures in their private worlds. The final point of this stage, where all opposites are lost in the sight of a traveler, is called absorption itself. Nasimi expresses this spiritual state of pleasure where all appearances have disappeared, in a typical style of immersion as follows:

> The place where I am has developed into no-space;
> This body of mine has completely become a soul;
> God's Sight has manifested Itself to me; and
> I have seen myself intoxicated with His meeting.

> A call has come to me from the Truth:
> "Come, O lover, you have intimacy with Us!
> This is the place of intimacy;
> I have seen you to be a faithful one!"

This is also the station where, like a wine glass, one becomes filled with and emptied of His love, loving and urging others to love Him madly. One who overflows with the gifts of this station regards any speech that is not about Him as being a mere waste of words, and any other consideration as being disrespect for Him. One desires that every word should essentially be about Him, every meeting should end with mention of Him, and everyone should talk about Him alone in the manner of a lover. How nicely one of His lovers says:

> I wish the people all over the world loved Him Whom I love;
> And all our words mentioned the Beloved One.

The fourth stage is journeying from God. This journey has also been called the fourth journey or coloring after self-possession. One who has got to this point, where one meets with God, turns towards the realm of multiplicity with new interpretations of the way of unity after having reached unity. In other words, descending while following the way of the Messenger, who descended after having ascended as high as "God's Presence," the traveler returns to be amidst people in order that others may also feel and experience what he or she has felt and experienced during some degree of meeting or reunion with God. Such returning travelers devote their life to saving others from worldly and other-worldly dungeons, causing them to rise to the holy Presence of God, attaining what they have attained, seeing what they have seen, and arousing in others a burning desire to meet with Him. Guiding those baffled by the depths of darkness to the light; guiding those bewildered about what lies beyond the corporeal world; educating those who have decided to follow the way to Him; making the hearts of those who aspire after His good pleasure content and at rest; assisting those who have found light to overflow with a knowledge of God; and allowing those favored with this knowledge to travel amid the hills of spiritual pleasures— all these are among the tasks incumbent upon the travelers upon their return to people from God. This is the state of the special apprentices of the Prophets, which some leading Sufi scholars described as subsistence by God and with God or distinguishing after absorption.

Those who have attained this horizon see unity in multiplicity and multiplicity in unity; they experience at the same time two depths with one dimension, and they set out for a new meeting with God at every moment with the pleasure of feeling His company and the pleasure of others whom they lead toward that meeting. They neither fall into confusion and make utterances of pride that are incompatible with the rules of Shari'a, nor do they show feigned reluctance to attract His mercy. Instead, they always breathe self-possession. They feel breezes of journeying in God in journeying toward Him, and they observe the truth of journeying from God in journeying in Him. They are in a state of having both found Him and lost Him, and of having both met with Him and departed from Him, and of feeling a nearness to and a distance from Him all at the same time.

Those travelers are the most perfect of travelers, the greatest of guides, and the masters of human education and upbringing. They cause the hearts of those who turn to them and follow them as masters of guidance to overflow with the feelings of belief, knowing God and loving Him. Modeling their actions on the Prophetic saying, "Make God loved by His servants, that He may love you,"[120] they both love God and are loved by Him. Their purity of intention and feeling, the profundity of their thought, their earnestness in their representation of Islam, and the refinement in their manners make them such a source of the water of life and a torch of light that everyone who aspires to the Divine gifts and radiance appeals to them, and every lover of Divine light takes refuge in their guidance. Because:

> Good actions originate in good nature and being virtuous;
> Traces of perfection are found in good nature and virtues.

Initiation means acquiring the ability to meet with God, living in constant consideration of journeying, which is regarded as an important means of being always together with Him, showing continuous resistance to bad morals, adopting good morals or a good nature and laudable virtues as one's character, purifying the heart, in which God is known to be as a "hidden treasure," refraining from worrying about and considering all else save Him, and of being in-

---

[120] Al-Tabarani, *Al-Mu'jam al-Kabir*, 8:91.

wardly prepared to entertain the Dearest of Guests. Concerning this, Ibrahim Haqqi of Erzurum says:

> The heart is the home of God; purify it from whatever is there other than Him. So that the All-Merciful may descend into His palace at night.

As mentioned before, the word initiation is used on its own to express the spiritual journey discussed, and it is also used together with journeying as in journeying and initiation. Sometimes the word spiritual is added and the concept is expressed as spiritual journeying and initiation. What is meant by all is that we should turn away from everything else save God, in the sense that we should not feel interest in or attachment to other things with respect to their own being and our worldly considerations, and that we should give our attention to Him exclusively. It also includes the guidance of those who represent the Qur'an and the Sunna perfectly in belief, thought and action, and appealing to them in cases of doubt, hesitation and bewilderment. Initiation also denotes living in perception of our absolute need for the Almighty in awareness of our helplessness, poverty, and neediness; having a heart overflowing and empowered with love and zeal, feeling with observation of the Divine manifestations, will-power and all other faculties with asking God for forgiveness, and praying so that inclinations to evil may be uprooted and inclinations to good strengthened.

Sincerity or purity of intention and perfect goodness or excellence (*ihsan*) are the two bases and the most important sources of power for journeying and initiation. When the initiates' heart beats with a feeling of sincerity and the consciousness of perfect goodness, they sometimes utter *There is no deity but God*, while having in mind several of the Divine Names, and therefore meaning "There is no Creator, no Provider, no Shaper... but God." At other times they open a window in the heart for each Name of the Bestower of Life, and set out to observe what is beyond the door that has been opened by the consciousness of perfect goodness. On occasion also they travel through reflection on the harmony of the qualities (color, scent, form, sound) manifested on things, or on the horizon of *Some fa-*

ces that Day shall be shining and radiant, gazing toward their Lord (75:22-23), and they burn with the zeal of meeting with Him. With a deep, mysterious desire of observation, which is impossible for any mental faculty to make, they try to rise to the heaven of knowledge of God from the launch-pad of belief. Then their love develops into a passion, which is strengthened with zeal. They fly into the depths of eternality on the wings of attraction and, with the feeling of being attracted by Him, rise towards the high towers of the angels, being welcomed by spiritual beings, reaching points that few can reach, seeing amazing things that few can see. But aware that what they seek in no way has any form, they regard every scene that greets their eyes only as a picture, a tableau, and remain devoted to the truth beyond:

> He is neither of bodily nor accidental existence,
> nor a substance, nor composed;
> He does not eat, nor drink, nor is contained in time:
> He is high above all such features.
> He is absolutely free from changing, transformation,
> and also from having colors or a form:
> All of these we spell out so that we can clarify what God is not.

Whatever level they reach, they always feel humble in acknowledgment, *We are unable to know You as knowing You truly requires*, and stress that the Divine Being cannot be perceived. To whatever extent they fulfil the demands of devotion to God, they admit: *We are unable to worship You as worshipping You truly requires*; and however deeply and sincerely they mention Him, they whisper their inability, saying: *We are unable to mention You as mentioning You truly requires.*

These travelers regard respect for God's commandments as the first and foremost means of approaching God, and piety and righteousness as the most blessed equipment for the journey. They train their souls and purify their spirits in devotion to the rules of Islam. They consider every effort for training and purification that is opposed to the rules of Shari'a as falling away from the religion, and if anything out of the way occurs at their hands, they see it as a sign that they are going to perdition. In every stage of journeying and initiation, the travelers pay exceptional attention to the safety of the journey and see this safety in their devotion to the essentials of the religion and religious life, and know that their worth in God's sight lies in piety and righteousness, and that only the pious, righteous ones can find God. "The final destination of the pious and righteous will be Paradise, and their drink, the drink of Paradise."

The author of *Gulshan-i Tawhid*[121] expresses this truth beautifully as follows:

> If you seek safety, know that piety and a righteous religious life
> Are the safest stronghold against all fears and danger.

Self-training, or the training of the soul, has been accepted as an extremely important element of all religions. The self or the soul mentioned here is the human soul or self, which is also mentioned as the speaking self, and is dealt with in seven stages according to some Qur'anic allusions to it:

If the speaking self or soul lives only a life of ease in the swamp of carnal appetites, it is the evil-commanding self; if it falters time and again while following the way of religion to attain piety and righteousness, but each time that it falters it criticizes itself and turns to its Lord, then it is the self-accusing self or soul. The self which always resists evil in devotion to God and is favored with certain Divine gifts in proportion to its purity, is called the self receiving inspiration. When it reaches the point where it has a relation with its Lord in perfect devotion and sincerity and when its consciousness is at rest, it is the self at rest. If it has reached the station where it abandons all its choices and is a representative of Divine Will, it is the self pleased with God. When its greatest aim is acquiring God's

---

[121] The author of *Gulshan-i Tawhid* is Shahidi Ibrahim Dede (1470-1550). He was among the famous Sufi masters belonging to the Mawlawi Order. He wrote in Persian and Turkish. *Gulshan-i Esrar* ("The Rose Garden of Secrets"), *Gulshan-i Tawhid* ("The Rose-Garden of Divine Oneness"), and *Gulshan-i Wahda* ("The Rose-Garden of Unity") are among his famous works. (Trans.)

good pleasure and approval and when it is always acting to this end in consideration of, "I am pleased with You, so be pleased with me," then it is the self with which God is pleased. Finally, the self which has the capacity to be completely adorned with the full manifestations of Divine qualities and Prophetic will-power and resolution is called the self perfected or the self pure.

A believer with an evil-commanding self is either unaware of the sins he or she commits or lives an uncontrolled life. Even if such believers perform the daily prayers and sometimes do supererogatory acts of worship, they are neither conscious of what obedience to God entails nor aware of what committing sins signifies. Such persons need to be assisted, aroused to become aware of the balance between fear and expectation, and made to deepen their knowledge, love and awe of God. It is the beginning of the major or greater *jihad* (striving) that such believers heed advice, engrave their errors in the memory so that they frequently criticize themselves, and are determined to regularly fulfill their religious duties and resist sins. So long as they continue to strive, some changes will begin to occur in their feelings and thoughts. They begin to see that not even their best deeds are sufficient and criticize themselves even for the least of their evil deeds. This is the second step in the self's journey, which is called the self-accusing self.

Those who have reached the stage of self-accusation intend to set out toward Him. However, they falter, making errors that stain their good deeds, and beautiful things follow ugly ones in their life. But whenever they stumble and fall, they pull themselves upright in remorse for the evils committed, cleanse themselves of sin by sincerely asking God for forgiveness and by trying to uproot their inclinations toward evil through prayer. Not content with these, they continuously accuse themselves, and suffer pangs of conscience. A time comes when they express these pangs with sighs from the depth of the heart, and when they put these feelings into invocations and tears in seclusion. Those with a self-accusing self advance along the intermediate corridor between carnal appetites and sins, and spiritual peace. They show great care in keeping their hearts upright in devotion to God and their thoughts travel between the outer and the inner worlds. They utter "There is no deity but God," they turn toward Him and display their yearning for Him, saying "There is none to be desired save Him," and continuously whisper "He is the Truly Desired One" and "the only One deserving worship."

In the sight of the self-accusing travelers who have deepened in spiritual attainment and reflection, the smallest errors and omissions begin to seem to them the greatest and most perilous lapses. When they rise to this point, they can more easily distinguish dark from light and good from evil, and when they think of the ugly face of sins, they feel repugnance, and when they think of good deeds, they moan with remorse and regret for not having done them. However, they are always hopeful and determined. It is of souls that have attained this point that God says: "Those who strive for Our sake—surely We will guide them to the ways to lead to Us. Assuredly, God is with those of perfect goodness who act consciously that We always see them (29:69)." God inspires in them all that is good and beautiful, and the things He approves of together with how they can attain them. The self that has traveled so far in order to reach God and has come to the point of receiving this inspiration is the soul or the self receiving inspiration.

Travelers who have attained this stage are preoccupied with Him and with consideration of Him. They breathe with observations everywhere of the matchless beauty of His making and look on everything as a beautiful scene of wonder, and they overflow with feelings of appreciation. While saying "There is no deity but He" with their voices, their hearts beat with the truth, "There is none deserving worship save He." Without being able to find the words to express their wonder in Him and His works, they can only utter "He," and begin to fuel the love and zeal in their hearts with every breath they inhale and exhale. While their spirit burns, their voices petition Him with the words,

> O cup-bearer, in the fire of love I have burnt away,
> so give me some water!
> Since I fell in love with a beautiful one,
> I have burnt away, give me some water!

In addition to the world losing its attractions, even those aspects of the hereafter that do not directly look to the Divine Being Himself, become of secondary importance to them. They seek welcome by Him in His Presence, they adorn their speech with yearning for Him and make their words more meaningful by arousing a yearning for Him in the hearts of others. They fill themselves with gifts that come from Him and try to distribute these, pouring the honey in their spirits into the hearts of those who yearn for Him. They frequently say, as Lamakani Huseyin Effendi[122] said,

> Clean the fountain of your heart when it is filled,
> Keep your eyes open when your heart becomes an eye for your heart.
> Drive out denial, and put the pitcher of your heart against that fountain;
> So that the pitcher may be filled with its exhilarating water.

When they get filled to the extent that they continuously overflow with the gifts coming from God, they pour them into the hearts of those around them, calling them as Muhammed Lutfi did:

> O you who are seeking God' gifts,
> come and join this circle (of dervishes)!
> O you who are passionately pursuing God's light,
> join this circle (of dervishes)!

Travelers who have attained this point eat, drink, and sleep little, and always feel wonder. Their interest in and occupation with worldly affairs is only because they live in the realm where cause and effect have a certain part. Fulfilling the responsibilities that are inherent in their rank and being thankful for the gifts of Truth, they sometimes breathe with the manifestations of the Divine Names and sometimes with those of the Attributes. However, if they cannot strictly continue their spiritual journey under the guidance of the Prophetic way or if they do not take refuge in the guidance of those who represent the Book and the Sunna, they may, due to the depth

---

[122] Lamakani Huseyin Effendi (d., 1625) was one of the famous Sufi poets and guides of the 17th-century Istanbul. *Wahdatname* ("The Book of Unity") and *Insan-i Kamil* ("The Universal Man") are his most well-known works. (Trans.)

of their devotion, go so far as to make utterances of pride that are incompatible with the rules of Shari'a; also they may display affectations instead of maintaining humility and self-possession in their relationship with God.

The final point that a soul who receives inspiration can reach is the ultimate point of certainty based on knowledge and the beginning of certainty based on observation. Until travelers reach this point, their belief that everything is from God and part of His creation is only a theoretical assertion. When they reach this point, they confess with all their being that everything is from God and a part of His creation. Every time they make this confession, they feel new breezes of contentment and begin to taste every commandment of God and everything pleasing to Him as if it were a dimension of their nature. This means that they are at the threshold of attaining the self at rest.

In the eyes of those who have reached the stage of the self at rest, all things, all colors and forms disappear with their peculiar features. They continuously think of and utter the truth of "There is no deity save God," and while doing so, they feel only Him as the true Self-Existence, they live surrounded by the light of this Existence, and experience with delight all creation as the manifestation of His Knowledge and Existence. In this state of pleasurable experience, they pronounce "There is no truly existent being save God," in the sense that every other existent being comes into existence by His giving it existence. This implies neither the Unity of Being nor the Unity of the Witnessed. It is a state of pleasure which those who do not experience it cannot perceive, and those who experience it cannot describe fully. In the hearts of the travelers who have risen to this point, all else save Him disappears under the light of His Existence, and the Holy Acts, Names and Attributes begin to appear wherever they look. The travelers who go on further and further become intoxicated with new signs of meeting with Him at every step, and feel that everything belongs to Him alone due to a certainty based on observation. These travelers attempt to make presents out of their existence which they see as a borrowed garment they have been made to wear, pronouncing: "I have found the most genuine, sweetest honey, so let my existence be plundered!"

These travelers are such that if they are asked to offer their souls, they stretch out their necks like a sheep in order to be sacrificed. They follow in the footsteps of the Prophet Ishmael, who is mentioned in the Qur'an, *(Ishmael) said: "Father, fulfill that which you are commanded, and you will find me patient, by God's will." So when they both (Abraham and his son Ishmael) wholly submitted (to God's will), and Abraham laid him prostrate on the side of his face (for sacrifice)* (37:102-03). They are extremely tender-hearted and unburden themselves with tears. They love everything, smell and caress everything, and especially feel a heart-felt interest in human beings, as they are polished mirrors that reflect the Creator. They exchange greetings with His manifestations in every color, taste, scent, and sound, and every exchange of greetings causes them to think and feel new things. They put the brake of self-possession and wakefulness on their pleasures and zeal. Fearing that they may fall into the error of thinking that all the spiritual pleasures, joy and delight that seethe in their spirit and pervade their whole being in waves originate in themselves and therefore belong to themselves, they pay no attention to these feelings, although many tend to sacrifice their souls for the same, but rather pursue only God's good pleasure and approval in every word and act of theirs. Like Yunus Emre, they always say: "I need and want You, only You."

At this point of the self at rest, God's gifts begin to pour abundantly on those with special capacities. In addition to several other characteristics, this rank is also the stage where those who have reached it are tested with spiritual discoveries and wonder-working. Sincerity requires that all spiritual discoveries and wonders which the travelers encounter should have no worth in their sight. They should even fear that these discoveries and wonders may cause their gradual perdition if they attribute them to themselves. At exactly this juncture, where a second nature begins to grow in them, the travelers' hearts expand and discover newer and newer truths and many secrets are revealed to them. At this stage, the veil is removed from their eyes with the result that the truths beyond things and events begin to appear in their own colors and dimensions, and where some become dazzled and feel dizzy, travelers with insight hasten to take refuge with the Sunna of the master of creation, and think and talk according to the fundamental principles of religion. They continue their journey, guided by the reflectors of the way which the Messenger and his Companions followed. Formerly, in the times after the Universal Teacher and Perfect Guide, upon him be peace and blessings, perfected guides who represented the way established by the Book and Sunna brilliantly and fully used to show the way to travelers. However, during times that have been deprived of such guides, many have been deviated and many others have been left stranded halfway.

The rank of the self at rest is also the station where an initiate journeys with or in the company of God, and the station which attracts particular Divine gifts. Some express these gifts with words that suggest incarnation and union; this is only because of a lack of suitable words or expressions. But it may cause a loss that leads the travelers to fall. Even though they may be at a summit, they can still fall into the abyss. Summits and abysses exist side by side. The higher one's rank, the deeper the abyss into which one can fall. One who falls from the apex of the tower of sincerity will fall into an extremely deep abyss. For this reason, as one covers distances along the way, reaching higher and higher points, one should become more and more self-possessed and wakeful. When the horizon or destination is within sight, travelers should supervise themselves more strictly, they should be more aware of their nothingness before God, and be conscious that whatever favor and blessing they enjoy is from Him and that they are only mirrors that reflect the same. They should turn more sincerely and deeply to the Source of those favors and blessings; they should affirm that the greatest favor and blessing is servanthood, and do so with a deep feeling and perception of their poverty, neediness, and helplessness; and they should pray in the manner of Uways al-Qarani:

O God! You are my Lord, and I am a servant.
You are the Creator, and I am the one created.
You are the All-Providing, and I am the one provided.
You are the Master and All-Owning, and I am the one owned.
You are the All-Mighty, and I am the one humble and abased.
You are the All-Wealthy, and I am the one impoverished.

According to some verifying scholars of Sufism, the final rank in the spiritual journey is the self at rest. Other ranks, such as being pleased with God, God's being pleased with the traveler, and perfection or purity, are different manifestations or evolved forms or dimensions of the being at rest. It is better to view these as the manifestations of feeling attracted toward God rather than different ranks or degrees.

However it is viewed or called, travelers who have reached the final point of being at rest receive fully—fully according to the capacity of a created being—the manifestation of the Divine Name the All-Living and become a polished mirror of It, only pursuing God's good pleasure as a requirement of the second nature that they have acquired. This summit is that of being pleased with God. Having attained this spiritual profundity, where they welcome with the same contentment whatever comes from Him—whether it be grace or reprimand—the travelers are freed from the influence of all the features of their corporeality, and gain a new existence in all its fresh aspects. This is the existence that comes with sobriety after self-annihilation, subsistence after annihilation, and certainty based on observation after certainty based on knowledge. In the sight of such a traveler, every particle becomes a voice which mentions Him in all the circumstances in which it exists. Every voice or sound is a tune that echoes from Him in a different way that is peculiar to it. Every color pours into the eyes and hearts, as if they were smiles from a clime of holiness. The traveler breathes with the truths of *There is none to be desired save Him* and *There is none to be worshipped save Him*. In proportion to their position, they take in these blessed words as if they were oxygen for their spiritual life, and send out, as if carbon dioxide, everything else that arises in the bodily existence that occasionally makes itself felt because of human nature. The travelers calm their nerves and irritations, things regarded as the remnants of the carnal self. When they feel stressed under the pressure of struggling with those remnants, they turn to their eternal Goal with supplicating tears, and experience their accomplishments as favors of God, saying as Muhammad Lutfi said:

> That which I have—I am not worthy of it;
> This favor and grace—why are they bestowed on me?

Their every word, act, and manner reveal the sincerity and depth of their being pleased with God the Almighty. Everyday they refresh the thought of resignation to God's will, without even being aware of the beauties that flow into the eyes of their hearts from the heaven of feeling that is attracted toward Him. They whisper:

> Whatever comes from You—
> be it a reprimand from Your Majesty or a favor from Your Grace;
> Both are a pleasure for my soul; both are pleasant—
> whether this or that is from You.

Having set up their thrones in such a world of approach and feeling, travelers advance through the manifestations of the Divine Names and Attributes toward the final point of certainty that is based on knowledge. Beyond this lies the peak of God's being pleased with them. Here they feel His pleasure and approval with the signs peculiar to this state, and which they know as witnessed by their sound, pure consciousness. This summit has been called by different names, such as the rank of God's special manifestation of His particular Names or absorption within absorption. Those who have reached it continue their journey on the summit of journeying from God in deep wonder and self-possession. With the Almighty acting as their eyes with which they see and their ears with which they hear, they can always see and hear correctly and they act endowed with most praiseworthy qualities. They overlook the evils done to them, ignore the imperfections they see in others, never cherish an ill-opinion of believers, embrace everyone with affection, and live in peace with all people because they know that they are all creatures of God. They always feel happy in their inner world (even though suffering with the afflictions of others) because they are pleased with God, Who is also pleased with them, and this converts everything into a confection in the workshop of their hearts, the abundance of which they then turn and offer to others. With their hearts always indicating God's good pleasure, they act in all places as those who direct their hearts to the One Who is Pleased with them. They love for God's sake, embrace for God's sake, smell for God's sake, and try to fulfill what is required by such a great favor, which is regarded as the beginning of the rank of the Truth of the Messenger as being Muhammad, and to deepen their relation with this rank.

The ultimate, indescribable point of the self at rest is the self perfected. Travelers at this point feel that Divine manifestations have pervaded all the created worlds to give them their color, and all other colors, forms and qualities have been wiped out, and they experience transformation after transformation in their inner world of pleasures and visions. This highest summit, where travelers continue their journey in journeying with God and experience unity in multiplicity and multiplicity in unity, belongs, first of all, to the Prophets. The pure scholars succeeding the Prophets in their duties can feel in their hearts only a reflection of this in loyalty to the Prophets. The most important characteristic of these scholars is wakefulness. They are aware of their place—where they are and why and with what mission. They distinguish between the whole and the parts, the universal and the particular, the origin and the shadow, and the ones who are leading and the ones who are led. They never fall into confusion. They are seen to neither make utterances of self-pride that are incompatible with the rules of Shari'a, nor do they display affectations such that God's attention may be drawn to them-selves. Neither do they see themselves as superior to others nor do they expect privilege. They attribute to Him whatever they have that is worthy of appreciation, and regard every effort to preserve the same as thankfulness to God for those things. They are exceptionally humble and modest. Without expecting anything in return, they are ready to shoulder further tasks and responsibilities.

The souls with such a degree of purity fulfill all their responsibilities in the manner and solemnity of performing their duties of worship and they cause every moment to overflow with a new delight in meeting with Him in the depth of their being. Their breaths reflect the breezes of His nearness, causing serenity wherever they blow. Their silence is a deep reflection that uncovers the meanings of things and events, and their words are sparks of wisdom from Prophetic psalms. Numerous eyes search for them. Their manners remind people of the Creator, and wherever He is remembered and mentioned, hearts are aroused to self-supervision, and boil like magma, burn like a furnace, and cry aflame:

> O nightingale crazy with love, do you cry again in pain?
> Do you head for a rose once more shedding such profuse tears?
> You hasten into fire like moths throwing themselves to light to burn;
> Or have you constantly been burning in the fire of love?

Besides the stages of the carnal self or soul, the Sufi scholars have also mentioned some degrees or ranks of depth and purity for the spirit. The inward dimension of the spirit is "secret," and the inward dimension of "secret" is "secret within secret." The most important dimension of "secret within secret" is "private," and its deepest aspect is "the more private." What is meant by "inward" is the essence or substance of a thing. These faculties are from the pure realm of Divine commands. The deepest, most abstruse and impenetrable of these faculties is the "more private." The "private" envelops the "more private" with its aspects belonging to the realm of Divine commands. "Secret within secret" surrounds them like a wall, and the spirit embraces all these faculties like an atmosphere and connects them to the heart. The development of these faculties depends on possessing a deep spiritual life to govern the human daily life. For this reason, it is not possible for unfortunate ones who have not been able to save themselves from their corporeality and to discover their real human faculties, to feel the gifts that flow into those who have risen to high levels of spirituality. The minimum conditions of feeling such are to have the necessary capacity and to make the required efforts to develop it, and then to be able to be saved from the domination of corporeality through periods of suffering.

> *May God guide us and you to the right, sound path. And let God's blessings be upon our master Muhammad, who was tender-hearted and compassionate, and on his family and Companions, the noble, godly ones.*

DERVISH (DERVISH)

Dervish is a word that means poor, destitute one. Even though it is used for the poor and helpless in worldly terms, in Sufi terminology it is used for those who are aware of their poverty and helplessness before God. Although poverty and helplessness in worldly terms are associated with beggary, travelers to God are not poor and helpless in that they do not ask anyone for anything. Heroes of truth, who have dedicated themselves to God, are content with what He has given them and are indifferent to all other things. Even in hunger and thirst they unburden themselves to God, without revealing their need to others. A dervish is also regarded as being the threshold to a door. This does not mean that dervishes humiliate themselves before people; rather, it means that they are humble and in their awareness of their nothingness before God attribute to Him whatever they may possess that is worthy of appreciation. They are also humble among people because of the Creator and always aware that they are a precious work of God's art with all the Divine gems inherent in their nature.

Sometimes perfect people are mentioned as being the dervishes of a certain guide. This is because it is important to stress the place of a dervish, both in the sight of God and of people. Besides, sometimes simple, humble, content, and lenient people are called dervishes, while there are some great, sagacious persons with a deep knowledge of God who are known as "a poor one with the heart of sultan," in that they are magnanimous even though poor.

The leading scholars of Sufism describe a true dervish as one who is abstinent, pious, righteous, patient, loving, tolerant, and steadfast, severing relations with all else save God from the heart, and devoted to His service with the intention and effort of reaching Him.

A dervish takes his or her first step by holding back from sins and by fulfilling obligatory and supererogatory religious duties. The second step is to be loving and tolerant toward everyone, to see the universe as a cradle of brotherhood/sisterhood, and to try to represent the nature and morals of Muhammad, and the truth of his being Ahmad, upon him be peace and blessings. The third step is to reach the horizon of sincerity and perfect goodness and to develop the theoretical knowledge and belief based on imitation into experience and verified truths.

At the first stage, dervishes are at the beginning of piety, and demonstrate that they are ready to understand the Qur'an and to start the journey to meet with the Almighty. They are awarded in proportion to their sincerity and purity of intention and advance toward piety and the summits of being pleased with God and finally into the Gardens of Paradise.

> God Almighty says: The great among you are those who are pious.
> The last abode of the pious will be Paradise and their drink will be kawthar.[123]

In the second stage, they build relations with all existence, living or non-living, (without, however, assigning their heart to any other than the Almighty) and appreciate each according to its position. They love and embrace everything, repel hostilities with love, and evil with good. Thinking that the road that they are to follow is the road of not showing resentment, but rather that of patience and tolerance, they run toward the rank of being pleased with God, and whisper like Yunus:

> You should be voiceless to one who curses,
> and handless to one who beats;
> A dervish should have no heart to resent,
> so you cannot be a dervish.

In the third stage, dervishes are persons of peace and spiritual vision, having entered the way of seeing, feeling, and knowing on-

---

[123] *Kawthar* is the name of a river in Paradise. (Trans.)

ly Him, and being faithful friends of Him. It makes no difference to them whether good comes from friends or evil from enemies. This is even more so if they have heard the voice of the Friend, then they will no longer feel breaths other than His, and will be freed from interest in and worries about any other than Him, acquiring a second nature that is determined by "secret." They know what they really should know and are freed from bearing a burden of unnecessary information.

Everyone can enter the way of being a dervish. No one who has taken a step on this way is denied. However, entering such a way has some requirements which one who is ready to take the first step on this way is expected to fulfill. Tokadizade Sekip[124] states that the door to being a dervish is open for everybody, but warns that this is the way of offering the soul to the Beloved and therefore requires sincerity and perfect goodness:

> The door to the Truth is open to a wakeful person,
> But those who know how to sacrifice their souls can reach God.
> I have seen many who have come to this dervish convent,
> Willing and ready to sacrifice themselves on the way of truth.

The Prophet Abraham is an excellent example to remind one that reaching God is possible by sacrificing one's soul in His way. He breasted the fire of Nimrod[125] in this way and, leaving his home and native land, set up his home in the desert. In utter submission to God, he took his wife and son and left them in a desolate valley. He offered the "fruit of his heart"—his son who had been bestowed on him in return for many years of desiring a son—to the Truth, as a sacrifice.[126] In short, he showed such resolution, power of will, and determination at every step, that except for the pride of human-

---

[124] Tokadizade Sekip was one of the Turkish poets and writers who lived in Izmir in the first half of the 20th century. He wrote in favor of freedom during the reign of the Ottoman Sultan Abdulhamid II, and was one of the founders of the Association of Defending the Basic Rights in Izmir. (Trans.)

[125] Nimrod was the title that was given to the Chaldaean kings in Iraq. (Trans.)

[126] Prophet Abraham, upon God's command, left his elder son Ishmael in the valley of Makkah together with her mother Hagar. (Trans.)

kind, he has no equal in human history. It is as if Sayyid Nigari[127] uttered the following couplet about him:

> Does one who seeks the Beloved struggle for his own life?
> And can another who seeks his own life be in quest of the Beloved?

So, being a dervish means aspiring to be a hero of meeting with the Beloved, which signifies devoting one's life to acquiring God's good pleasure and approval in the consciousness of the meaning and purpose of the religious commandments. It has also been described as being in quest of the Truth under the guidance of love and zeal and by dominating one's voice, heart, and carnal soul. This description is also significant. Riza Tevfik, a late Turkish poet and philosopher, presenting the characteristics of being a dervish, enlightens this point as follows:

> Being a dervish means dominating one's essence;
> One who is a captive of his ego is not a dervish.
> It is adopting love as a guide and finding God;
> It is not sweets, an axe, a staff, a needle or a skewer.

> Do not sit absentminded in the name of devotion;
> Do not shout, nor dance violently, nor beat your breast!
> Nor foam by crying "O He, O All-Living!"
> Mentioning God is not a part of digestion.

> Learn the secret about God from your heart;
> It is the heart which sees the Beloved through love.
> What causes a wakeful one with knowledge of God to feel that pleasure,
> Is not henbane, nor wine, nor opium, nor anything else.

> Do not expect wonder from the stone of Najaf,[128]
> Nor separate from human beings, your brethren.
> You cannot see the Truth from graves or tombs;
> A true man of God is a sultan, not a hermit.

---

[127] Seyyid Mir Hamza Nigari was a Sufi poet from Azerbaijan. He wrote lyrical poems to express God's love. (Trans.)

[128] Najaf is a city in the southern Iraq, which bears holiness for the Shi'te Muslims. (Trans.)

Everywhere are heaps of crude souls,
What is your relation with them?
Take refuge in your heart that tends to seclusion!
The world is not as spacious as the heart.

In the beginning, a dervish is a student who studies theoretical knowledge; his or her practicing what is learned is representation; then, feeling and experiencing more deeply what is known and practiced—by each according to his or her capacity—is certainty. The first stage can also be regarded as theoretical Shari'a, the second as practical Shari'a, and the third as Shari'a experienced in truth. A traveler is a dervish during the whole of the journeying, through all of its stations, from the beginning to the end.

Some exacting scholars of Sufism regard being a dervish as an essential condition on the way to meet with God. According to them, being a dervish has the same meaning and importance for the cleansing of the carnal self, the refinement of heart, and the purification of spirit and its acquiring transcendence as treatment, diet and abstention from harmful habits, food and drink do for health. As a doctor's advice is essential for the cure of diseases, spiritual diseases also require the advice and direction of a spiritual guide. The character of an individual is important in the diagnosis and treatment of bodily diseases, which is why modern medicine advises that every patient requires individual attention. This is also true for spiritual diseases and treatment. Each disease may require a treatment which is different, at least, in its details.

For example, for an initiate who cannot be saved from the pressure of corporeality or bodily desires, or reach the level of life lived in the heart and the spirit, austerity is essential. A guide who knows the person and can diagnose his or her disease well, will advise renunciation of the world and whatever in it relates to the pleasures of the worldly life. If the initiate has fully concentrated on the pleasures of the other world without considering the Truly Desired and Eternally-Besought One, the guide will urge renunciation of the other world with its pleasures and concentration on the Truth. If, on the other hand, neither the world nor the hereafter can keep an initiate from the main goal of the journeying, if both serve to improve concentration on eternity, the guide will open the doors on the world and the hereafter wide for the initiate. Concerning this, Jalal al-Din al-Rumi says:

> The world means heedlessness of God; it does not mean possessing silver coins, clothes, or a family. Our Prophet praised wealth earned in lawful ways and used for the revival and uplifting of Islam, and said: "How good is any wealth earned in lawful ways for a righteous one!" If enough water finds its way into a ship, it causes it to sink, but if it is under the ship, it causes it to float. If you do not put the love of wealth in your heart, then you can swim safely in the ocean of spiritual journeying and initiation.

True dervishes, from the time of Adam until today, have thought and acted in such a way. Even though they were not called dervishes, we can regard the People of the Suffa—the poor Companions who stayed in the antechamber adjacent to the Prophet's Mosque in Madina—as the first dervishes of the Muslim Umma. They observed both the balance between the world and the hereafter and the Divine rights to a degree that no one else has been able to, and they became heroes of resignation (to God's will).

After the Companions, all the people of journeying and initiation who have journeyed on the way to God under different titles, such as asceticism or Sufism or being a dervish, have performed great tasks, as if they were the soul and blood in the veins of the society, so long as they have had no interest in politics and concentrated all their efforts for belief in God's Unity and maintaining the Islamic life in this belief. When they have acted to the contrary, they have both harmed society and ruined themselves.

Using being a dervish, which, in fact, is a state based on humility and a feeling of nothingness, for worldly benefits is such a means of contamination of the spirit that nothing other than a special Divine grace can clean it.

Let Mawlana Jalal al-Din al-Rumi have the last word:

A luxurious life is a shame on dervishes; a burden in their hearts.
How nice is feeling destitute before Him;
And being in need of Him on His way.
For pomp and luxury on the way to the Beloved
Are like thorns; they hurt the feet of dervishes.

O God! Make full of blessings my religious life, which is the guarantee of my innocence, and my other life, to which I am bound to go, and my world, in which I can be perfected.

And bestow Your blessings and peace on our master Muhammad, and on his family and the Companions altogether.

SALIK (INITIATE)

A *salik* (initiate) is a traveler who follows a way to a goal and makes efforts to meet with God. The way of traveling differs according to the capacity, abilities and gifts with which each individual has been favored. Some are extraordinarily attracted and taken by God Himself to the ranks of loving and being loved by God and being pleased with Him and His being pleased with them, without having to observe some of the rules that must be observed during journeying. Such are mentioned as those who are attracted by God. They can reach, through the blessings of the Prophet's Ascension, in a few minutes, hours or days the states and stations that others can reach after many periods of suffering, and become purified of carnal dirt. Their hearts are refined in the shortest way possible and, reaching their Beloved and Desired One at a speed that is not possible through other efforts, they are able to feel all the spiritual pleasures of being favored with His company. They have reached the horizon of "a perfect human being," which is regarded as the point where the outward and inward have been united.

These perfect ones, who are attracted by God toward Him, are the hidden treasures of the Divine mysteries, the centers on which the lights of the Divine Knowledge and Existence are focused, and those who offer the water of life to believers for the health of their spiritual life, a water with which they will quench their thirst for eternity. They revive dead hearts with their speeches, open blind eyes with their glance and attentions, and cure the spiritual wounds of those who are in their aura. They live intoxicated with ever new gifts and favors, and cause those around them to experience the most dazzling of observations. With their seeing directed by their insight, and their speaking dependent on their hearts, they are enraptured with the colors and lines which pertain to Him, and which they see in everything they look at, and they scatter pearls and coral whenever they open their mouths to speak. Since they are dazzled and enchanted by even a half-seeing of Him, those who do not know them think that they are insane or intoxicated. Ruhi of Baghdad[129] describes their state very well:

> Do not think that we are intoxicated with the wine of the grape;
> We are among the intoxicated from eternity in the past.

If some temporarily go into ecstasies with the initial signs of Him, they immediately come to their senses because of their nature, and they take refuge in wakefulness and self-possession, continuing on their way to meeting God in wakefulness. There is nothing in their feelings, thoughts or acts which causes people confusion; nor are there utterances of pride incompatible with the rules of Shari'a, nor any affectations, nor relaxed behavior. They advance toward being pleased with Him and His being pleased with them in reliance on Him in the atmosphere of *The eye did not swerve, nor did it stray* (53:17).

Some others complete their spiritual journey by observing its heavenly rules, reaching the horizon of attraction toward God with the support of Divine help and feeling as if their will-power has been connected to a sacred center of attraction. They continue their future life connected to that center in the manner of those who have let themselves go in the current. You can find in such people, who have taken off toward nothingness and carnal non-existence, neither anxieties, worries, nor grief. They are occupied with the Eternal Friend, they feel His intimacy, and live free from uneasiness and troubles because of the peace they find in His presence. The following verses of Niyazi Misri[130] indicate this horizon in one respect:

---

129 Ruhi of Baghdad (d. 1605) was one of the important figures in the Ottoman-Turkish classical literature, who usually wrote about moral issues. (Trans.)

130 Mehmed Niyazi Misri (d., 1694) was a Sufi poet who was born in Malatya (Turkey), educated in Egypt and lived in Istanbul and Edirne. (Trans.)

Having renounced the worldly worries,
And taken off to carnal non-existence;
Zealously flying without ceasing,
I call, "O Friend, O Friend!"

There are still some others who constantly make an effort, from the beginning to the end, and, without expecting any return, sincerely fulfill their duties of servanthood. They neither feel attraction nor are attracted toward God, nor do they display any affectations, nor have any superiority or inferiority complexes or fancies and fantasies. They show great will-power and patience, observing even the least important rules of devotion without any show and being extraordinarily steadfast in His way. They prefer living an Islamic life over wonder-working and pleasures, and never adopt Paradise and what lies beyond it as a goal of their devotion. Regarding believing and devotion as the greatest blessing of the Lord, they live in thankfulness for such gifts in utmost humility and modesty. With his particular style, Mawlana Jalal al-Din al-Rumi describes being favored with this blessing as follows:

Happiness has come and held us by the skirt,
And set up our tent in the heaven.
Yesterday the Beloved asked me:
"How do you do with this unfaithful world?"
I answered: "How can one be who,
Has seen the fortune of the fortunate state?
Thanks that I have found in the bottom of my teeth
The sugar that Egypt cannot see even in her dreams."

The first thing an initiate must do is to turn to God in repentance and contrition, in determination to emigrate to what God is pleased with from what He is not, to what He asks us to do from what He does not, and to a life in the heart and the spirit from a carnal life. So long as their efforts are supported by such a high degree of refinement of the carnal self, purification of heart, and good morals, initiates feel that they change both inwardly and outwardly while their horizons become gradually enlightened. To the extent of their sincerity and purity of intention, they begin to present an example of straightforwardness in acting, with the mechanism of their consciousness becoming gradually radiant. With belief developing into conviction, and conviction deepening with increasing knowledge of God, and knowledge of God being transformed into love, and love growing into burning passion, and passion ending in constant wonder, a human being, who has been created of dust, of wet clay, becomes the focus of attention for the inhabitants of the heavens. Those dwelling in the pure realm of the Divine dominion regard it an honor to follow the example of such humans. Whoever turns to them for guidance intends to be guided to the truth, and whoever holds fast to them intends to grasp a strong rope.

This "greatest copy and pattern of creation", who has become a source of radiance in the inner depth of his or her self, turns into a center of Divine gifts and a storeroom of favors, becomes a blessed one who offers everyone the water of life. Each of the different mansions which such a traveler passes through during the journey upward is called a "state," and the relatively stable point to which his or her abilities develop, and which we may describe as the "arch of perfections" of a traveler, is called a "station." "The gifts and radiance of everyone is in proportion to his or her capacity."

Every traveler to the Truth ends the journey at a certain peak and observes all the worlds, materially and spiritually, from this summit or pinnacle. The final point which every traveler reaches according to his or her capacity is the peak particular to that individual, and therefore each peak is of a relative height. The highest, the only real peak, which separates the mortal from the Eternal or the contingent from the absolutely necessary, which is mentioned in the Qur'an in "or nearer" in the statement *a distance between the strings of two bows adjacent each other or even less* (53:9), which describes the nearness of God's Messenger to God, is the one belonging to the master of creation, upon him be the most perfect of blessings. All other heights are defined, in comparison with one another, with such expressions as "lower" or higher" or "greater" or "less" and belong to those whom God has made near to Him, and the godly are relative and in proportion to the capacity-capital of everyone and the Divine gifts with which they are favored.

When the initiates step on their individual horizon of perfection and make their heart into a polished mirror to the sacred Divine gifts, that heart becomes familiar with the Divine look and the breezes of Divine inspiration, and they begin to feel and view creation differently, according to the individual's level. They burn with the excitement of demonstrating to others what each sees and feels.

Those initiates always think of Him and mention Him as "The One to be worshipped is He—God", breathing the truth of "The One to be sought is He—God", pondering their inner world and the outer world, respiring with "The One to be known is He—God" and relating everything to the truth of the Divine Being around the axis of Names and Attributes, developing their belief, first based on acceptance without seeing what is believed in, into a conviction based on a seeing by the heart, supported by a state of spiritual pleasures. They experience verbal and physical devotion with such delight that it is as if they have entered Paradise and been favored with a vision of God. Haqani[131] says:

> What behoves an initiate is to proclaim:
> We worship but God alone.

They hold back from everything which they think is not approvable in His sight, and think of Him only. They reflect deeply on a profound understanding of the fields that He allows.

Initiates who have come to the end of their journey think only of Him, consider Him, know and concentrate on Him with His title of "He." They consider and concentrate on Him because of Him and because they must do so, and they consider all else than Him—whether relating to this world or the next—only in accordance with and in proportion to His permission. For one who has

---

[131] Haqani Mehmet bey (d., 1606) was an Ottoman Turkish poet. He spent his whole life in Istanbul. *Hilya* ("The Portrait") and *Miftah-i Futuhat* ("The Key to Conquests") are his well-known works. (Trans.)

focused on Him only and considers all else save Him because of Him, the only thing to be sought and desired is He and His good pleasure. Let us listen to Mawlana once more:

> O you who are seeking the world; you are like a day laborer in this world;
>> And you, lover of Paradise, are also far distant from truth.
> O you, who are unaware of the truth and pleased with the two worlds,
>> You are excused, for you have not felt
>> the pleasure of suffering for the Beloved' sake.

In short, initiates who have determined their goal well and who are aware of the horizon where they are, leave both their bodies and souls, with which others are most concerned, on the bench where corpses are washed for burial, and scatter all their capital of being before the door of their heart. Freed from all concerns of everything save Him that may keep them from their way, they turn to their heart and try to understand its voice. They put their eyes and ears under the command of their insight, they plunge into the pure world of metaphysical considerations. It sometimes occurs that they can transcend space in one attempt, and make their voices heard by the inhabitants of heavens in another.

This point, where the heart turns completely to the invisible speaker in it, is like a launch pad from which initiates can rise to the door of eternity in one leap. A step forward, with their head and feet having met at the same point, the heroes of ascension (to God) and descent (to return to being amidst the people) become like a ring. In such state, where the "bird of petition" should be sent to God, lips and voice fall silent, and only the warm sounds of the heart are heard. The head bends itself down to lean ever increasingly on the heart, and whispers to itself: *Worship your Lord until certainty comes to you (by death)* (15:99).

> *O God! I ask You for Your love and the love for him who loves You, and for the deeds which will cause me to get near to You.*

> *O God, bestow Your blessings and peace on Your beloved one and the Messenger, Mustafa, and on his family and Companions, who were appreciative and faithful.*

ANOTHER WAY OF JOURNEYING
AND INITIATION

Some make spiritual journeys by refining and developing the inner faculties, while others purify the carnal self within, causing it to take certain steps. In both these ways, suffering for certain periods is essential to reach the rank of perfection and to become a perfect human being. Yet there are other ways, different from these two ways, to reach the ranks and stations and the favors and blessings that come through spiritual journeying and suffering. Among these ways, there is one which is based on the way of the Prophet's Companions and may be regarded as a manifestation of the truth of Messengership.

Helplessness, poverty, affection, reflection, zeal and thankfulness are the basic elements of this way. Helplessness means being aware of one's inability to do many of the things that one wants to do, and poverty denotes the awareness of the fact that it is God Who is the real Owner and Master of everything. Embracing everybody and everything because of Him is affection, while reflection is thinking deeply, analytically and systematically about and meditating on the outer and inner world, with a new excitement everyday. Zeal is the great, ardent desire and yearning to reach God and to serve in His way. Always thanking God for His bounties and proceeding to Him in full consciousness of all His blessings during the journey is thankfulness.

According to Bediuzzaman Said Nursi,[132] this way is more direct and safer. Helplessness is a path of light leading to being loved

---

[132] Bediuzzaman Said Nursi (1877-1960) is the most famous and one of the greatest Muslim thinkers and scholars of the 20*th* century. He wrote about the truhts and essentials of the Islamic faith, the meaning and importance of worship, morality, and the meaning of existence. He is very original in his approaches. *Sozler* ("The Words"), *Mektubat* ("The Letters"), *Lem'alar* ("The Gleams"), and *Sualar* ("The Rays") are among his famous works. (Trans.)

by God that is safer and quicker than love; in it the more one perceives one's helplessness, the more quickly one will reach one's goal. Poverty is an inexhaustible treasure which, to the extent of one's consciousness of it, will lead one to the protection and direction of the All-Merciful and His infinite Power much sooner and more safely than the greatest discipline, efforts and endeavors could. Affection is deeper and more sincere than love. No traveler having this feeling, which is a manifestation of Divine Compassion, has ever been left halfway. Reflection is the way of the enlightened spirits who relate everything to wisdom through study and the observation of one's inner world and the outer world. As for zeal, it is the characteristic of those who are always conscious of the points or senses of reliance and asking for help that are innate to them. These two senses always remind of God. Those endowed with zeal never become desperate or disappointed. And finally, thankfulness is returning with gratitude all the blessings of God that we receive almost gratis.

The essence of the way can be summed up as: "I am helpless, You are the All-Powerful; I am poor, You are the All-Wealthy; I am needy and in straitened circumstances, You are the All-Compassionate; I am bewildered and seeking a way out, You are the only Goal Which is sought and to be reached." It is not possible for those who are aware of their helplessness, poverty, neediness and bewilderment to see themselves as pure or of being of any rank, thus it is not possible for them to be heedless or forgetful of God while knowing that whoever forgets Him is forgotten and bound to forget him or herself also. Nor is it possible for them to attribute to themselves the accomplishments with which God has favored them, using the pretext of their endeavors, nor to ascribe their evil and sins to Destiny, thus regarding themselves as existing independently of God.

According to Bediuzzaman, this way can be dealt with from the viewpoint of the following four disciplines:

- Making efforts to see the carnal self as not being purified and sinless, as against its innate tendency to see itself as pure and sinless.

- Being careful and resolved to forget oneself when and where one should forget and remember oneself when and where one should remember.
- Being well aware of the fact that God creates everything—good and evil—and is the only source of all good. Thus, one should attribute to oneself all one's sins and evil as being caused by one's own person, albeit it is God Who has created them, and all good and all accomplishments should be attributed to God, and one should be thankful.
- Whatever state one is in and whatever rank one reaches during one's journey, one should know that both one's existence and merits are but a shadow or a shadow of the shadow of the lights of Divine Existence, and that all aspects of one's existence are a mirror of the manifestations of His Knowledge and Existence.

Now let us explain these points in accordance with the approach of Bediuzzaman:

The first discipline: The carnal self in its nature is fond of itself, and only loves and has relations with others because of itself. The self-love of the carnal self is so great that its adoration of itself is like the adoration of God felt by a sincere believer devoted to the One Who absolutely deserves worship and who should be sought. It never shows inclination to acknowledge its errors and always sees itself as being pure and free of error. So, one should wage the major (greater) jihad against such an attitude, always criticizing and questioning it, softening and melting it in the blast-furnace of self-criticism and self-supervision in order to re-shape it. One should never see oneself as free and absolved of errors and sins, and the acceptance of this is, in fact, the tap under which it should and can be cleaned. Only by doing so can one's innate positive potentialities be developed.

If we continuously seek purification in seeing ourselves as prone to evils and errors, angels and other spiritual beings will greatly appreciate our decency and cleanliness, and, as stated in a Prophetic saying,[133] they will come down from all sides to shake hands with us. If, by contrast, we are so heedless that we see ourselves as clean and infallible, we will inevitably be representatives of a loathsome nature from which even devils will keep aloof in disgust. As Mawlana said, human beings are such that sometimes they become like the Devil under the influence of satanic impulses, and sometimes they are on a par with angels at the summits of spiritual life.

The second discipline: A person with an unpurified, evil-commanding carnal self may be forgetful of the most vital matters, which should never be forgotten, and such a person does not even want to recollect them, while pulling up from the heart matters that should never be remembered. Human beings should always think of serving God's cause, of being earnest in their deeds, of their responsibilities to the people around them, and of death and what lies beyond it. They should uproot from their spirit hatred, jealousy, worldly ambitions, greed, and carnal desires. Only by doing so can human beings keep their innate tendency toward spirituality alive, and hold themselves back from rousing the satanic tendencies within them.

We, travelers on the way to God, should see belief in God and living along the line of His good pleasure as a blessing, and concentrate on how we can please Him with all our thoughts, feelings, and actions. We should also try to lead our lives in His company, and by virtue of this company, we should continually seek new means to be always in close relationship with Him. We should always be aware of what Mawlana reminds us of: "There is a hidden One here; O heart, do not see yourself as alone." Based on our relationship with Him, we should strive to transcend our limited nature in order to advance toward infinity, developing our drop-like existence into an ocean, and seeking the mysteries of the universal in our particular existence. If we lead such a life, the things that are seen as impossible to do are done and obstacles that seem insurmountable are surmounted. Particulars become reflections of and mirrors to the universal, and what we see as non-existent takes on

---

[133] Al-Muslim, "Tawba," 12-13; Al-Tirmidhi, "Qiyama," 59.

the color of existence, a dew-drop excels the moon in reflecting the sun, earth becomes as elevated as the heavens, and our particle-like natures expand to the extent of the universe.

Mawlana, the prince of the lovers of God, advises us to transcend the corporeal dimension of our existence and discover the mysterious potentialities of our spirit, saying:

> A pitcher which has found the way to the sea:
> Rivers prostrate themselves before it.

The third discipline: A carnal self that has not yet been able to step on the way to refinement through journeying in itself and the outer world, ascribes to itself whatever good and achievement it is favored with, while imputing evils and failures to either external factors and causes or its incorrect, stunted concept of Destiny. Instead of overflowing with thankfulness for whatever favors it receives, it inwardly collapses because of self-pride, conceit, and arrogance, and extinguishes its feelings of thankfulness to and praise for God. It contaminates its horizon with the filth of such bad morals, and ruins itself. Whereas, if the carnal self is able to attribute to God all the good and achievements and impute all evils, shortcomings and failures to itself, then it would be favored with blessing after blessing, even in the most unfavorable circumstances. What is necessary is that the carnal self should see that its perfection lies in its perception and acknowledgment of its imperfection, and that it should always be humble before and devoted to God. The carnal self should also overflow with thankfulness and zeal by perceiving and acknowledging that its power comes from its helplessness, and its richness lies in its innate poverty.

It is extremely important for us as believers to know that all our merits and accomplishments are from God, while all our imperfections and errors are from our own selves, and that we should keep our system of self-interrogation and self-control alive and active. So long as the travelers to God can do this, they will always yield fruit, even in the most unfavorable circumstances. Whereas, from the moment when aridity arises in the spiritual world of the carnal self, due to certain erosions, then only thorns will grow, even in the most favorable circumstances, and it will hoot like an owl, lamenting its loss.

If human beings were only physical beings, their concerns and worries about corporeality would be meaningful. Seeing a noble being as consisting only of a physical body means reducing it to the level of flesh, which is bound to disintegrate and rot away and be food for microorganisms. This is the most abominable form of despising the noblest and most honorable of all creation. But the actual fact of the matter is that humankind, by virtue of their creation, endowment, and potentials, are more valued and sublime than even the angels. Human beings are much more than being mere body; they are endowed with heart, spirit, and other inward spiritual faculties, with consciousness, intellect, perception, intelligence and other outer and inner senses and feelings. Human beings are an assemblage of values that transcends the physical dimension of their being. Human beings are such precious and well-endowed creatures that they can sometimes fly so high that even the angels desire to catch up with them; sometimes they can reach the peaks which separate the realm of mortal beings from eternity and infinity. Using their mental faculties to the utmost degree, they arrange travel to celestial bodies, and transfer sounds, voices and images from great distances, offering us the most beautiful melodies of time and space shrinking at great speed.

However, despite the extent of their capacity and exceptional nature, humans can fall into a net of hatred, grudges, greed, and lust, becoming the most wretched and abased of all beings. They can be wretched slaves and beggars, despite their nature and capacity to be the masterpieces of creation; they can become nothing more than worms creeping on the earth, despite their potential to be heavenly beings. But if they turn completely to God with all their inner dynamism, overflowing with thankfulness for all the good He has bestowed on them, and impute to themselves all the evils they may commit and shortcomings they may suffer, they can become perfected and be saved from those shortcomings through awareness and wakefulness, and by being cleansed under the taps of self-control and supervision. Then humankind can set up the tent of true humanity on the debris of evil feelings and passions, and express themselves through accomplishments, without ever losing their humility and feelings of nothingness before God. This also means discovering themselves anew at every attempt, being fully aware of themselves in their own depths, and experiencing a new revival at every moment. Mawlana sees this as the feet of the soul being freed from the fetters of corporeality and the spirit starting to become heavenly. A spirit which has become heavenly also attempts to arrange its own, inner world with its whole power of perception and consciousness, makes incessant efforts to repair the defects standing in the way of its perfection. Such a spirit travels sometimes in the realm that stands before the veil over existence and sometimes beyond it, and goes into ecstasies at every seeing of the depths of its heart. Every such seeing arouses in it a new desire to grow into perfection, and every desire a new zeal for self-renewal. It sees its heart as a home of God and utters:

> The heart is the home of God; purify it from whatever is there other than Him,
> So that the All-Merciful may descend into His palace at night.

The truly and fully human beings cleanse the heart of foul concepts and images, adorn their "secret" with knowledge of God, illuminate their "private" with the torch of love and zeal, and make their "more private" utter loyalty. They are always occupied with the Beloved One, and ready to sacrifice themselves for His sake. This is their affliction, which is preferred to all cures; they are exhausted with the excitement of being on the way to Him. However, their affliction is sweeter than all cures, and their exhaustion is preferable to every rest or repose. Their affliction causes them to travel through deserts in quest of greater afflictions, saying:

> I used to seek a cure for my inward affliction;
> They said: "Your cure is the affliction itself."
> I used to seek something to sacrifice in the court of the Beloved;
> They said: "Your soul is the thing you seek to sacrifice."

> (M. Lutfi)

The soul also utters, as many have uttered:

> I used to seek a cure for my affliction;
> I have come to know that my affliction itself is my cure.
> I used to try to find that which is hidden in my origin;
> I have come to know that my origin is that which is hidden.

(Niyazi Misri)

Many have sung melodies of love about Him, and of separation from Him and yearning to meet with Him with all of their being, as if each part of their bodies were a flute.

Concerning this, Mawlana says:

> O heart! You and your suffering for Him exist; ah, how nice it
> is always to be concerned with Him and suffering for Him!
> That suffering is, in fact, your cure. So, bear with all the afflic-
> tions and troubles coming from Him, without making the least
> complaint. So does He decree. If you have been able to tram-
> ple your bodily desires, then you have killed the dog of your
> carnal self, which is the thing that should be killed.

The fourth discipline: The carnal self sees itself as if it were a being which exists independently. It sometimes adopts a manner so
refractory and abased that every attitude and act it performs is disobedience and hostility to Him Whom it must unquestionably worship. In reality none other than Him has an independent existence
of itself. Every existing being or thing, living or non-living, functions as a mirror to the Names of the Most Exalted Creator with respect to the level of life with which it is favored. Even though the human carnal self has an exceptional nature and capacity particular to
itself among other beings, its existence with whatever it has is from
Him, and subsists by Him alone. For this reason, with respect to
itself, it is a zero in the face of Eternity, a shadow in the face of the
Original Being, and is nothing in the face of the Truly Existent One.
Its perception of this is the first step to the attainment of true existence, while thinking otherwise is a lethal stumbling. When one sees
oneself as an independent being existing and subsisting by oneself,
one rolls headlong into the dark abyss of non-existence. Yet, when

one functions as a polished mirror to the Truth (having whatever is good and valuable as only a reflection from Him), one is en route to eternity. One smashes the tight frame around one and finds the light of the Existence of the True Being. Concerning this, Muhammad Iqbal[134] says:

> In your essence, there is a substance from the Existence of God,
> and a ray from His manifestation. But for His ocean, I do not
> know where we would have been able to find this "pearl."

The following couplet, whose author is not known, relates the matter to the famous saying, "He who knows himself, knows his Lord:"

> Know your own self, if you desire to have knowledge of God;
> Only he who knows his own self, is one who has knowledge of God.

Mawlana sums up the matter as follows:

> So long as a servant is annihilated with respect to his ego and conceit,
> It is impossible for him to attain true belief in God and His Unity.
> Unity does not mean union with God; it means freedom from ego.
> Whoever says otherwise, speaks a lie and cannot make falsehood truth.

To sum up, it is possible to say that, other than the way composed of love, suffering and similar essentials by which one can reach God, there is another way; this is the way of one's perception and the acknowledgment of one's own helplessness and poverty before God, and of affection and reflection. This second way is safer and more direct than the former one.

Travelers following such a way in consciousness of their helplessness turn to the One of Infinite Power with all of their being, each saying: "Hold me by the hand, hold because I cannot manage without You." The more aware they are of their poverty, the more

---

[134] Muhammad Iqbal (1877-1938) is one of the most outstanding Muslim thinkers and activists of the 20th-century Muslim world. He studied in England and wrote many books. *The Reconstruction of the Islamic Thought* is the most well-known among them. (Trans.)

sincerely they take refuge with the Divine Wealth, and attribute to Him whatever in their possession is good and praiseworthy. They are in constant thankfulness and act zealously where others stumble because of their self-pride and utterances that are incompatible with the rules of Shari'a. Those who study deeply and reflect on their inner world and the outer world do not fall into pride (by ascribing any accomplishment and the favors they have received to themselves,) nor do they fall into mental and spiritual confusions by imputing evils to external causes or Destiny. On the contrary, they attribute to God all of their accomplishments and the favors they receive, rely on Him, and enjoy the pleasure of dependence on Him. As for evils, they ascribe them to themselves and turn to God with repentance, penitence and contrition, feeling pangs of separation from Him and pleasures in the expectation of again meeting with Him. Since they regard their existence as a shadow of the light of the Divine Existence, they never consider that they have independent self-existence, nor do they need to be preoccupied with such notions as Unity of Being and Unity of the Witnessed. With the conviction that their existence, with all its attributes and potentials and whatever endowment they have been granted, are all from Him, then they live with the pleasure or the hope of His company, and act in thankfulness for being on the way to Him. They never value or esteem easy behavior or utterances that suggest self-pride and self-complacency.

The basic essentials of this way were once expressed by the present author as follows:

O friends, come and listen, O friends!
Our way is the way of zeal;
The comrades satisfied with belief,
Thorns are roses for us.

Thanks to Him, we have seen the Face of the Truth,
And found the very essence of everything;
We have adopted His every word as a principle;
And His Speech is evidence for us.

All strength by which we are strong is His;
We are known for His Name, by Which we act,

And travel, going beyond the summits;
All difficulties are easy for us to surmount.

We have no wealth but are extremely wealthy;
And are noble and honored by relation to Him.
Reflection is our way; and everything, wet or dry,
Is a source of knowledge of God for us.

Plains, residences, and deserts,
All voices mention Him throughout the universe,
Roses of all colors that have opened,
Each is a message to us from Him.

You know us from serving God with utmost zeal;
Our work is always thinking of Him,
And what we will always do and declare:
His Book is the guide for us.

We have found Him and submitted to Him;
And been saved from grief and despair;
We were sullied but have been cleaned;
His Mercy is the ocean in which we were cleaned.

O Lord, accept my repentance, and clean me of the dirt, answer my prayers, secure my place in religion, guide my heart, make my voice always speak the truth, and root out all kinds of hatred and envy from my heart. And bestow Your blessings and peace on our master and support Muhammad, and his family and Companions altogether.

A DISTANCE OF TWO BOWS' LENGTH

This metaphoric Qur'anic expression concerns God's Messenger' unparalleled nearness to God during his Ascension. From the viewpoint of Sufism, it denotes rising beyond the horizons of Divine acts and Names and reaching the peak of Attributes or even going beyond it. Reaching the peak of Attributes is called Nearness relating to the Attributes, and going beyond it is Nearness related to the (Divine) Being Himself. However, we should point out that this nearness is our nearness to the Being Who is nearer to everything than itself, and is self-annihilation in the lights of His Existence through freedom from duality in the state of spiritual pleasures. Travelers who experience this cannot see, know or feel anything other than Him, see what they see as His making them see, feel what they feel as His making them feel, hold what they hold by His making them hold, and obtain what they obtain by His making them obtain. With all the atoms of their bodies, they become eloquent voices speaking of Him.

This nearness is the fruit of ascension toward God. In the universal level it was represented by him whose existence is the ultimate cause for the creation of the universe, upon him be peace and blessings. Those performing spiritual travel under his guidance can have a share in it, each according to his or her rank. A traveler, the elements of whose bodily existence come from stone, dust, clay, air and water, enters the way of being perfected through belief, righteous deeds, sincerity and pursuing God's good pleasure. Freed from imprisonment in the dungeon of corporeality and traveling on the horizons of life in heart and spirit, the traveler is saved from the loneliness and solitude that originate from being distant from God, and reaches the point of friendship with God. In other words, as the traveler was originated by God in the beginning, so finally he or she returns to Him. One's being originated or sent to the world is a descent and called the arch of descent, and one's returning to God through Him and acquiring nearness to Him is ascension and called the arch of ascension. Since the picture formed of these two (curved) arches resembles two archery bows facing one another (separated only by the thickness of two adjacent lines), this has been described as the distance of two bows. Rather than distance, it denotes that the Messenger reached as far as the line or boundary of the realm of mortality and contingency, which adjoins the (Divine) realm of eternity and absolute necessity.

The expression "or nearer" signifies that the two (hypothetical) lines or boundaries, one belonging to the realm of mortality and contingency and the other to the (hypothetical) Divine realm of eternity and absolute necessity, have joined each other and become as if one boundary. It therefore refers to the furthest point of nearness to God as far as that which a created being can reach in journeying toward God. This nearness belongs only to God's Messenger, upon him be peace and blessings.

As mentioned before, every human being is caught up in two movements, one of descent and the other of ascension. The Sufis call the former the arch of descent, and the latter the arch of ascension. Although some Muslim philosophers have viewed this as a cycle based on the theories of Divine emanation and appearance, which are likely to open a door to heretical doctrines such as monism, incarnation and union, in reality this cycle is the education, purification and development of the spirit, making it into a polished mirror to God by means of belief, righteous deeds, sincerity, purity of intention and struggle against the carnal self. This is another title on the way to becoming a perfect human being. It is a way that everyone can follow. That is something that Nadiri expresses most memorably:

> What does it mean that we have taken up our residence
> at the highest point of rising, or at a point nearer (to Him)?
> We have made the way leading to the station of
> two bows' distance a straight and easy path, like an arrow,
> by treading it time and again.

THE UNIVERSAL MAN

Also known as the perfect man, the universal man is the brightest mirror of God's acts, Names, Attributes, and even His Essential Qualities that qualify Him as God. There is a rule that when an attribute is mentioned without it being specified who the one or ones that have it are, then such an attribute belongs to the one who has it at the most perfect level. So, when we talk about the universal man, we mean, first of all, Prophet Muhammad, upon him be peace and blessings. Then come other Messengers and Prophets, and the greatest spiritual guides who are known as "means of Divine help" (*ghaws*) and "pole" or "axis" (*qutb*), and "those made near to God" (*muqarrabun*), and godly ones (*abrar*), and other saintly people, each according to their rank or degree.

Each group being based on their particular considerations, philosophers, theologians, and Sufis approach the universal man by a different rubric. In the language of philosophers and some theologians, he is the first intellect, the universal intellect, the comprehensive word, the encompassing point, the point of unity, the Divine mystery, the mirror of the Divine mystery, the greatest means, and so on; while he is mentioned by some Sufis with titles such as the guide, the one leading to truth, the perfect scholar, the perfecting one, the mature and perfect, and the greatest cure, etc. All these definitions or titles can be summed up in a single sentence, which is that the universal man is the mirror of the Divine Existence and the two worlds. Being the essence, juice, voice, and translator of existence, he not only demonstrates "the hidden treasure" in all realms of existence and connects everything to the Divine Being, but he is also an articulate expression of the Being that is in the depth of his consciousness and the richness of his nature.

The universal man is such a polished mirror that God's Essential Qualities qualifying Him as God are reflected in him at almost every moment, beyond all concepts of modality, and the earth becomes more valuable than the heavens because it is his residence. The universal man functions in effect as the intellect, heart and spirit of existence, without whom nothing can be understood correctly, no information can be developed into knowledge about God, and the mystery of the life of any thing cannot be perceived. The whole physical realm when not viewed from his perspective is devoid of spirit, and any part of time which is not enlightened by him is in darkness. So, those who live in such a realm and at such a time are deprived of the light and the true life with respect to the heart and spirit, and cannot develop their human nature to its true and full potential.

People have only been able to continuously turn to God without failure by means of universal men. Masses have discovered their true goals under their guidance and interpreted things and events correctly by means of the lights that they have disseminated. For this reason, those who have found and followed them have found the truth and those who have been able to penetrate their inner world have observed the Face of the Truth to the extent of the transparence of their heart and spirit.

The universal man is an example in the name of religion and religious life. Belief, Islamic life and perfect goodness constitute his way; obtaining God's good pleasure, his goal; loving God and making Him loved by others, his duty; Paradise and God's vision are the surprising fruit of his thought, belief and life, provided he is not cast in the role of the goal of his devotion.

The universal man always pursues a way to help others and to increase his knowledge of God. Since he lives in accordance with good morals, he always displays good and excellence. He always sees things from a beautiful perspective and therefore as beautiful, he thinks and acts beautifully, and speaks beautiful, useful things. In quest of God's approval and good pleasure in all his acts, words, and manners, he always feels His company. He thinks of Him, mentions Him, speaks about Him, reminds others of Him with all his attitudes and expressions, and lives as the most articulate voice of truth. The greatest of the universal men, the master of creation, was foremost in having every good quality that could be found in a universal man. Seeing him once was enough for an unbiased one to be able to discern the Divine mystery lying in the essence of Islam. As stated by ʿAbd al-Karim al-Jili,[135] there has never been nor ever will be a second one qualified with human perfections to the degree of Prophet Muhammad, upon him be peace and God's blessings.

If perfection lies in purifying the spirit and cleansing the carnal self with the Divine Revelation and inspiration, and in developing the human faculties, overcoming bodily appetites and animal impulses, and attaining subsistence by the subsistence of His particular blessings in utmost submission and obedience to Him, so as to become thereby the most polished mirror to the Divine Names, Attributes, and Essential Qualities, then the only one who was able to achieve all these without the least imperfection, and whose servanthood or devotion was at the level of "the distance of two bows," is the master of creation, upon him be the most perfect of blessings and salutations. He is foremost and unparalleled in perfection and, in the words of Bediuzzaman, the pride of humankind and the whole of creation, and the seal of Prophethood.

In the language of Sufism, the universal man is a substance or an essence which has combined in his being without any contradiction the spiritual or metaphysical and physical realms of existence, as well as its original and the shadowy or reflected, and its particular and universal, and its substantial and accidental dimensions. According to Sayyid Sharif al-Jurjani, the holy person who is the pride of humankind was such a mysterious and precious book, and such a missive containing the truths related to Divinity and creation, that no one other than the fortunate who have been able to be purified of all corporeal dirt can perceive and recognize him perfectly. We see the universe as the macrocosmos, but in truth and in God's

---

[135] ʿAbd al-Karim ibn Ibrahim al-Jili (1365-1417 ?) is the writer of the famous book, *al-Insan al-Kamil* ("The Universal Man"). He was from Baghdad. In his Sufi teachings he generally followed Muhy al-Din ibn al-ʿArabi. (Trans.)

sight, humanity is greater than the universe. In the words of 'Ali, the Fourth Caliph, his nature is more sublime than even the angels, with the worlds hidden in it. The fact that the universal man is a comprehensive mirror to God's Existence and Essential Qualities, that the inner side or dimension of his being is the focus of the manifestation of all the Divine Names, Attributes and Essential Qualities, and that the outer dimension of his being, with all its words, lines and paragraphs, is a summary or index of all existence, in part explicitly, and in part allusively. As the Holy Existence is manifested on him in the universal, detailed form, that is, as he car ries a couplet or a word from everything, even if in a very abbreviated form, every being is in one respect immanent in the mirror of his being. He finds the Divine Being in his heart as a hidden treasure. It is highly probable that one of the reasons why angels were commanded to prostrate before the first universal being—Prophet Adam—was because of the rich attributes he had in his being. Such richness as this required that the one endowed with it should respond with serious devotion. This was manifested as religion and religious life, which is a representation of the Divine way of acting and of His laws in the universe. God attaches special importance to us, and in return, we should try to please Him by practicing Islam in all its dimensions throughout our lives.

With respect to his relation with existence and events, the universal man is the vicegerent of God on the earth, who observes and knows the meaning of His acts and orders, and is His witness. God looks at His creatures through his eyes, hears them through his ears, and gives them support through his hands. He is a man of perfect compassion, who embraces everyone in need of attention, support and maintenance. He feels compassionate toward everyone, and like blood circulating in all the veins and arteries, his compassion is present in the body of society, keeping an eye on it to protect it against all harmful things and to meet its needs, controlling all its activities like the soul. As declared in the Qur'an, *We have not sent you save as a mercy for the whole creation* (21:107), and *We have not sent you save as a bearer of good tidings and warner for the whole humankind* (34:28),

God's Messenger, who is the greatest of the universal men, upon him be peace ad blessings, is a mercy for all creation, living or non-living, and a guide and leader for all humankind, and a bearer of good tidings (in return for belief and good deeds) and a warner (because of humankind's deviations in belief and their evil deeds). As for other universal men, each of them is, in adherence to the Messenger, also a mercy for all creation, and a guide and leader for humankind.

The universal man radiates the spirit of the people, enlightening them concerning their nature and God, guiding them to the truth, purifying their spirits and cleansing their carnal selves, and awakening their faculties to the Truth. People find their "direction" through him, and know their goals in life and advance straight to them with his guidance. He leads to perfection the souls that have aptitude for perfection. Anyone who is favored with recognizing him and entering his aura will have entered the way leading to God, closing up the distances in their nature between them and Him. Everyone who overcomes their corporeality by such guidance, feels at heart His nearness beyond all concepts of modality, and according to their capacity are able to taste the pleasure of the "seeing" of Him with their insight, attaining His friendship with their spirit. Although everyone who has the necessary capacity and aptitude can feel certain degrees of pleasure of nearness to and friendship with Him, only the universal man favored with the universal manifestation of Him can be a perfect, spotless and bright mirror to Him.

As all conscious beings feel the mysteries of Divinity in the universal man, the Divine Being, in a particular sense, observes all His manifestations in the other mirrors in that one polished mirror. This means that the universal man is such a comprehensive mirror that reflects the All-Permanent One among mortal beings that one who sees him knows what it means to have seen the Truth, one who loves him knows what it means to love the Truth, and one who follows him knows what it means to be on the way of devotion to Him. We should point out once again that all these distinctive excellences belong, first of all, to God's Messenger in the universal, perfect form. All other universal men can be favored with them in his footsteps in particular forms and degrees. They are heirs to God's Messenger in learning, knowledge and in their love of God, in zeal, in feeling, in attractiveness to others and their attraction to God. Being called by the Messenger to the table where all these Divine blessings are offered, they call others to join them.

God always observes Himself and has others to observe Himself in different mirrors on the earth. Since the universal man is the most comprehensive and brightest mirror that perfectly reflects the acts and Essential Qualities of the All-Merciful, he functions as one who "sees" and causes others to "see" Him. The places where and the times when there is not a universal man are orphaned in one respect. For this reason, every time and space needs the universal man as much as it needs air and water. Since God manifests Himself in the most comprehensive way, it is extremely important for existence that a universal man should be present in every time and place. For such a one is the mirror of the Divine Being, with his knowledge being a ray of His Knowledge and himself being a mysterious key to His secrets.

One who finds the universal man and shares the same atmosphere with him attains many mysteries and lights that others cannot, and becomes a source of lights for others. The universal man is aware of his position and task. He sees himself like a mirror reflecting the Divine lights, and never attributes to himself his abilities and merits, or the tasks he performs. He attributes to God his every accomplishment in sincere conviction of the fact, *You did not kill them but God killed them* (8:17), and feels deeply in his consciousness the meaning of *When you threw, it was not you who threw, but God who threw* (8:17). Not merely attributing to God all his accomplishments, merits, and abilities, he rather regards them as His extra favors, saying:

> That which I have—I am not worthy of it;
> This favor and grace—why are they bestowed on me?

He never deviates into believing such doctrines as union and incarnation. In fact, in order to assert such doctrines, there must be two independent, self-existent beings, whereas, the universal man is not a self-existent being independent of God. The Divine Being is absolutely independent and Self-Existent, while all other existing beings exist and subsist by the lights of His Existence. Regarding any created, mortal being as God's incarnation or as one united with Him in the name of exalting that being is sheer deviation.

The universal man is perfectly conscious that he is one created by God and is extremely aware of his being a servant. He never utters words of pride because of the favors he receives, nor does he fall into the error of regarding himself as being identical with God because of his being a mirror to Him. He regards, feels and experiences whatever blessing he is favored with as a manifestation of the Divine Names or Attributes and is humble to the utmost degree before God. This is the state of his annihilation with respect to the carnal self and egoism and the attainment of a new existence in heart and spirit. We can regard this as one who is not self-existent tasting the true existence by His Existence. In his *Diwan*, Mawlana Jalal al-Din al-Rumi says about the heroes of this favor:

> In that station, one who exists has seemed to me as non-existent,
>   And another one who does not exist as existent.
> Beyond the world which has the characteristic of a soul,
>   I have seen many dazzled and intoxicated with love of Him,
>   All of whom are beings of pure faithfulness and delight.

The universal man is a polished mirror for the True Being and, in his relation to other beings, is like a star which stands still in its place or rotates around itself, and around which satellites turn. While rotating around himself, he flies around his axis in utmost devotion to Him and, as stated in the verse (16:16), *As well as various other means of finding direction, and by the stars they guide themselves*, he guides others to the straight path and directs them along it. Like a compass, he causes others to find their direction, and like a door or window he shows others the truth, and like a bridge he makes others pass from the darkness of their own world into the spacious world of eternity. When people enter his aura, they begin to feel the breezes of friendship with God; on reaching that door, they quiver with calls from the realms beyond, and on crossing that bridge, they rise to the horizon of having a relationship that consists of worshipping servants and the Sole Object of Worship with the Unique, Besought-of-All in the perfect manner. This horizon signifies God's Throne (of absolute dominion over all things) in the universal sphere with respect to His manifestation of all His Names throughout the universe, and the human heart (which corresponds to God's Throne) in the particular sphere with respect to His manifestation of His particular Names on particular things. The most important food of the travelers to this horizon is maintaining the purification of their hearts, and hunting the special Divine gifts and favors in prostration on their rugs in the mysterious world of nights that are regarded as blessed times when no one sees us. Concerning this, Ibrahim Haqqi says:

The heart is the home of God; purify it from whatever is there other than Him.
So that the All-Merciful may descend into His palace at night.

Mawlana also has something beautiful to say concerning the corridor or spiral of nights which extends to the Hidden Treasure:

If you seek that peerless Sovereign, and have set out to reach Him,
You should not sleep during that journey.
Good, fortunate ones sleep in the shadow of God's love and mercy.
O brother, beware that you should not sleep in another place.

We should spend nights, which draw us to deep thoughts and heavenly considerations, in humble devotion by standing, bowing, prostrating, and reciting His Names and making humble petitions to Him.

According to some Sufis, everything has an outward, visible aspect, which is called the outward. This material world is the outward or external world. It has also an inner or inward aspect, which we call the inward. It consists of all metaphysical worlds, including the spiritual ones and the hereafter. There is another (intermediate) world which has both the inward and outward aspects and which lies between them and the Divine Names, separating the two (outer and inward) worlds from each another. This intermediate world is the world of the universal man. God's knowledge of Himself is the true, substantial mirror to Himself, and the Divine Being is manifested and known in that mirror beyond all concepts. The knowledge of the universal man is a mirror to himself that is dependent on Divine Knowledge, and he is manifested and known in that mirror of his knowledge. Nevertheless, whatever he has, including his knowledge, is a gift to him and therefore does not belong to him. For this reason, with whatever he has he indicates the One Who has everything absolutely and originally.

A human being is indicative of the Divine Being, while his or her attributes are indicative of the Divine Ones. The restriction and particularity of human nature and its attributes (as humans being created and of relative character) indicate the universality, originality and infinity of the Divine Being and His Attributes (as the Divine Being being the Creator and of absolute character).

It is because of this type of relation with the Divine Being that a traveler who has reached the rank of universal man is considered to have reached the rank of perfect vicegerency of God. Above this rank is the station of "or nearer" that lies between the Necessary and the contingent. The only one who has reached this station and who has represented it throughout the whole of human history is the master of creation, who represents the greatest rank which any mortal being can reach and the (most) perfect manifestation of the Divine Names as concentrated on a single being. He has reached this greatest rank because of his most laudable virtues or matchless excellence in spirituality and morality, the straightforwardness of his acts, the depth of his relations with his Lord, the perfect balance he was able to establish between the affairs of this world and the next, and his insight into the mysteries of Divinity and creation. The perfection of all other perfected beings is relative when compared to his and is dependent on allegiance and submission to him. All other Prophets and Messengers, who rose in the heavens of humanity, diffused the light only before he honored the world. Pointing to the fact that that greatest being is like the sun and all the other Prophets and Messengers are like its satellites or "stars" which diffuse light only before it rises, Busayri says:

> Surely, he is the sun of virtues with others being stars,
> Giving out light for human beings only when it is night.

As the master of creation, upon him be the most perfect of blessings and salutations, he is both the seed and the fruit of the Tree of Creation. The Tree of Creation has always been related with him from the beginning to the end, and has grown in connection with him. More than being the seed and fruit of the Tree of Creation, he is also its essence and spirit. He can also be viewed as the basic element of the "soup" of existence.

> As the basic aim in the creation of the universe,
> That most exalted sun came into existence.

The heavens and earth shrank from being a mirror to the abstract nature of Divine Existence, which comprises all of the Divine Names, because they were unable to reflect it. Yet, humanity was endowed with the potential to do this. Thus, humanity was given external (material) existence in order to realize this aim. However, most people are ignorant and are caught up in wrongdoing, in that they cannot fulfill this task of reflection; in order for a human being to not be an ignorant one or a wrongdoer, he or she should be extremely careful, sensitive, and conscious of the responsibility of being a mirror to Him. In other words, a human being will make good the gap of ignorance and wrongdoing in his/her nature by setting his/her mechanism of consciousness to move in harmony with the Divine Revelation, and so change the field of loss into a market of profit. The following Qur'anic verse (33:72) expresses this fundamental task of humanity: *We offered the Trust to the heavens and the earth and the mountains, but they declined to bear it, and shrank from it, but humanity undertook it. Surely, he is a wrongdoer, and ignorant.*

Nothing in the universe—whether it be the heavens or the earth and the mountains—except humankind has a heart, will-power, consciousness, internal senses, or faculties, all of which are essential to seeing, making others see, and reflecting the greatest truth in existence. They have neither the ability nor physical possibility to represent and reflect that truth. It is only humankind who, by reinforcing and deepening their innate endowment from God by fulfilling their religious responsibilities, can perform this mission. Those among human beings who can do this are saved from ignorance and wrongdoing.

It is true that, in practice, every human being has not been and is not able to succeed in fulfilling this task. But it is also true that there have been and are many who are conscious of the aim of their creation and who improve themselves by fulfilling their religious responsibilities on the way to becoming a universal human being. They develop their potential and knit the laces of eternity to fulfill the Divine purpose for their creation out of belief in God, knowledge and love of Him, yearning, zeal, the feeling of attraction and being attracted toward God, and spiritual pleasures. Those conquerors of hearts who have set up their thrones at the intersection of the worlds, of both this and the next realm, have gained a second, transcendent nature beyond their own, with souls that are extremely alive and active through the breezes of the All-Beloved, and their horizons airy with breezes of friendship with Him. In his enchanting style, Mawlana depicts these mythical birds of the heaven of perfection as follows:

> Heroes of journeying on the way to God are alive
> with a soul other than that known soul;
> The birds that fly on the air that "emanates" from Him
> have nests other than the nests known.
> Do not try in vain to see them with those eyes of yours;
> with these you cannot see them.
> They dwell in another realm beyond both this world and the next.

One can have knowledge of God through His acts and Names, and the Names are manifested on things and events. Humanity is both the seed and fruit of existence. As for the universal man, he is the essence and spirit of everything. For this reason, it is not possible to have a perfect knowledge of God without considering existence as far as its beginning or seed is concerned, or without turning to the horizon of the universal man, who is a comprehensive voice of the Divine Being, Attributes, Names, and acts. He is also a pattern of existence that contains all the ranks as he is the final link in the chain of existence. We can therefore say that the Almighty can be known and felt only through the universal man in accordance with His Grandeur and Majesty, and the universal man sees, knows, and holds everything by Him and builds relations with others in dependence on Him. The unique, greatest representative and hero of all instances of seeing, knowing, holding, and being in relation is Prophet Muhammad, upon him be peace and blessings, while all other universal men can attain what they will attain only in his footsteps. For the truth he represents—his truth as being Muhammad or the Truth of Muhammad—has its origin in God's manifestation of all His Names throughout the universe, which comprehends all truths. God—Allah, the proper Name of the Divine Being Which comprises all the Divine Names and Attributes—was his private tutor or Lord, Who brought him up especially. Since the proper Name of the Divine Being—God (Allah)—comprises all the Divine Names and Attributes, the master of creation, upon him be the most perfect of blessings and salutations, is the most polished or brightest mirror to the Divine Essential Qualities and Attributes and Names, as he is the most comprehensive mirror to Him reflecting all His Names and Attributes. The saying, "God is always seen in the mirror of Muhammad," is a reality. Other universal men, including all the other Messengers and Prophets, have not been and will not be able to receive the same degree of favor, for God bestows His blessing upon him whom He wills (62:4).

Each of the other universal men may have been and may be favored with the manifestation of one or a few Names and Attributes; the part of each one in the manifestation of each Name and Attribute differs according to his capacity. However great the moons and stars of the heaven of the Prophethood and the sainthood, the capacity of each restricts him. They will reach the final point of their rising when they have fully realized their potential. As saintly people differ in their knowledge and love of God and in their spiritual pleasures, the ranks of the universal men also differ according to the extent of their being favored with the manifestations of the Divine Names. This is one of the reasons why saintly people, pure scholars of religion, godly ones, and those made nearer to God by God Himself may also differ in their views and interpretations concerning the secondary matters of religion, which are open to different interpretations.

The difference of ranks between Messengers and Prophets, which is indicated in (2:253), *Those Messengers: some We have exalted above others (in some respects)*, also arises from the manifestations of the Divine Names in different wavelengths and the degree of each being favored with them. For example, Adam in the brief or summarized knowledge of all things given to him, Abraham and Ishmael in the knowledge, forbearance and leniency with which they were favored, and Jesus in the (spiritual) power with which he was endowed, are higher in degree than others. As for the master of creation, upon him be the most perfect of blessings and salutations, he was honored with the full and detailed manifestations of all the Divine Attributes and Names, and therefore is the highest or most advanced of all in all virtues.

Each universal man is perfect according to his capacity and the degree of his knowledge of God. All of them have combined in themselves the knowledge of Divine Revelation, scientific and theological, or intellectual and spiritual proofs, and a knowledge of God in certain degrees. Lacking in one of these would be an important defect or imperfection in the name of perfection. The Qur'an and Sunna (Revelation) are the foundation, reasoning and logic or intellectual activities are the means with which one approaches the goal, and a knowledge of God and wisdom are the fruit of walking straightforwardly on the way.

> O ascetic, do not think that everything is finished
> with fasting, prayer and pilgrimage;
> What is necessary to be a perfect one is knowledge of God and wisdom.
>
> (Niyazi)

Our Lord, Our Master, the Goal of our endeavors! I implore you, O God, not to burn me in the Fire! We seek refuge in God from the chastisement of the Fire; and we seek refuge in God from all seditions, plain or hidden. And bestow Your blessings and peace on our master Muhammad, the intercessor for our sins, and on his family and Companions, so long as days and nights continue, afternoons follow each other, the moon reappears after its complete disappearance, and the Farkadan (the two stars b and Ursae Minoris) coincide.

INDEX